Religious Belief and Popular Culture in Southwark c.1880–1939

S. C. WILLIAMS

OXFORD
UNIVERSITY PRESS

OXFORD

UNIVERSITY PRESS

Great Clarendon Street, Oxford OX2 6DP

Oxford University Press is a department of the University of Oxford.
It furthers the University's objective of excellence in research, scholarship,
and education by publishing worldwide in

Oxford New York

Athens Auckland Bangkok Bogotá Buenos Aires Calcutta
Cape Town Chennai Dar es Salaam Delhi Florence Hong Kong Istanbul
Karachi Kuala Lumpur Madrid Melbourne Mexico City Mumbai
Nairobi Paris São Paulo Singapore Taipei Tokyo Toronto Warsaw

and associated companies in Berlin Ibadan

Oxford is a registered trade mark of Oxford University Press
in the UK and in certain other countries

Published in the United States
by Oxford University Press Inc., New York

British Library Cataloguing in Publication Data

Data available

Library of Congress Cataloging in Publication Data

Data applied for

ISBN 0-19-820769-7

1 3 5 7 9 10 8 6 4 2

Typeset in Minion
by Regent Typesetting, London
Printed in Great Britain
on acid-free paper by
Biddles Ltd., Guildford and King's Lynn

PREFACE

This is not a book about the Church, which so often takes centre stage in religious history. It is a book about people and the nature and expression of their religious ideas in the day-to-day life of a community. The Metropolitan Borough of Southwark forms the focus of this study, providing a window through which to consider popular religion not merely as a hangover of some previous rural and pre-industrial era, but as an integrated facet of the modern urban environment. While concerned largely with details and individuals, this subject has enormous ramifications for the study of religious history as a whole. By emphasizing the centrality of participant accounts of religious behaviour and belief and the formative role that religion played in the creation and perpetuation of local popular culture, this study critically re-evaluates the theory of secularization, which has continued to shape the ways in which historians have understood socio-cultural and religious change. It also develops a methodological framework through which to consider the elusive and eclectic dimension of religious belief. This is done by drawing on the work of anthropologists and sociologists and on the advances made by social historians working in the field of popular politics, class, and popular culture. These groups, in their efforts to re-evaluate the relationship between the economic base and the cultural superstructure, have gone further than historians of religion in developing a methodology through which to interpret patterns of communal belief. In particular, their concentration on language and cultural symbolism offers an effective approach which has been incorporated into this study. A wide range of written and oral source material has been drawn on in this respect. The perspectives of churchmen, such as those interviewed by Charles Booth's team in 1898–9 and contained in the Booth Collection at the London School of Economics, are examined alongside, for example, the Burnett Collection of working-class autobiographies at Brunel University; a hitherto unused collection of artefacts and writings by the folklorist Edward Lovett, deposited at the Cuming Museum in Southwark; the transcripts of the Essex Oral History Survey; and my own interviews with former inhabitants of Southwark. This breadth of material allowed different types of religious language to

be examined as a means of exploring the complexity of popular religious experience. The anomalies and subtleties of belief are emphasized throughout and its simplistic treatment in both the study of religious history and popular culture is challenged. Some headway is made towards the creation of a methodological bridge between the relative neglect of religion in studies of popular culture on the one hand, and the tendency of historians of religion to isolate their analyses from the dimension of popular culture on the other.

A recurrent theme of the book is the exploration of oral evidence as a medium through which to examine the dimension of personal religious belief. And it is with this in mind that I turn first to acknowledge my gratitude to all those at the Camberwell and Walworth Age Concern Day Centre and the Beornude Centre who trusted me with their memories. Some of those I interviewed are no longer living and I hope that in some way this book will be an enduring memory of their lives.

I want to thank Jane Garnett for her ongoing commitment and encouragement both in the supervision of the thesis on which this book is based and throughout the process of preparation for publication. I am also grateful to all the members of the Department of Theology at Birmingham University for awarding me the Research Fellowship that has given me the time and space to finish this book and for providing such a stimulating environment in which to work. In particular, I would like to thank Hugh McLeod for his support and help at each stage.

I am grateful to John Walsh and Roger Laidlaw for their help at strategic moments along the way and to Stephen Humphries and Nicola Smith at Southwark Local Studies Library and Caroline Ellis at the Cuming Museum. For permission to cite unpublished material my thanks go to: Alan Bartlett; Paul Thompson, 'Family and Work Experience before 1918'; the Department of Sociology, University of Essex; Brunel University; Ruskin College Oxford; Southwark Local Studies Library; and the British Library of Political and Economic Science.

The wise comments of Michael Beaumont and Gabriele Braun were particularly timely during the final stages of this project. I am grateful to Harriet Harris and Clare Griffiths for their suggestions and encouragement. My thanks also to Janet Soppitt, Ann Luke, Mary Williams, Jennifer Rees Larcombe, Joy and Charis Pollard, Rachel Beavis, and Emma Coles for hours of help and kindness. My greatest debt of gratitude is to my husband, Paul.

CONTENTS

ABBREVIATIONS

The following abbreviations are used throughout.

EOHA	Essex Oral History Archive
Int.	Interview
LSE	London School of Economics
n.d.	No date of publication known
n.p.	Unpaginated
SLSL	Southwark Local Studies Library
SCW	Initials used to denote my own oral interviews

The place of publication of printed works is London, unless otherwise stated.

NOTE ON THE TRANSCRIPTION OF TAPED INTERVIEWS

Round brackets are inserted to indicate a parenthesis or an aside in the course of narration and Q and A are used for question and answer.

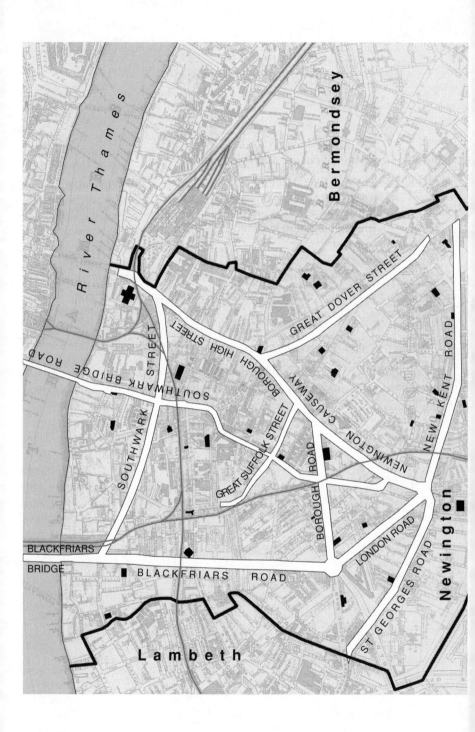

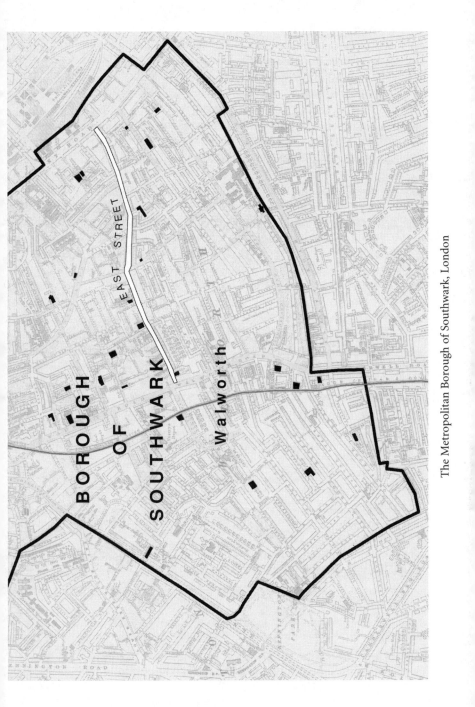

The Metropolitan Borough of Southwark, London

1

Religious Belief and Popular Culture

> To count up the churchgoers and chapel-goers and argue that the neighbourhood is without religion or to estimate the proportion of children and young persons in places of worship and then say 'religion has no hold on them' . . . is a serious error. It is a confusion of formal outward signs and inward spiritual graces. Many of the poor rarely attend church, not because they are irreligious but because they have long since received and absorbed the truths by which they live; while the idea that attendance at public worship is a duty doesn't occur to them and does not seem credible when suggested . . .[1]

When the district nurse Margaret Loane ventured into the homes of working-class families in London at the end of the nineteenth century she encountered what historians and anthropologists have since called popular religion. Far from matching the typical irreligious caricature ascribed to them by most Victorian religious commentators, the working families with whom she spent time adhered to their own distinctive styles of religiosity. These regulated ethical behaviour and provided a symbolic system whereby individuals and communities made sense of their world. Yet until relatively recently, historians of the nineteenth century have neglected these more subtle and nuanced dimensions of belief. They have focused predominantly on the 'formal outward signs' or institutional expressions of religiosity and they have excluded from their definition of the religious realm those patterns of popular belief expressed in the homes, streets, and alleys as well as in the churches and mission halls of this period.

Influential writers such as E. R. Wickham and K. S. Inglis set the tone for this neglect. Their books *Church and People in an Industrial City* (1957) and *The Churches and the Working Classes in Victorian England* (1963) laid the foundations for an orthodox interpretation of the relationship between urban life, the working class, and irreligion which

---

[1] M. Loane, *The Queen's Poor* (1906), 26.

has proved remarkably resilient. Like many of their nineteenth-century predecessors, both historians ascribed lower levels of church attendance in the industrial towns to the alienation of the working classes from the churches. Working-class non-attendance was judged to be symptomatic of a profound spiritual malaise and it was on this basis that the religious life of the cities was measured.

The simplistic identification of religion with institutional church practice remained implicit in much of the work done during the 1960s and 1970s. The incorporation of the secularization thesis into historical interpretations gave this tendency a theoretical underpinning. By the end of the 1970s the arguments put forward by Wickham and Inglis were caught up in a wider theoretical schema in which the inevitable diminution of religious values, sentiment, and institutions was envisaged as part of the transformation of traditional agrarian communities into the modern associational state. Early formulations of this thesis propagated a theoretical relegation of the dimension of religious belief by denying the self-claims of religionists and seeking an alternative explanation for the form and content of religion within social phenomena. The effect of this approach was to undercut attempts to consider the formative role of belief in the interpretative processes whereby individuals ascribe meaning to environment and action. It also gave precedence to the analysis of socio-structural change over and above an examination of the actual content of religious ideas. The consequence of this was the consideration of religion, no less than class, in terms of the realities of the material life, the dismissal of religion in studies of the urban environment as either a waning force or as an interesting pre-industrial hangover, and the analytical supremacy of social context, social forces, and a new sociological determinism. One has only to look at the work of Gilbert, Horsley, and Currie[2] to see the development of this line of thinking in the writing of religious history. These writers specialized in counting up the numbers of church- and chapel-goers and thereby quantifying the extent of religion from 1700 onwards.

Today, as a result of over a decade of revisionism, few historians would commit the 'serious error' of confusing 'inward spiritual graces' with 'formal outward signs' in an unqualified manner. Most would nod in assent at Loane's emphasis and agree that the sum total of church- and

---

[2] A. D. Gilbert, *Religion and Society in Industrial England: Church, Chapel and Social Change 1740–1914* (1976); *The Making of Post-Christian Britain* (1980); and R. Currie, A. Gilbert, and L. Horsley, *Churches and Churchgoers: Patterns of Church Growth in the British Isles since 1700* (Oxford, 1977).

chapel-goers is an inadequate gauge of religious fervour and even point to the importance of popular religion in the daily lives of working-class people within the urban environment.[3] But it none the less remains the case that a concentration on formal religious behaviour so outweighs a consideration of the more intangible expressions of belief that popular religion continues to elude us as a serious subject of enquiry in its own right. Even within the revisionist camp there are very few who are pre-pared to carry this tacit assent into an active understanding of the nature of these 'inward spiritual graces' and to explore the concept of religious duty which excused individuals both from public worship and from the label of 'irreligion'. Furthermore, the revisionist work that has been done remains inhibited in a number of important respects. It has failed fully to liberate itself from the enduring legacy of secularization because of its preoccupation with the question of religious decline. Despite the heavy critical fire to which the secularization thesis has been subject, the model continues to shape the agenda for the historiographical debate. Its theoretical framework still creeps into the writing of religious history, perpetuating the picture of popular religion as a mere concomitant of institutional creeds or as a corrupted version of orthodoxy.

Revisionist writers, no less than those of the orthodox school, have devoted their attention to assessing the timing, the extent, and the causes of religious change. They have arrived at some radically different answers to the questions concerning the place of religion in society. The picture of weak ineffectual churches failing to respond adequately to the chaotic social and economic changes which marked the nineteenth century has given way to an appreciation of both the variety and the vibrancy of church life at the close of the Victorian era. Much of the work of the last decade has been directed towards attacking the secularization thesis for its perpetuation of 'simplistic historical myths'[4] which are seen to substitute for grass-roots, empirical analyses of local churches. Writers such as Jeremy Morris,[5] Simon Green,[6] Jeffrey Cox,[7] Callum Brown,[8] and

---

[3] See e.g. H. McLeod, 'New Perspectives on Victorian Class Religion: The Oral Evidence', *Oral History*, 14 (1987), 31–50; *Piety and Poverty* (New York, 1996).

[4] C. G. Brown, 'Did Urbanisation Secularise Britain?', *The Urban History Yearbook* (1988), 1.

[5] J. N. Morris, *Religion and Urban Change: Croydon 1840–1914* (Bury St Edmunds, 1992).

[6] S. J. D. Green, *Religion in the Age of Decline: Organisation and Experience in Industrial Yorkshire 1870–1920* (Cambridge, 1996).

[7] J. Cox, *The English Churches in a Secular Society: Lambeth 1870–1930* (Oxford, 1982).

[8] C. G. Brown, *The Social History of Scotland since 1730* (1987); 'Did Urbanisation Secularise Britain?' *Urban History Yearbook*, 15 (1988), 1–15.

Mark Smith[9] have stood against the assumption of a necessary correlation between urbanization and secularization of the kind made by Gilbert, Horsley, and Currie. They have reassessed the response of the churches to the urban environment in terms which stress the achievements rather than the failures of the institutions. Green, for example, attacks the application of an inevitable universal process of social change as a means of explaining the decline of the church. He looks instead to the crisis of the associational ideal within the local church community as the specific source of its weakness in Yorkshire in the early decades of the twentieth century. The consideration of evidence such as statistical material on the occupational composition of churches and chapels has reinforced this approach. Mark Smith's work on Oldham and Saddleworth suggests that most congregations in the area had a larger working-class component than is traditionally assumed.

Yet, for all their innovation in relocating the extent and causes of religious change, these writers have continued to allow their agenda to be shaped by questions of decline, often at the cost of developing new avenues of enquiry and considering interpretative approaches which are able to give insight into the more elusive dimensions of popular religious culture outside the churches. Hugh McLeod's recent book *Piety and Poverty* (1996), for instance, seeks to 'define the nature, the extent and the causes of the secularization of the working classes during this period and to explain why these varied so considerably between the different parts of Western Europe and North America'.[10] The comparative approach adopted by McLeod, along with his use of a range of hitherto under-used sources, such as oral history, permit a far more nuanced and detailed picture of the relationship between the churches and the working classes but the basic framework employed in the book remains unaltered. Popular religious belief emerges in the description as one further factor by which to gauge the relationship between secularization and urbanization and to measure the extent of religious decline in the different areas. It is introduced like a trump card into an old debate, forcing new conclusions from those offered in the 1960s but repeating in the 1990s the same questions which are themselves in need of reconsideration.

If we are to understand 'popular religion' as a cultural phenomenon with its own parameters, concerns, and definitions we need to be willing

[9] M. Smith, *Religion and Industrial Society: Oldham and Saddleworth 1740–1865* (Oxford, 1995).
[10] H. McLeod, *Piety and Poverty* (New York, 1996), p. xix.

to move away from these familiar lines of questioning and to begin to explore belief in new and wide-ranging ways which will inevitably take us beyond the urge to measure and quantify religion whether in favour of or in reaction to a linear scale of secularization. One of the barriers to the development of these new avenues of enquiry has been the continued preoccupation of orthodox and revisionist writers alike with measurable, outward, and tangible signs of religiosity. For some this has been the product of a particular theoretical stance. Callum Brown, for instance, undertakes his critique of the orthodox school from the point of view of the social scientist adhering to the materialistic categories which are themselves so problematic. His definition of religion is based on observable forms of religious behaviour which leave untouched the more amorphous aspects of religious culture. Long-term trends of religious adherence and practice form the basis of Brown's examination and, although he recognizes that religious statistics are not the only measures of the social significance of religion, he none the less argues that 'there are probably none better to be had in the realms of religion'.[11] This search for religion in social phenomena means that belief itself continues to elude us. It remains a dependent variable of some more obvious reality such as social class, just as it did in traditional formulations of the secularization theory.

For other revisionist writers this preoccupation with outward measures of religiosity is more a matter of focus than theory. In the work of Jeffrey Cox and Alan Bartlett, for example, 'inward spiritual graces' are considered merely as they merge with 'formal outward signs' and overlap with the facilities, sacraments, and teachings of the church. Cox makes reference to the 'spectrum of beliefs encompassed by diffusive Christianity',[12] but in practice he isolates the 'Christian end'[13] for consideration, while the culture of which these beliefs were a part is not really considered. Alan Bartlett has in many ways gone further than Cox in attempting to correct the external perspective of studies of working-class religion.[14] His use of oral interviewing in particular allowed a deeper examination of working-class religious belief, but he too explores popular religion primarily at the points at which it touches the institutional church. His focus is on the work of the churches within the

[11] C. Brown, 'A Revisionist Approach to Religious Change', in S. Bruce (ed.), *Religion and Modernisation* (1992), 36.

[12] Cox, *The English Churches*, 97.

[13] Ibid. 95.

[14] A. B. Bartlett, 'The Churches in Bermondsey 1880–1939' (Birmingham University Ph.D. thesis, 1987).

Borough of Bermondsey and towards the reaction of the community to this work rather than on the beliefs of that community *per se*. His oral interviewees were drawn from among former working-class church-goers. Yet such church-based aspects of religion remain unconsidered as part of a far broader range of popular beliefs which both included and extended beyond the sphere of the church and which cannot be under-stood simply in terms of orthodox criteria.[15] Folk customs and traditions were not confined to the traditional rural setting nor were they just hangovers of an earlier era. They continued to be expressed within the local urban subcultures of London as important elements of popular culture. These customs included a number of rituals and practices used to avert misfortune and to attract prosperity. They involved the employ-ment of specific objects such as charms, mascots, and amulets in order to effect these purposes or to act as preventative or curative guards against various kinds of disease. Folk wisdom and medical lore also combined with more overt expressions of folk superstition which sought to manipulate and control the super-empirical sphere and to bring order and predictability to the local human environment. Cox's brief dismissal of aspects of folklore in urban Lambeth as mere survivals of semi-pagan magic, reflective of a purely general belief in luck, does not do justice to this material. Folk beliefs continued to combine with more official dimensions of religiosity and overlapped to form a distinct pattern of religious expression. The complexity of religious ideas within popular culture cannot be understood without appreciating the coalescence of these different types or languages of belief and without extending the parameters of our questioning to include popular culture as a setting for religious expression alongside the church.

This book is devoted to exploring these kinds of belief. It does so with-in the context of a local study of the London Borough of Southwark. By the 1880s this area had developed an identity which remained character-istic until the Second World War. The cries of street sellers, and the barrows and market stalls of the costermongers filled the byways of the borough. The pearly kings and queens added their distinctive presence, while the music-halls and ramshackle theatres epitomized the colourful but less salubrious side of London culture. The borough's working-class inhabitants were famed for low levels of church attendance and tarred with the brush of lamentable irreligion. Yet the 'poor who rarely attended church' in this area at the end of the nineteenth century and in

---

[15] S. C. Williams, 'Urban Popular Religion and the Rites of Passage', in H. McLeod (ed.), *European Religion in the Age of Great Cities 1830–1930* (1995), 216–39.

the period prior to the Second World War, certainly did receive and absorb the truths by which they lived, as Loane suggests. They continued to attend church on occasions such as weddings, baptisms, funerals, and watch-night services to celebrate New Year. They sent their children to Sunday school with dogged determination, sang hymns in one another's homes, prayed in private, and continued to separate the sabbath from the rest of the week by a series of rituals and observances which broke the normal rhythm of life. Orthodox rites and images formed a vital part of their sense of heritage and tradition, not merely as a residue of a former 'golden age' or, as Jeffrey Cox puts it, 'the best that a millennium of protestant indoctrination could achieve'.[16] They were expressed along-side a range of folk customs, beliefs, and practices usually associated with English villagers and earlier periods.

However, to tap such belief and to attempt to enquire into the character of these 'inward spiritual graces' necessitates the development of a method which is able to yield a nuanced account of both personal belief and popular culture. The preoccupation of religious historians with the debate over religious decline has inhibited the development of these areas. Methodology has to form a key priority in the questioning of religion in this period. There is much to learn in this respect from recent developments in the field of social history. In this discipline a search has taken place for an appreciation of the ways in which the historical actor constructs the meaning of social structures and values. An attempt has been made to move beyond the external consideration of social structures and institutions to consider the dimension of mentality and culture. The symbolic interactionists have been a formative influence in this regard. They, and their successors the ethnomethodologists led the way in challenging the treatment of belief and its ascribed role in the modern world. Herbert Blumer, for example, focused his analysis on the interpretative methods by which actors assemble the meaning of social structures in their day-to-day activities. The notion of social reality as external to the individual, constraining him to behave in typical ways and forcing upon him certain modes of conceptualization was challenged by these writers in favour of an approach which regards the meanings that are attached to and derived from social interaction as the primary agents in the construction of social value systems.[17] Studies

---

[16] J. Cox, *The English Churches in a Secular Society: Lambeth 1870–1930* (Oxford, 1982), 95.

[17] H. Blumer, *Symbolic Interactionism* (Engelwood Cliffs, NJ, 1969); P. L. Berger and T. Luckmann, *The Social Construction of Reality: A Treatise in the Sociology of Knowledge*, (New York, 1966); K. Dixon, *The Sociology of Belief* (1980); J. A. Hughes, *The Perspective of Ethnomethodology* (1983); and H. Garfinkel, *Studies in Ethnomethodology* (New York, 1967).

such as Louisa Passerini's *Fascism in Popular Memory* (1987) took this perspective on board and incorporated the analysis of symbolic and cultural phenomena such as self-representations, myths, and stories into the reconstruction of political behaviour and experience among the Turin working class during the Fascist regime. She emphasizes the conflicts of power which took place on a cultural and symbolic plane rather than concentrating merely on those which took place within the narrow political sphere.[18] Similarly, Joanna Bourke in her recent book, *Working-Class Cultures in Britain 1890–1960* (1994), is concerned with the subjective dimension of class identity. She constructs her definition of class on the basis of the label individuals gave themselves and which emerged from the routine activity of daily life rather than from economic determinants, status, or institutional affiliation. Bourke, like Passerini, highlights the symbolic expressions of power in social relationships over and above the purely material realities.

In other studies a strong emphasis is placed on the notion of popular culture as an alternative interpretative model by which to describe political, social, and economic configurations to those based on class and class consciousness. Eugenio Biagini and Alastair Reid, for example, in their book *Currents of Radicalism* (1991) follow in the tradition of Gareth Stedman Jones[19] and stress the importance of reconstructing the language and thought of those participating in popular radical movements at the end of the nineteenth century. They begin from the assumption that it is vital to approach political radicalism from within rather than in terms of its consistency with external norms of revolutionary rhetoric or with teleological models of historical development.

What ordinary people thought and the way in which they expressed it matters and ought to be taken seriously by historians: what the politically active among them demanded cannot be assessed in abstraction from their own needs, desires and capacities.[20]

---

[18] See also L. Passerini, 'Work, Ideology and Consensus under Italian Fascism', *History Workshop*, 8 (1979), 82–108.

[19] G. S. Jones, *Languages of Class 1832–1982* (Cambridge, 1983); see also J. Epstein, 'Understanding the Cap of Liberty; Symbolic Practice and Social Conflict in Early Nineteenth Century England', *Past and Present*, 22 (1989), 75–119; J. R. Cronin, 'Language, Politics and the Critique of Social History: Languages of Class', *Journal of Social History*, 20 (1986), 177–84; W. Reddy, 'The Language of the Crowd at Rouen 1752–1871', *Past and Present*, 34 (1977); J. Thompson, 'After the Fall: Class and Political Language in Britain, 1780–1900', *Historical Journal*, 39/3 (1996), 785–806.

[20] E. F. Biagini and A. J. Reid, *Currents of Radicalism: Popular Radicalism, Organised Labour and Party Politics in Britain 1850–1914* (Cambridge, 1991), 5.

In the same vein Patrick Joyce has considered ways in which the social order has been represented other than on the basis of class, by looking at varieties of language and inclusive universalizing cultural discourses such as the concepts of nation and people which he includes within the category of populism.[21] Joyce argues that the 'search now is for how meanings have been produced by relations of power rather than from external or objective class structures or other social referents'.[22] Instead of human subjects being seen as the centre of multiple identities imposed by the external environment, human subjectivity is itself regarded as an historical creation worthy of study.

This wide-ranging reconsideration of notions of industrial, economic, and class development has profound implications for the study of Victorian working-class religion, yet this challenge to modernization theory by social historians has not extended to a thorough re-evaluation of the role and dimension of religion in modern popular culture. In Patrick Joyce's recent book, *Visions of the People* (1991), for example, little more than lip-service is paid to the dimension of religion within the development of popular concepts and social identities and to the forms in which these concepts are constituted in terms of popular discourse and language. Likewise, Joanna Bourke dismisses religion altogether in a brief discussion of the failure of the church to provide a centre for social communion in working-class areas.[23] Yet religion needs to be considered not merely as it impinges upon the examination of popular politics,[24] but as an integrated and formative factor within studies of popular culture.

These approaches suggest a number of possibilities for the establishment of a method through which to explore popular religion. First, they highlight the need to reconsider understandings of religiosity on the basis of criteria of the religious behaviour and experience adopted by the actors themselves, rather than merely viewing them in conformity with institutional codes, dogmas, and practices. Secondly, they suggest the need to treat these explanations as an indispensable part of the final account of belief, not merely as the product of causal social explanations which are in some sense more fundamental. Furthermore, they point to the importance of the language of those engaged in varieties of religious activity as a means of understanding how belief is constructed in

[21] P. Joyce, *Visions of the People: Industrial England and the Question of Class 1840–1914* (1991).
[22] P. Joyce, 'The End of Social History', *Social History* (1995), 82.
[23] J. Bourke, *Working-Class Cultures in Britain 1890–1960* (1994), 145–8.
[24] P. Joyce, *Work, Society and Politics: The Culture of the Late-Victorian Factory* (1980), 176–8 and 243–8.

different cultural settings. By giving participant criteria a central place in defining the parameters of that which is considered to be religious one can escape from many of the problems associated with establishing a definition of religion which is wide enough to embrace all dimensions of popular religious experience. The tendency when defining religion is to create distinctions such as natural and supernatural, Christian and unchristian, orthodox and unorthodox, high and low, élite and plebeian which may make theological or analytical sense to the historian or the observer but which impose categories alien to the actors themselves. This is particularly pertinent when considering popular religion, where the interaction of theoretically distinct religious idioms forms a central characteristic of the phenomenon. In Southwark a consideration of participant accounts of belief alongside institutional descriptions, revealed the multidimensional character of religious experience. Church rituals, for example, were performed for the social benefits conferred as well as for spiritual or magical efficacy. Both the social sentiment and the spiritual formed parts of a single religious expression which was too closely interwoven to be separated. Likewise individuals could insist on the regular attendance of their child at Sunday school and still cut a lock of hair of that same child, place it between two pieces of bread, and give it to a passing dog as a cure for the child's whooping cough.[25] The religious professions of the vicar and the ritual practices or remedies of the local fortune-teller could both be ascribed validity in this way. In urban Southwark the popular religious response was characterized by a defiance of many of the analytical categories frequently imposed by contemporary observers and historians. Orthodox and folk religion cannot be crudely juxtaposed as two separate spheres. Folk elements of belief operated, as David Clark suggests in his study of the Yorkshire fishing village of Staithes at the end of the nineteenth and beginning of the twentieth century, as part of unofficial aspects of doctrine, theology, and worship found within the church as well as outside it[26] while church-based religion in turn was appropriated into the symbolic structure of popular culture. John Rule highlights a similar pattern of interwoven religious idioms in Cornwall between 1800 and 1850.[27] He describes the convergence of popular Methodism with the indigenous beliefs of the

---

[25] S. C. Williams , 'Religious Belief and Popular Culture: A Study of the South London Borough of Southwark *c*.1880–1939' (Oxford University D.Phil. thesis, 1993), 38.

[26] D. Clark, *Between Pulpit and Pew: Folk Religion in a North Yorkshire Fishing Village* (1982), p. viii.

[27] J. Rule, 'Methodism, Popular Belief and Village Culture in Cornwall', in R. D. Storch (ed.), *Popular Culture and Custom in Nineteenth-Century England* (New York, 1982), 48–70.

people. Popular religion included a conception of Christian doctrine which, as he argues, was 'adapted and transformed as it moved from the church to the cottage'.[28] Village people, therefore, possessed a background of beliefs which were partly Christian and partly magic against which they sought to understand the realities of the human situation. As Clark argues, the religion through which the villagers made sense of their lives consisted of a combination of 'official' and 'folk' religion. Clark highlights the divergent traditions from which these two kinds of religiosity sprang but argues for their complex interconnection in the social setting into which the ordinary villager was born: 'The highly complex interconnections between official and folk religion reflect their symbiotic relationship'.[29]

Popular religion is more appropriately defined, therefore, as a generally shared understanding of religious meaning including both folk beliefs as well as formal and officially sanctioned practices and ideas, operating within a loosely bound interpretative community. These formed part of a particular value orientation or culture: a generalized and organized conception of nature, of man's place in it, of man's relation to man and of the desirable and non-desirable as they relate to man's environment and interpersonal relations.[30] They did so in a manner akin to the ways in which a community possesses a verbal repertoire[31] with a variety of linguistic codes or types of language. The inhabitants of the borough were exposed to a range of religious idioms, perspectives, or discourses which in combination constituted popular religion. The voice of the vicar can be described as one 'field of religious experience' as Lawrence Taylor argues in his study of south-west Donegal.[32] This church-based, official or orthodox religious discourse embodied a series of shared meanings, attitudes, and values through which a regime of truth about the world was structured and communicated. It involved a particular conception of nature and of the human world, of man's place in it and of his correct and incorrect behaviour towards his fellow man. It was distinguished by the prescription, regulation, and socialization of these values via the medium of specialized

[28] Ibid. 62.
[29] Ibid. 166.
[30] C. Kluckholme, 'Values and Value Orientation in the Theory of Action', in T. Parsons and E. Shils (eds.), *Towards A General Theory of Action* (New York, 1962), 388–433.
[31] In his study of socio-linguistics, *Socio-linguistics* (1974), Peter Trudgill has argued for the use of different linguistic varieties in different situations and for different purposes.
[32] L. J. Taylor, 'Languages of Belief', in M. Silverman and P. H. Gulliver (eds.), *Approaching the Past* (New York, 1992), 146.

institutions or orthodox doctrine. The church-based religious discourse, thus defined, may be equated with Robert Towler's and David Clark's description of 'official religion'. Both Towler and Clark use the term official religion to refer to all aspects of religious belief and practice which find a warrant in the formal teachings of any church, denomination, or sect.[33]

In contrast, magical remedies, rituals, and explanations which were passed down by word of mouth from one generation to the next may be seen as an alternative narrative or folk religious discourse. This included a variety of beliefs and in some cases a more overt concept of the supernatural. This discourse was far more eclectic and thematic than that of church-based religion. It was not systematic and the absence of any formal institutional base meant that it was subject to a greater degree of personal and local interpretation. None the less it remained a way of seeing and interpreting the world and of acting towards it in response.

These religious perspectives or discourses both formed part of the popular religious repertoire. At an event such as an infant baptism the two narratives could operate in conjunction with one another, not merely in terms of a crude opposition between the vicar and the participant but within a range of beliefs held by the single actor. For the participants, the two discourses were intermeshed. They may well have been able to employ an orthodox narrative to explain their motives in bringing a child forward for baptism. This was not merely adopted to placate or appeal to the vicar or the lady visitor on the doorstep, nor was it solely an instrument of *embourgeoisement*. The participants may have believed sincerely in the efficacy, the validity, and the importance of the content of that narrative, and yet at the same time they may also have acted and justified their behaviour as part of a folk discourse in which certain other expectations and assumptions were operating to constrain them to act in a certain way.

The dual operation of these two dimensions or languages of belief did not necessarily diminish the depth of each component part. Christian hymns, orthodox rites and symbols continued to hold an evocative power in Southwark in this period, while elements of folk belief had not been fully depersonalized nor had they degenerated into mere luck as some suggest.[34] Furthermore, this overlap of different discourses was not simply reserved for certain specific events such as the watch-night service

[33] Clark, *Between Pulpit and Pew* (1982), p. viii; R. Towler, *Homo Religiosus* (1974), 148.
[34] Cox, *The English Churches*, 94.

or the infant baptism; it also operated in popular definit.
meant to be truly religious, to sin, and to be moral.   ;hat it

By letting go of the instinct to view official and unofficial r.
monolithic and immutable entities and considering instead the as
related character of different patterns of belief, it is possible to esc.
from the often repeated misconception that popular religion is alway,
rural, primitive, and traditional as opposed to urban, civilized, and
modern. Instead, the dynamic role of popular forms of devotion which
encompassed both official and non-official religion, can be appreciated.

Furthermore, this approach allows popular religion to be defined as
primarily a cultural phenomenon in the Geertzian sense of a system
which gives meaning to the world.[35] This has the corresponding
advantage of releasing the notion of popular religion from too close an
association with ideas of class. Social historians of the nineteenth century
have tended to confuse symbolic communities, based on the creation
of cultural meaning, with more straightforward analyses of structural
communities based on social processes.[36] Communities do undoubtedly
possess both these components, but they each demand different interpretative approaches if they are to be adequately understood. On the one
hand one is dealing with the interpretation of symbolic meaning and on
the other with social structures. The mixing of these approaches can be
particularly problematic when one is seeking to decipher the role of
belief. In Southwark a symbolic or popular cultural community bound
by a common set of beliefs, values, and norms was apparent at the end
of the nineteenth century through to the Second World War. Religion
formed part of the symbolic system of meaning by which this community was constituted. The community was not simply the product
of structural processes determined by social and economic criteria: its
foundations lay in the expression and experience of a common world-
view. When religion is simply interpreted in structural terms on the basis
of class these essential phenomenological aspects tend to be overlooked
in the endeavour to establish the extent to which religion, along with the
structural group, has or has not withstood the onslaught of social
change. Religion tends thus to be typified, like the structural community
itself, as uniquely traditional, surviving only in the context of certain
pre-industrial social relationships and necessarily excluded from the
social forms of the modern exemplified by the impersonal, urban,

[35] C. Geertz, 'Religion as a Cultural System', in M. Banton (ed.), *Anthropological Approaches to the Study of Religion* (1966), 1–46.
[36] A. P. Cohen, *The Symbolic Construction of Community* (1992).

and classed-based social structures of industrial society. The
correlation of symbolic communities of this kind with the
ctural analysis of class prevents us from understanding the new,
ried, and complex ways in which religion continues to help establish
cultural meaning and identity in modern social situations.

Although this study of Southwark takes the non-elite and the poor as
its starting-point it does so simply to establish some kind of limit on
what would otherwise be an unrealistically huge undertaking. It is not
intended to imply that 'popular' should simply be equated with the
'working class'. This starting-point makes sense for the straightforward
reason that it is this social group around which the historiographical
debate has revolved since the days of Horace Mann, the Registrar-
General who constructed the report on the Religious Census of 1851.[37]
The report, which was not published until 1852, caused intense contemporary debate. It revealed not only that about 40 per cent of church-
goers in England attended non-Anglican churches but also that on the
day of the census only 7.26 million of the 17.92 million inhabitants of
England and Wales attended religious worship of any kind. The findings
focused attention on the religious condition of the working poor who
were blamed for these statistics. The connections which Mann made
between urban life, the working class, and irreligion remained the prevailing view throughout the nineteenth century and they have continued
to inform the assumptions of the twentieth-century historiographical
debate. The 'working classes' are treated here not monolithically but as a
group within which there was division based on belief, culture, and
world-view. Of those considered in Southwark, some identified themselves specifically with the church, employing the language of the
regenerate and the unregenerate, the believer and the unbeliever. Others
(although very few in Southwark) defined themselves in terms of an
ideological commitment to a creed of secularism. The 'popular religious
community' often defined itself both in opposition to those who
formally allied themselves with the institutional churches whether
through conversion, confirmation, or church membership and in opposition to secularism. In practice this meant disassociation from those
who failed to drink with the 'herd' at the local public house[38] or from
those who did not participate in the informal network of neighbourly

[37] H. Mann, 'Religious Census of 1851'. Results published in *Parliamentary Papers*,
1852–30, 89 (England and Wales), 1854, 59 (Scotland).

[38] R. Samuel, *East End Underworld: Chapters in the Life of Arthur Harding* (Oxford,
1986), 243.

support. This cultural community established its own definitions of who was bad and who was good, who was unChristian and who was genuinely religious, and these attributes were not strictly defined by class. As Patrick Collinson points out in his Ford Lectures on sixteenth-century protestantism, 'The friction between the godly and the ungodly could arise within and not necessarily between social classes'.[39] The criteria which separated them was one of world-view or culture while personal experiences and issues of gender and of age played their part alongside more general economic determinants. It is the boundary of this community which this study seeks to reconstruct.

In adopting this kind of method it becomes essential to draw participant definitions out of the historical material available and to consider the language itself as it reveals the cultural symbols used by individuals. It is often the difficulty of finding appropriate material through which to reconstruct popular religion which prevents the development of these lines of questioning. The challenge here is to discover, as the sociologist Victor Branford pointed out in 1914,

. . . some method of observing and recording what the French call *état d'âme*—the thoughts and emotions, the habits of mind and life of persons in their interior and ultimate relations with one another and with their surroundings. The sort of question this more intense study has to put before itself is how can we decipher and record people's ideals, their characteristic ideas and cultures and the images and symbols which habitually occupy their minds.[40]

This problem is all the more complicated as most of the material upon which we rely consists of the comment of middle-class observers who attributed a set of meanings to these beliefs on the basis of their own presuppositions. Charles Booth's *Life and Labour of the People of London*, completed in 1902, Sir Hubert Llewellyn Smith's *The New Survey of London Life and Labour* (1931), works such as *Across the Bridges* (1911)[41] written by the philanthropist Alexander Paterson, the annual reports, reminiscences, and writings of local churchmen, all consist primarily of the expression of the opinions of others on the beliefs of the working

---

[39] P. Collinson, *The Religion of the Protestants: The Church in English Society* (Oxford, 1979), 193.

[40] V. Branford, *Interpretations and Forecasts: A Study of the Survivals and Tendencies of Contemporary Society* (1914), 72.

[41] See also C. M. Davies, *Unorthodox London* (1874) and *Orthodox London* (1873), J. E. Ritchie, *Days and Nights in London* (1880) and E. J. Orford, *The Book of Walworth* (1925). Local newspapers such as the *Southwark Annual*, the *South London Chronicle*, the *Southwark Recorder*, the *South London Press*, the *Daily Graphic* and the *Bermondsey and Rotherhithe Advertiser* also provide an additional source of observation and opinion.

16   *Religious Belief and Popular Culture*

classes. Booth's *Life and Labour* provides a particularly rich example of these problems. This work was intended as a comprehensive survey of the industrial and social status of the population of London. The first series—'Poverty' (first published in 1898)—consisted of a study of the social conditions of the inhabitants of every household in London. Evidence was drawn from the records of school board officers and checked against police records, poor law statistics, and the personal observations of the investigators. The second series—'Industry' (first published in 1900)—attempted to connect the conditions of life with the occupations of the people. It consisted of a review of work trade by trade, an enumeration of the age and gender of the employed, and a description of the social conditions of the employees. Having completed the 'Poverty' and 'Industry' series Booth undertook a survey of the 'Religious Influences' acting on the lives of the inhabitants of the capital. This appeared in 1902 and consisted of an appraisal of the effects of the agencies which sought to influence the people of London, most notably the churches. The fourth volume on the 'Religious Influences' gives detailed descriptions of the Southwark area and the summary given in volume vii included conclusions based, in part, on the evidence drawn from interviews with churchmen in the area.

Booth's inquiry provides a valuable corrective to the statistical approaches of Richard Mudie-Smith[42] and Robertson Nicoll.[43] It offers a glimpse of the wider social impact and the influence of religion on the people, but it does so by relying purely on the official perspectives of churchmen and philanthropists. Booth's staff of five interviewed the head of every religious and social agency in London. Their opinions were then weighed against a visit to the church and the comments of other church leaders. There was no attempt, however, to include the opinions of the beneficiaries of these religious institutions. The product was a characterization of the religious beliefs of the people based on descriptions selected and mediated by Booth's personal value criteria. The 'people' are characterized as, above all, indifferent to religion. The descriptive terms, 'indifferent', 'vague', 'ignorant' and 'uncommitted' are used throughout the third series, to describe the beliefs of the less articulate sections of the population in relation to a standard of orthodoxy arising from the perspective of the institutional churches. These terms are also highly generalized. Booth specifically used the widest possible variety of opinion in order to identify the extraordinary

---

[42] R. Mudie-Smith, *The Religious Life of London* (1904).
[43] *The Religious Census of London*, reprinted from the *British Weekly* (1888).

and to define the consensus. His concern was to escape from the sensationalism and subjectivity of previous attempts to analyse social behaviour, but the third series presented particular problems. The lack of equivalent sources to the records of relieving officers and school-board visitors which were used in the first and second series rendered the application of a statistical yardstick impossible. Booth had, therefore, to rely on second-hand observation and impression, the evaluation and selection of which was subject to his personal discretion. He did not lay out a systematic methodological foundation for the 'Religious Influences' and the result was a concentration upon oversimplified stereotypes which Robertson Nicholl described as 'Religious gossip served up in a miscellaneous manner'.[44]

This problem was fuelled further by Booth's reliance on characterizations of the male as representative of the working people as a whole. Booth himself argued that the habits of the home were stronger than the precepts of the school and the influence of the churches but he did not examine the female dimension of religiosity in any detail. His assumption was that accounts of male attitudes and opinions were sufficient to reflect adequately the outlook of the social group as a whole. The divergent material, social, and cultural worlds of contemporary males and females makes such neglect peculiarly problematic[45] as does the fact that women played a key role as conduits of belief and culture in working-class homes.[46]

Yet despite these problems, *Life and Labour* should not be laid to one side as an historical source.[47] The beliefs described, often in a derogatory and dismissive manner, can be reinterpreted and understood through a perspective other than that of Booth and of those professionally involved in equating religion simply with the institutional structures of which

---

[44] *British Weekly*, 2 Apr. 1903.

[45] The separation of the male and female environments is highlighted by Ellen Ross, 'Survival Networks: Women's Neighbourhood Sharing in London before World War I', *History Workshop*, 15 (1983), 4–28; 'Fierce Questions, Angry Taunts: Married Life in Working-Class London 1870–1914', *Feminist Studies*, 8 (1982), 575–602.

[46] E. Roberts, *Working-Class Barrow and Lancaster 1890–1930* (Lancaster, 1976); *A Woman's Place; an Oral History of Working-Class Women 1890–1940* (Oxford, 1984); 'The Working-Class Extended Family: Functions and Attitudes, 1890–1940', *Oral History Journal*, 12 (1984); and *Women and Families: An Oral History 1940–1970* (Oxford, 1995); see also Bourke, *Working-Class Cultures in Britain, 1890–1960* and C. Chinn, *And They Worked all Their Lives: Women and the Urban Poor in England 1880–1990* (Manchester, 1988).

[47] R. O'Day and D. Englander have recently argued in favour of the value of the inquiry as an historical source in *Mr. Charles Booth's Inquiry: Life and Labour of the People of London Reconsidered* (1993).

they were a part. To do so two primary methods are used in this study. The first is to adopt a strategy of cross-verifying the descriptions of socio-religious observers such as Booth against a series of impressions drawn from a wide range of fragmentary material; the second is to examine the cultural symbols used by individuals to interpret meaning in both written and spoken language. The endeavour is, as Lucien Febvre wrote,

... to make mute things talk, to make them say things which of themselves they do not say, or about the societies that produced them, in order to build up between them the vast network of mutually supporting relationships which make up for the absence of the written document.[48]

Oral history, autobiographies, popular ephemera, street literature, local newspapers, music-hall songs, folklore, and the manuscripts of the original Booth Collection are drawn alongside socio-religious comment such as Booth's. The Booth manuscript material, for example, containing the original lists, letters, maps, and interview notebooks reveals Booth's impressions and descriptions as well as the structure and the intention of the questioning in individual interviews. It allows the quotations contained in the published volumes of *Life and Labour* to be attributed and located within the broader context of the interview rather than merely within Booth's argument. Much of this material counterbalances, challenges, and elaborates on the material found in the published editions. By considering his comments in the light of a range of fragmentary evidence, the points at which his opinions are inappropriate to the criteria of religiosity and meaning employed within popular culture are revealed and their validity as characterizations of the beliefs of non-church-attending sections of the population can be assessed. The perspectives of the actors are thus able to elucidate or even contradict impressions given elsewhere.

Oral history played a particularly important part in this process. Interviewing allowed a centralizing of participant accounts of behaviour and belief while the twenty-nine interviews carried out in Southwark were specifically directed towards exploring the language, symbolism, and imagery employed among those on the edge of church-based culture and to communicate their experience of life.[49] Religious historians have tended to use oral history to support studies of the institutional church

---

[48] P. Burke (ed.), *Lucien Febvre—A New Kind of History* (1975), 34.

[49] See Luisa Passerini's vindication of the use of oral history in this way in 'Work, Ideology and Consensus under Italian Fascism', *History Workshop*, 8 (1979), 82–108.

and as a tool with which to extract additional factual information on such issues as church attendance.[50] It is all too easy to go into an interview and raise topics in a way which suggests that one merely wishes to hear what the interviewee thought about formal church services and how frequently they attended them. This has its place of course, and there is no doubt that the perspective given by oral material allows a glimpse of an otherwise hidden life. Yet, the sense of abundance which one feels when one begins to work with the oral source, can lead to a preoccupation with the detailed reconstruction of everyday life, where thick description becomes the sole life-blood of research. This approach can produce a naïve realism, that goes to the interview seeking only the reality content of the oral text and neglects to consider the more fundamental issue of what that text reveals about the symbols and images through which reality is communicated. If this deposit of historical truth is all we seek in the oral testimony then we are likely to spend much of our time separating the factual core from the impediments of rhetorical excess, political bias, or personal hindsight, while crucial issues of factual reliability and the representativeness of the source will present major obstacles. However, when the focus of the endeavour becomes the way in which memory is constructed and the manner of the telling is treated as equally important as that which is told, then the way is opened for the source to yield its unique value, which lies in the first instance in its expression of culture.

Social historians using oral history have been moving in this direction for some time now. The approach has been pioneered in Italy by Luisa Passerini and Alessandro Portelli and recently publicized more widely in Raphael Samuel and Paul Thompson's book *The Myths we Live By* (1990). James Fentress and Chris Wickham in their excellent book *The Social Memory: New Perspectives on the Past* (1992) make 1960s oral history their chief target of attack. They challenge the methodological naïvety of the early work of Paul Thompson and Jan Vansina in his book, *The Oral Tradition as History* (1985), arguing that social memory is least reliable at the level of information, but most informative when used to consider shared meanings and remembered images. They argue that even at a stylistic level the devices used to make the narration of a story memorable and which may apparently vouch for its reliability, may

---

[50] This point is made by Hugh McLeod in his article, 'New Perspectives on Victorian Class Religion: The Oral Evidence', *Oral History*, 14 (1986), 31–50, where he argues that oral history may be used as a means of exploring personal and private dimensions of religious belief.

at the same time serve the function of detaching the account from its historical context. Similarly, Lusia Passerini argues that,

The subjective dimension does not allow a direct reconstruction of the past, but it links past and present in a combination which is loaded with symbolic significance. When the oral sources have been placed in a proper framework they are highly relevant to historical analysis. These testimonies are first and foremost statements of cultural identity in which memory continually adapts received traditions to present circumstances.[51]

Psychological research supports this approach. It suggests that the memory itself falsifies distinctions based on truth and untruth, for what the memory retains are not specific data but concepts. Psychologists such as Alan Baddeley, for example, argue that people remember in terms of their previous assumptions and beliefs and that subjects will try to make sense of a given incident by recalling their feelings and inter-pretations rather than what they actually and literally observed.[52]

Religious history has much to learn from these approaches. In particular, oral history offers a medium for assessing the language in which social meaning is created which is, as yet, under-exploited as a means of understanding religious belief. The free-ranging life history interviews carried out in Southwark allowed religion to emerge (or not emerge, as the case might be) within a structure dictated by the inter-viewee and as part of a discussion of a wide range of topics. In this way the participants themselves were given room to establish the contours of what they considered to be religious, and the associations, assumptions, and the types of language used to structure popular belief systems could be analysed. A distinct language was identified in which beliefs were formulated and conveyed, which was common to many, although not all, of those interviewed. The parameters of the cultural group could be discerned on the basis of this common formulation or conventionaliza-tion of belief.[53] Assessing the language in which social memory is created also provides a medium through which to consider varieties in cultural

---

[51] L. Passerini, *Fascism in Popular Memory: The Cultural Experience of the Turin Working Class* (Cambridge, 1987), 18.

[52] A. Baddeley, 'The Limitations of Human Memory', in L. Moss and H. Goldstein (eds.), *The Recall Method in the Social Sciences* (1979), 4–35.

[53] i.e. on the basis of social memory as defined by J. Fentress and C. Wickham, *The Social Memory: New Perspectives on the Past* (Oxford, 1992), *passim*. Fentress and Wickham give a valuable description of the character and construction of social memory but their book does not examine in detail the conventionalization of memory as it relates to the dimension of belief nor do they develop the distinction between male and female patterns of recollection and narration.

symbolism, not only between individuals and groups but also between genders.

The connections made between events, beliefs, symbols, and values, for example, provide insight into the role of particular memories. Certain events in an individual's life were often formative in establishing or changing a particular pattern of belief. In a number of the interviews memories of specific incidents led on to the recollection of particular beliefs. An act of hypocrisy on the part of a vicar, for example, could engender a specific statement of unbelief which was anchored in the memory with a particular moment in time. One interviewee's recollection of a limelight concert precipitated a discussion of her belief in the person of Christ. Her description of a particularly vivid slide show led on to a description of how she and her sisters returned home to catch a glimpse of what they believed to be the figure of Jesus standing in their bedroom. The discussion then continued as Mrs Luke described the powerful sense of fear which she associated with a belief in the immanence of Jesus. Her discussion of this belief was punctuated by sharp recollections of the bruises incurred when she made a rapid descent from the bedroom on that particular evening.[54] Memories of Sunday school frequently triggered memories of specific hymns which in turn evoked a sense of nostalgia associated with the home and particularly with the mother. Such associations were informative when considering the place of religious ideas within the mental framework of the interviewees. The connections made between events, beliefs, symbols, and values are vital to the reconstruction of the role and impact of the memories which are recorded. The subtleties of these kinds of evidence can be overlooked in the examination of other types of source material. As David Vincent argued in the case of autobiographical material, these sources have the potential to tell us not merely what happened but the impact of an event upon an actor in the past.[55]

Likewise this kind of interview gave access to the ephemeral world of the joke, the rumour, and gossip which are valuable in revealing the attitudes of the observed.[56] A community's verdict on the local churchman or on a regular church attender in a local street could be gleaned from an incidental comment, a throw-away remark, or an anecdote included in the course of recollection. Stan Hall, the son of a bus con-

---

[54] SCW, Int. 6.

[55] D. Vincent, *Bread, Knowledge and Freedom: A Study of Nineteenth Century Working Class Autobiography* (1981), 6.

[56] G. E. Evans, *Where Beards Wag All: The Relevance of the Oral Tradition* (1970), 22–3.

ductor, who was born near the Elephant and Castle in 1901, recalled the Metropolitan Tabernacle in Southwark in relation to the rumour which circulated in the Borough concerning the hand print of Jesus which was believed to be impressed on the wall in blood. The recollection of the chapel's impressive façade was given in relation to the fact that local boys were afraid to play near it in case the rumour proved true.[57] Specific memories can in this way be reconstructed within an emotional and personal context and in relation to both the impact felt and the role which incidents play within an individual's understanding of the past.

By bringing the perspective of the actor to bear upon the types of activity observed and the meanings attributed to those acts by the observer, the oral testimony can reveal, for example, the reasons given for non-church attendance within popular culture and the justification adopted for having one's child baptized or sending one's children to Sunday school and participating in prayer and hymn singing at the local mothers' meeting. In so doing it can demonstrate the gap which existed between the perspective of the socio-religious observers and the observed.

In addition, the evidence permits a reconstruction of the rich oral folk culture which persisted within the urban community in this period; as Bernice Martin calls it, 'the ritualised repetition of wisdom in oral form'.[58] Verbal folk wisdom of this kind formed a framework of assumption and belief underlying the use of a range of folk artefacts found in the Lovett Folklore Collection. The meaning and the distribution of the artefacts were gleaned from the autobiographies and oral testimonies. Some of the charms, mascots, rituals, and practices which the folklorist Edward Lovett (1852–1933) collected and deposited at the Cuming Museum in Southwark were mentioned in passing by interviewees or were tucked in as incidental asides in written reminiscences. The use of coral necklaces as a charm and cure for minor throat complaints was corroborated, for example, by a number of interviewees, as were the sayings and rituals to which Lovett refers in his articles and books. Mentioning specific artefacts such as these often stimulated recollection on themes which might otherwise have lain dormant and such comparative techniques shed light on rich seams of folklore, folk custom, and superstition.

Oral testimonies thus provided an alternative form of evidence in which interpretative and phenomenological dimensions are stressed.

[57] SLSL, A. S. Hall, 'Reminiscences' (1988), 5.
[58] B. Martin, *The Sociology of Contemporary Cultural Change* (Oxford, 1981), 65.

When used together with the folklore, ephemera, and autobiographies, this material can challenge simplistic descriptions of the irreligion and indifference of infrequent church attenders as caricatured by Booth. It demonstrated the vibrant and distinctive character of an alternative form of religious expression which drew on church-based religious discourse in a selective and conditional manner. Furthermore, when used alongside the Lovett Folklore material, the oral evidence qualifies a crude association between popular religion and orthodox religiosity by highlighting the folk discourse which remained in the modern urban environment.

Whilst stressing the character of the language through which beliefs, ideas, and attitudes are expressed, this study also seeks to relate this analysis, as far as possible, to the local historical context and to avoid the dangers of what has been called 'the semiotic dissolution of history'.[59] The social milieu is considered alongside the content, form, and expression of beliefs without suggesting that an account of the social context explains why the beliefs were held. Thus the analysis of religion to follow begins with a consideration of the Metropolitan Borough of Southwark.

---

[59] See e.g. D. Thompson, 'Languages of Class', *Society for the Study of Labour History Bulletin*, 52 (1987), 54–7; J. R. Cronin, 'Language, Politics and the Critique of Social History: Languages of Class', *Journal of Social History*, 20 (1986–7), 177–84; J. Epstein, 'Understanding the Cap of Liberty: Symbolic Practice and Social Conflict in Early Nineteenth Century England', *Past and Present*, 122 (1989), 75–118. See in addition, P. Trudghill, *Sociolinguistics* (1974), 32 and G. M. Spiegel, 'History, Historicism and the Social Logic of the Text in the Middle Ages', *Speculum*, 65 (1990), 59–87.

2

The Metropolitan Borough of Southwark

The characteristics for which Southwark was famed during the nineteenth century were low life, criminality, and heathenism. The social environment of the borough was described by James Greenwood in the late 1860s as the 'very nest and nursery of crime . . . Here are to be found the lowest of the low class of beer shops in London and probably in the world, the acknowledged haunts of "smashers", burglars, thieves and forgers. There is hardly a grade of crime the chief representatives of which may not be met among the purlieus of the Borough.'[1] Hollingshead wrote of the area in similar tones as: 'A vast and melancholy property . . . lighted up at intervals with special markets of industry or budding into short patches of honest trade, sinking every now and then into dark acres of crime and covered everywhere with the vilest sores of prostitution'[2]

By the time Charles Booth finally published *Life and Labour* in 1902, Southwark was known as 'a maze of small streets and courts crowded in many parts with a low-living population'.[3] By this date, however, contrary to the claims of some commentators,[4] Southwark was by no means an anonymous place. It contained a series of vibrant and homogeneous subcultures with their own self-defined communal traditions which remained relatively stable until the 1950s.

The Metropolitan Borough was formed in 1900 from the amalgamation of the civil parishes of St Saviour's Southwark, St George's, Christ Church, and St Mary Newington. It was bounded on the north by the River Thames, upon which the area remained economically dependent, and it included the southern approaches to Blackfriars, Southwark, and

---

[1] J. Greenwood, *The Seven Curses of London*, ed. J. Richards (Oxford, 1981), 111.

[2] J. Hollingshead, *Ragged London* (1861), 166.

[3] C. Booth, *Life and Labour* (1902), 'Religious Influences', iv. 7.

[4] See, in particular, W. Besant, *South London* (1899), 319; Booth, *Life and Labour* (1902), 'Poverty', i. 272.

London Bridges, by which it was connected with the City of London. On the west was the Borough of Lambeth, the irregular boundary line passing near St George's Circus and skirting Kennington Park. On the south lay the Borough of Camberwell and on the east the Borough of Bermondsey. The northern part of the borough was crossed by a network of wide thoroughfares, such as Blackfriars Road, Southwark Bridge Road, Borough High Street, St George's Road, and Great Dover Street, which carried the cross-river traffic to the southern centres. Most of these roads met at St George's Circus or at the Elephant and Castle.

The population of the civil parishes at the time of amalgamation was somewhere near its peak of 202,479.[5] This had risen from 173,900 in 1861[6] and it had fallen again by 1931 to 171,695.[7] The area had experienced rapid urban development during the first half of the nineteenth century. The 1851 Post Office Directory Maps show the concentration of urban life which clustered around the river and provided the scene for the squalid courts and alleys described by Charles Dickens in *Oliver Twist* (1837), by Greenwood, and by Hollingshead. Much of the hinterland at this date, however, was still relatively free of urban development. Open farmland, for example, was found beside stretches of the New Kent Road and near the Grand Surrey Canal rolling south to the communities of Camberwell and Peckham. Railway development during the latter half of the century extended the scope of urbanization further south and increased overcrowding in sections of northern Southwark.

Such development overlay a considerable degree of continuity in terms of the basic historic character of the area. Throughout this period the borough remained principally a residential area with the exception of a thin strip of industrial and commercial concentration on the immediate banks of the Thames. Above all else it continued to form an entrance and exit to and from the metropolis, relying heavily for economic vitality on the river and the large industries which clung to its banks. Seventeenth- and eighteenth-century cottages along with the terraces, flats, and tenement blocks of the late nineteenth century wove their way in among local industries and warehouses such as the cart and wheel works near Harrow Street, the essences and flavourings factory on Southwark Street, and Heywood Brothers Architectural Iron-Mongers in Union Street. The wharves and warehouses of the riverside gave way to printing manufacturers, stationers, engineering works, and brewers,

---

[5] *Census for England and Wales 1901, County of London* (1902), Table ix.
[6] Ibid.
[7] *Census for England and Wales 1931, County of London* (1937), untabulated.

which provided employment for a large percentage of males at the turn of the century and an increasing number of females during the First World War and interwar period.[8] The Barclay and Perkins Brewery was situated in the heart of the borough, while Courages lay over the border in Bermondsey near Tower Bridge. The leather factories on the edge of Southwark and Bermondsey and the food-processing industries in Bermondsey such as Sarson's Vinegar and Cross and Blackwell formed similar economic focal points in the area. Hat making employed a number of people in the Blackfriars Road area, as well as in Bermondsey, while Borough High Street was dominated by the offices of hop traders and brewery middlemen as well as commercial establishments. Both the 1911 and the 1921 censuses show the large number of charwomen and office cleaners who lived throughout the borough and crossed the river each day to take up their employment in the City.[9] Among them were the mothers of Mrs Scott from Villa Street, Walworth[10] and of D. M. Doniton, born in 1909 in the north of the borough. Mrs Doniton describes in her reminiscence how her mother would rise each day at five o'clock to clean the offices on Borough High Street and in the City in order to support her family of eleven while her husband, a sailor, was away at sea.[11] Further south in the borough some factories were found on the banks of the Grand Surrey Canal. These had accompanied the development of the canal between 1801 and 1822. The traditional local industries of the more outlying parts of Southwark, such as fish-curing in Walworth, continued undisturbed until the interwar period.

The area to the south of the Elephant and Castle could claim more confidently to be predominantly residential. In these areas street trading was the overriding occupation of the inhabitants. Yet by 1921 more than twice the number of males enumerated in the Metropolitan Borough of Southwark worked outside the area. A similar pattern, if not so extreme, was apparent among female workers. By 1901 Booth wrote that

The bulk of the workers travel at any rate to and often across the river to their daily task. Morning and evening see the bridges crowded with those who pass their working day in London so much so that it is difficult to cross at all against the stream which sets northwards in the morning and southwards at night. It is so with the casual no less than with the regular work.[12]

[8] *Census for England and Wales 1901, County of London* (1902), Table xxxv.

[9] *Census for England and Wales, County of London 1911* (1914), Table xxiii; *Census for England and Wales, County of London 1921* (1922), Table xviii.

[10] SCW, Int. 19.

[11] Brunel University, Burnett Collection, D. M. Doniton, 'Reminiscences', n.d., n.p.

[12] Booth, *Life and Labour* (1902), 'Poverty', i. 276–7.

Mr Wheeler was an example of this. He lived with his family in Castle Street, one of the courts off Borough High Street. He worked as a fish-curer and haddock-smoker in Billingsgate. His daughter, Margaret, recalls in her reminiscence how an old man by the name of Dan Paton awoke her father early each morning in time to set off at dawn on the journey over the river and towards the City to work.[13] Similarly, Emma Reynolds, born in Red Cross Street in 1911, described how her father would rise each morning at five o'clock to take up his employment as a butcher in Battersea,[14] and Mrs Scott recalled how her father would cross the river each day from Walworth to work as a compositor in the City.[15]

Casual workers who looked to the metropolis for employment or who sought it at the riverside could not live beyond walking distance from the wharf or factory, or from the bridge which they had to cross each day.[16] The luxury of the tram or railway fare was one which few could afford before the First World War. A man employed irregularly at the docks and his wife in office cleaning, to cite a frequent example, would have had to work hours which made residence in Southwark inevitable. So far as this type of citizen was concerned, the 'dormitory suburb solution' was unavailable.[17] The result was the concentration of a particular economic and social culture which radiated out from the river and which was marked above all by the homogeneity of its poverty and over-crowding: 'There is a deplorably low level in all parts which lie near the sources of work and this low level tends to perpetuate itself, for no sooner does anyone rise and get a bit decent than he may be expected to move out to Clapham or elsewhere'.[18]

The demolition of courts and alleys as a result of railway and ware-house development added to the poverty and isolation of these areas and extended their scope as displaced populations spread south to areas such as Walworth. When the demolition of a street took place, groups of families tended to move together to another area, thus recreating the distinct social and cultural conditions elsewhere in the borough.

These trends account for the fall in population in the northern parts of the borough throughout the period 1860–1939. The wards of Christ Church, St George-the-Martyr, St Michael and St John all experienced

[13] SLSL, M. Fish, 'Reminiscences of Southwark' (1985), 8.
[14] SCW, Int. 4.
[15] SCW, Int. 19.
[16] Booth, *Life and Labour* (1902), 'Poverty', i. 277.
[17] T. Barclay and T. Perry, *Report and Survey of Housing Conditions in the Metropolitan Borough of Southwark* (1929), 8.
[18] Booth, *Life and Labour* (1902), 'Poverty', i. 277.

falls in population between 1911 and 1921, while the southern wards remained fairly constant.[19] Similarly, Christ Church and St Saviour saw a sharp fall in population between 1891 and 1901, while Newington and St George-the-Martyr saw an increase,[20] thus accelerating a more gradual pattern that had started in these areas in the 1850s.

By the 1930s, therefore, old courts and alleys in the north were hemmed in by industrial and railway development. They continued to exhibit a distinct social character for most of the period, which was merely re-emphasized by their growing isolation. Redevelopment tended to extend their boundaries to residential areas south of St George's Road, the Elephant and Castle, and the Newington Causeway; while the relentless depopulation of the urban middle class, along with wealthier sections of the working class, continued to reinforce the character of these areas.

Here old local attachments continued to predominate even after the amalgamation of the civil parishes into a single metropolitan borough in 1900. The process of amalgamation itself precipitated a fierce parochial response throughout the civil parishes. The *Southwark Annual* claimed that 'only on special occasions would the parochial Jews have dealings with the despised Samaritans'.[21] Among the administrative élite this narrow parochialism gradually gave way to a new public spirit which was heralded by the *Annual* as a sign of genuine progress: 'the public weal eventually predominated over private desires'.[22] But among the inhabitants of Southwark, in general, parochialism remained. As Sir Hubert Llewellyn Smith pointed out in 1931, local attachments were not so much towards the borough, which was purely an administrative entity, as towards the social centre of a district, usually much smaller and often possessing an old local name.[23]

In Southwark these attachments centred on three principal focuses: first, the area in the north around Borough High Street, historically known as the Borough; secondly, the Elephant and Castle; and thirdly, the eastern part of Walworth in the immediate vicinity of the East Street Market. Like the neighbourhoods described by Donald McKelvie in his study of urban Bradford in the late 1950s and 1960s, these centres operated as 'ingrown communities which over a long period of time

[19] *Census for England and Wales 1911*, Table xxx and *1921*, Table, xviii.
[20] *Census for England and Wales 1901* (1902), Table ix.
[21] The *Southwark Annual* (1902), 39.
[22] Ibid.
[23] H. Llewellyn Smith, *The New Survey of London Life and Labour* (1931), vi. 241.

have become an idea in the minds of the successive generations which have lived in them, quite as much as a physical entity occupying a number of streets or lanes or squares'.[24]

The area known as the 'Borough' consisted, so far as it is possible to define its rough boundary lines, of the area immediately surrounding Borough High Street extending as far south as Borough Road and Union Road. This included most of St George-the-Martyr parish and much of the ancient Trinity ward in Newington. It was usually taken to include the area to the west of Borough High Street about as far as Southwark Bridge Road. Its focal point was the High Street itself.[25] Booth argued in 1902 that the parish of St Saviour's which covered the northern part of the borough was the poorest in the whole of South London.[26] Of the 33,000 inhabitants living between Blackfriars Bridge and London Bridge, 68 per cent belonged to Booth's category of 'the poor'.[27]

Poverty combined with a high rate of overcrowding. In 1905 the parish of St George-the-Martyr had a population density of 212 people per acre, a death rate of 30 per 1,000, and an infant mortality rate of over 200 per 1,000.[28] The mean annual death rate remained high throughout the period: 13.8 per cent in 1931, the third highest figure of all the boroughs examined in *The New Survey of London Life and Labour* (1931),[29] although the infant mortality rate became indistinguishable from those of the other boroughs in later decades.[30] The lack of public open space, a mere 20 acres per 1,000 inhabitants in 1931,[31] aggravated this problem and elevated the importance of church gardens and graveyards as well as the public houses as recreational focuses in the area.

This population was described as the 'despair of those who work amongst it'.[32] It consisted mainly of poor, rough waterside labourers and market porters mostly of irregular employment, including 'thieves and

[24] D. McKelvie, 'Aspects of Oral Tradition and Belief in an Industrial Region', *Folklife*, 1 (1963), 78.
[25] The phrase 'the Borough' was used originally as a nickname for Borough High Street.
[26] Booth, *Life and Labour* (1902), 'Poverty', i. 279.
[27] Booth, *Life and Labour* (1902), 'Poverty', ii. 31.
[28] Dr MacNamara, 'The Physical Condition of the People', in W. T. Stead (ed.), *Coming Men on Coming Questions* (1905), iii. 7.
[29] Llewellyn Smith, *The New Survey of London Life and Labour* (1931), vi. 400.
[30] Ibid.
[31] Ibid. 399.
[32] Booth, *Life and Labour* (1902), 'Poverty', i. 279.

bullies who live on the earnings of prostitutes',[33] and whom the London City Missionary for the Borough Market area described as 'lifted up today and down again tomorrow'.[34]

There is in this part a great concentration of evil living and low conditions of life that strikes the observer and leads almost irresistibly to sensational statements. It contains a number of courts and small streets which for vice, poverty and crowd-ing are unrivalled in London and as an aggregate area of low life form perhaps the most serious blot to be found on our map.[35]

Norman James, who grew up in the heart of this area in Union Street in 1921, described the inhabitants of his street as 'most of them burglars and wanted people'.[36]

The character of this area remained basically unchanged throughout the period. Llewellyn Smith cited Collinson Street and Scovell Road, Melcote Street and Little Suffolk Street, between Blackfriars Road and Borough High Street,[37] as areas of particular poverty and overcrowding. These formed a network of small alleys and streets, which were noted by a number of writers not only for their appalling condition but also for their communal character. Most of the inhabitants were indigenous south Londoners rather than immigrants from abroad or from rural or surrounding areas.[38] The census material suggests that an increasing number of males and females enumerated in the borough had been born in London. In 1881, 69.8 per cent had been born in London, 29 per cent elsewhere in the United Kingdom, and only 1.2 per cent abroad.[39] In 1911, 80.4 per cent of those enumerated in Southwark had been born in London and only 18.2 per cent in the rest of the UK, and 1.4 per cent abroad.[40] And in 1921, 83.2 per cent had been born in London, 15.2 per cent elsewhere in the UK, and 1.3 per cent abroad, compared to 70.7 per cent, 24.9 per cent, and 4.4 per cent for the county of London as a whole.[41] The predominantly English character of the area was a feature which struck C. F. Garbett, the Bishop of Southwark from 1919 to 1932, when he described it in 1931,[42] while Booth's description of the book-

[33] Booth, *Life and Labour* (1902), 'Religious Influences', iv. 9.
[34] LSE, Booth Collection, B270, 73.
[35] Booth, *Life and Labour* (1902), 'Religious Influences', iv. 7–8.
[36] SCW, Int. 16.
[37] These streets are among those highlighted on the map.
[38] Booth, *Life and Labour* (1902), 'Religious Influences', iv. 8.
[39] *Census for England and Wales, County of London 1881* (1882), Table vi.
[40] *Census for England and Wales, County of London 1911* (1914), Table xxx.
[41] *Census for England and Wales, County of London 1921* (1922), Table xxi.
[42] C. F. Garbett, *In the Heart of South London* (1931), 1–8.

binding, paper, and printing industry as the most 'essential of London occupations'[43] underlines the indigenous character of Southwark, in which stationery works were concentrated.

Southwark, unlike other parts of London, lacked strong immigrant communities. In 1901 a mere 610 male European immigrants were found in the area and half that number of females, while those from the rest of the world did not total more than 100. This figure is surprisingly low when compared to areas such as Stepney.[44] Similarly, Southwark did not possess a distinct Irish community like its neighbour Bermondsey. Although by 1911 nearly 2,000 males and females had emigrated from Ireland to Southwark, they were for the most part integrated within the local community. By this date very few of Southwark's Irish inhabitants had actually been born in Ireland. Of a total male population of 95,532 and 96,375 females, 75,428 of the males had been born in London and 76,810 of the females; and in 1921, of the 89,653 males enumerated in Southwark, 85,944 had been born in England and predominantly in London and only 575 had come from Ireland; of the 94,751 females, 91,338 had been born in England and 602 in Ireland.[45] The Irish in Southwark saw themselves, like the rest of the local population, as cockneys. Even in Red Cross Street, the area which housed most of the Irish population, Emma Reynolds, a former resident, claimed that the overwhelming character of her street was certainly Catholic but not really Irish. The inhabitants, she argued, were above all cockneys:[46] 'I wouldn't say we had so many Irish down there, we was all bred and born down there'.[47] Norman James, who grew up in nearby Union Street, argued: 'they're all cockneys, let's get it right, cockney area, all cockneys'.[48] He pointed out that the Borough Market consisted largely of stalls run by local Southwark families who had lived in the area for a number of generations.[49] James's own parents had been born in the Old Kent Road and his grandparents not far away in Deptford.[50]

The indigenous character of the area combined with a strong familial and communal focus. When asked if the inhabitants of his area did their

---

[43] Booth, *Life and Labour* (1902), 'Industry', v. 28.

[44] *Census for England and Wales, County of London 1901* (1902), Table xxxvii.

[45] *Census for England and Wales, County of London 1921* (1922), Table xxi.

[46] SCW, Int. 4.

[47] Ibid.

[48] SCW, Int. 16.

[49] Cf. M. Young and P. Wilmott, *Family and Kinship in East London* (1957). They argue that in the markets and in printing the right to family succession was formally acknowledged (p. 79)

[50] SCW, Int. 16.

shopping in Bermondsey New Road the Revd W. H. Longsdon, the Vicar of St Michael's Church, Lant Street from 1893 to 1906, replied, 'It is the other side of Borough High Street and therefore a world away, we are very local in our habits and many of the parishioners are old inhabitants'.[51]

In the area slightly to the east of St George-the-Martyr parish church one family in particular could trace the family back several generations, all of whom had lived in the area;[52] while many of the inhabitants of a single street were connected by cousinship and by marriage.[53] Slightly further south in Massinger Street, just off the Old Kent Road, Lilian Tims described how her mother's three sisters and one brother all lived with their respective families in the same street along with their parents who had also been born in the area.[54] A vital network of economic and social support based on these working-class kinship groups persisted in urban communities,[55] which supports the claims made by Michael Young and Peter Wilmott in their study of family and kinship in East London.[56] Far from having been destroyed by the industrial revolution, the extended family survived as a unit, not merely of social and economic utility, as Michael Anderson argues,[57] but as a web of affective familial bonds of duty, mutuality, love, and loyalty.[58] In the 'Religious Influences' Booth gave a detailed description of Moss Alley, a narrow and badly ventilated street which gave way at one end to Bankside, and of St Margaret's Court which was situated between Red Cross Street and Borough High Street, 'where', he said, 'in some places there is almost village life'.[59] As in Bethnal Green, 'The one time villages which have elsewhere been physically submerged and their boundaries obliterated . . . live on in people's minds'.[60]

Similarly, St Margaret's Court consisted of two passages with antiquated houses and cottages off them.[61] These formed a secluded and highly individual sub-community within the network of similar courts

[51] LSE, Booth Collection, B269, 69.

[52] Booth, *Life and Labour* (1902), 'Poverty', i. 280.

[53] Ibid.

[54] SCW, Int. 23.

[55] Cf. E. Roberts, *A Woman's Place: An Oral History of Working Class Women 1890–1940* (1984).

[56] Young and Wilmott, *Family and Kinship, passim*.

[57] M. Anderson, *Family Structure in Nineteenth-Century Lancashire* (Cambridge, 1971).

[58] Cf. E. Roberts, 'The Working-Class Extended Family: Functions and Attitudes, 1890–1940', *Oral History Journal*, 12 (1984), 48–55.

[59] Booth, *Life and Labour* (1902), 'Religious Influences', iv. 10.

[60] Young and Wilmott, *Family and Kinship*, 87.

[61] Barclay and Perry, *Report and Survey of Housing*, 17–18.

and alleys which extended on either side of Borough High Street and around Borough Market. Typical of these were Layton's Buildings and Balin Place which consisted of narrow courts of four two-roomed cottages surrounded by garages and factories. The cottages were dark and airless, with yards of about ten feet by three feet and the water closets were insanitary.[62] This type of housing also characterized the Lant Street area. Courts such as these were often reached by means of an archway which further emphasized their secluded character. Caravan Terrace, between Surrey Row and Pocock Street to the west of this area, is an example of this kind of residential pattern. It was surrounded by factories which were plagued by rats. There was only one dustbin and two taps for ten cottages, the court was lit by only two street lamps, and there were no wash-houses even as late as the 1920s.[63] It was in this area that Thomas Morgan grew up, who was interviewed by Thea Thompson as part of the Essex Oral History project. Morgan was born in King's Bench Street, a court off Pocock Street, which was specifically mentioned by Mr J. Conners, the London City Missioner for the Borough Market area at the turn of the century, as one of the worst streets in the area.[64] Morgan's description is similar to that of E. Balne who was born in St Margaret's Court in 1895 and then lived subsequently in the Southwark workhouse for most of his childhood.[65]

The better streets within the parish of St George-the-Martyr housed mechanics and small tradesmen. In his autobiography, C. E. Joel records his life in Trinity Street near Borough High Street between 1910 and 1920. His mother and aunt owned a shop on the Borough High Street and his father worked as a labourer in the Bermondsey Leather Warehouse.[66] By 1921 a number of new modern block dwellings had been constructed to the east of St George-the-Martyr church in the area formerly known as the Mint. These consisted of self-contained flats of reasonable quality, such as the postwar London County Council Tabard Gardens Estate of 1910, and small blocks of Church Army Flats on the corner of Tabard Street and Weston Street. They were comparable in the 1920s to the London County Council Estate around the Oval Station. The rents ranged from between thirteen to twenty-one shillings a week. These

[62] Ibid. 17–18.

[63] Ibid. 17–18.

[64] LSE, Booth Collection, B270, 187.

[65] Brunel University, Burnett Collection, E. Balne, 'Autobiography of an Ex-workhouse and Poor Law School Boy' (1972), n.p.

[66] Oxford, Ruskin College, Working-Class Autobiographies, C. E. Joel, 'Autobiography' (1906), n.p.

prices were high enough to ensure an elevated sense of respectability among inhabitants and to force the less affluent sections of the working classes into the increasingly overcrowded neighbouring slum courts to the west of St George's Church off Borough High Street.[67]

The tight-knit communal character of these streets and courts is thrown into sharp focus by the contrasting character of the huge tenement blocks which interspersed the old courts along Borough High Street. Buildings such as Stanhope and Mowbray in Red Cross Way and Douglas Buildings in Marshalsea Road acted as temporary staging posts for a transient and shifting population among whom the pattern of community life was far less defined. These buildings are described as anonymous places, housing an estimated 6,000 people of 'nomadic propensity'.[68] The Revd W. J. Somerville, the vicar of St George-the-Martyr parish Church on Borough High Street, wrote that 'When I was first appointed to the charge I visited every tenement there. Seven months later half of my new acquaintances had gone.'[69]

In his interview for the Booth Survey in 1899 Revd Father G. Newton, the Roman Catholic vicar of the Church of the Most Precious Blood in Red Cross Street, announced his dislike of the effect of this block system of dwellings on the inhabitants: 'They have no public opinion, no conscience. People come in and leave and the rest of the occupants are none-the-wiser, neither glad nor sorry, the most part ignorant of the change.'[70] Newton specifically contrasted these tenement blocks with the courts of the area: 'But with a court it is different, everybody knows. Public opinion may not be of a high order but it is there'.[71]

The presence of these tenement blocks did not diminish the communal character of the surrounding courts. They wove their way in among the distinct indigenous communities which were preserved in this part of the borough alongside railway and industrial development. At the turn of the century it was still possible to find those who rarely, if ever, went outside their borough boundaries 'just as country folk do not leave their own villages'.[72] Individual streets, courts, and alleys continued to form tight-knit communities in which a distinct popular culture thrived. As Ellen Ross has argued, 'Powerful links between men and their work mates, women and their kin and neighbours—links which often

---

[67] Barclay and Perry, *Report and Survey of Housing*, 8.
[68] St George-the-Martyr, *Report and Statement of Accounts* (1898), 6.
[69] Ibid.
[70] LSE, Booth Collection, B270, 171.
[71] Ibid.
[72] Llewellyn Smith, *The New Survey of London Life and Labour* (1934), i. 191.

involved substantial exchanges of service and money—wove together individual conjugally-based households into the quite cohesive cockney culture'.[73]

This was the case in particular with the costermonger community which inhabited the area to the south of St George's and St Saviour's around Friar Street between Pocock Street and Borough Road. This area was judged by Booth to be even worse than those areas which surrounded Borough High Street. The pattern of secluded and 'murky' courts and alleys persisted as a prominent feature in this area. Contemporary descriptions give a vivid picture of the half-washed clothes which dangled across the streets; costermonger barrows; trestles for street stalls on Saturday nights stacked in every vacant spot, and the foul smell of rotten refuse, boiled bones, and smoked haddock which clung to the air.[74] The predominant characteristic of the area, however, as of those previously described to the east, was its social cohesion: 'There is still a communal class hanging around these badly lighted poverty-stricken streets'.[75]

This communal class consisted largely of the costermongers[76] of the area. They formed homogeneous communities within this defined geographical location which dominated whole streets and alleys such that 'Sometimes the whole adult population of one street will engage in pitched battle with the inhabitants of another when bricks, bottles, pokers and even knives will be frequently used'.[77]

They patronized certain beer shops, such as The World Turned Upside Down in the Old Kent Road[78] which, as Goulden argued, they tended to prefer to their own homes.[79] By the end of the century in areas such as these, the costermonger community had formed close-knit clans which banded together to form protective groups which could ensure the reservation of street and market pitches for local traders before the

[73] E. Ross, 'Survival Networks: Women's Neighbourhood Sharing: London before World War 1', *History Workshop*, 15 (1983), 5.

[74] St Alphege Mission, *Twenty Years Work Among the Masses* (1893), 6–7.

[75] St Alphege Mission, *Annual Report* (1883), 6.

[76] The term 'costermonger' was used to refer to street traders of various kinds. E. J. Orford explained this term by pointing out that: 'Long ago such folks were known as "costard-mongers" or "apple-sellers" whence costermonger, or, in everyday language, costers pronounced "causters"'. Orford, *The Book of Walworth* (1925), 10.

[77] St Alphege Mission, *Twenty Years Work Among the Masses*, 7.

[78] This pub was referred to as a base for coster gatherings in the oral testimony of Lilian Tims, SCW, Int. 23; and P. F. Brooks refers to it as the headquarters for the Pearly Kings and Queens Guild in his book, *Pearly Kings and Queens of England* (1975), 42.

[79] St Alphege Mission, *Annual Report* (1883), 41.

advent of official licensing by borough councils in 1927. Each of these clans had a leader who became known as the coster king; and his wife became the queen. Under the leadership of the coster king they kept outsiders away and safeguarded the interest of members. This phenomenon may have accounted for some of the pitched battles described above and it provided the basis for the distinct pearly culture of the late nineteenth and early twentieth century.

Pearly culture was symbolized above all by clothing. Apparel had always acted as a symbol of communal solidarity within the costermonger community. Henry Mayhew described the costermonger community in the mid-nineteenth century in relation to a distinct style of dress,[80] as did E. J. Orford in the early years of the twentieth century.

The coats of these men were nearer to the fashions of Queen Anne's time than those of polite society, while the women wore dresses of startling mauves and purples. Add to these pearly buttons (not pearl buttons), bell bottoms and feathers and the distinctiveness of the costume was assured.[81]

This distinct style of dressing reached an elaborate pitch at the end of the nineteenth century with the fashion for pearl jackets. A road sweeper, Henry Croft of Summerstown, introduced the fashion for smoked mother-of-pearl buttons to London in the 1870s. In 1880 he appeared in a suit encrusted almost entirely with pearl buttons and within the space of a few years the authority of costermonger leaders in twenty-eight of the London boroughs was delineated on the basis of the quantity of pearl buttons sown on the jacket. Each borough had a royal family and lesser kings and queens who often inhabited a single location such as a street. It was believed that only the son of a pearly king could succeed to the title as only he had been sufficiently immersed in the cultural values of the costermonger community[82] which were passed down from one generation to the next.

Overcrowded accommodation in areas such as these ensured that the street itself remained a principal focus of play, gossip, and relaxation. The domestic lives of the inhabitants were of necessity both public and communal. E. J. Orford described how, in Walworth on a summer's evening,

One must either endure the stifling seclusion of one's own apartment or be at ease as one of the throng, there is no hesitation in sitting outside in the street, on

---

[80] H. Mayhew, *London Labour and the London Poor*, 3 vols. (1851), i. 40.
[81] Orford, *The Book of Walworth*, 10.
[82] Brooks, *Pearly Kings and Queens*, 20.

the window sill, or on chairs and gossiping with neighbours while the children play everywhere—the spirit of the village green asserting itself in the most unpromising surroundings.[83]

A strong sense of social cohesion is a recurrent feature of the oral and written testimonies. Molly Layton was born in 1911 to the south of St George-the-Martyr in South Street, Walworth. Her family, which included both parents and grandparents, knew everyone in the street, and in the summer 'If it was hot weather we'd all sit outside the doors, my mum and all them would sit out the doors'.[84] Social cohesion was inseparable from the feeling of trust which existed between the members of a single court or street.

. . . and as for having a key you wouldn't dream like, only at night if you went to bed. There used to be a string in the door you could just pull and go in you know or if you went shopping my old granny would just shut the door wouldn't dream of locking it.[85]

Norman James described how even the 'burglars, thieves and wanted people' of Union Street trusted one another sufficiently to leave their doors unlocked.[86] This emphasis on trust within the local street community is a common theme of most of the interviews carried out in Southwark. Molly Layton went on to point out that 'my grandfather would rise at six to go to his docks and where we lived he used to light the fire before he went to work and that street door would be open till the time he came home and we never used to close that door until ten at night'.[87]

This kind of communality involved shared values and identities which, as Ellen Ross has shown in her study of women's neighbourhood sharing in London,[88] were reinforced through the exchange of material goods, favours, and money between neighbours and through the operation of a highly localized form of 'public opinion'. Like G. Newton,[89] C. H. Simpkinson, vicar of St Paul's Lorrimore Square in the western part of Walworth from 1887 to 1894, used the term 'public opinion' to denote a code of practice which was enforced through the approval or dis-

---

83 Orford, *The Book of Walworth*, 77.
84 SCW, Int. 20.
85 Ibid.
86 SCW, Int. 16.
87 SCW, Int. 20.
88 Ross, *Survival Networks, passim.*
89 Ibid. 80–1.

approval of the community.[90] This unspoken lore of the community was sufficient to establish an authoritative standard of behaviour, to force individual offenders out of the area, and to alienate outsiders. Dora Bargate, the daughter of a city office cleaner from Rotherhithe, describes how even in a more anonymous tenement block, residents would combine to enforce the eviction of one woman who left her children alone at night while she went to visit her male friends.[91] The informal mechanism by which this pattern of communal life thrived was through gossip and rumour: '. . . news travelled fast from neighbour to neighbour and was exchanged at the butcher's or over the backyard fence. Forthcoming pregnancies, marriages, engagements and day-to-day gossip were grist to the mill'.[92]

Communication was by word of mouth and this word, it is important to remember, was culturally distinguished by a strong cockney accent. 'Real cockney values'[93] were thus transmitted from one generation to the next and perpetuated through sayings, proverbs, and stories and at times enforced through the consensus of the community. In the Walworth area, for example, in the years before the First World War, 'old wives' tales' still held an authoritative place within the community and appear to have acted as a barrier to the introduction of modern medicine and hygiene and the advice of the district visitor.[94] This phenomenon established a personal link with the past, as local history was passed down by word of mouth from one generation to the next.

At the heart of these patterns of communal culture in Southwark were local institutions such as the pub and the music-hall. The legal suppression of older, more traditional forms of popular recreation such as cock-fighting and bear-baiting left the pubs largely unrivalled as recreational focuses. Norman James pointed out in his oral interview that, 'nearly every street had a pub, where you lived, next door . . . '.[95] It was here, among the men in particular, that social interaction took place, gossip was exchanged, and sport discussed.[96] 'These public houses are still the community centres where everyone meets, arranges most of his

[90] C. H. Simpkinson, *A South London Parish* (1894), 14.

[91] Brunel University, Burnett Collection, D. Bargate, 'Memories', n.d., n.p.

[92] H. Blacker, *Just Like it Was: Memories of the Mittel East* (1974), 97.

[93] J. Dash, *Good Morning Brothers* (1969), 13.

[94] L. J. Carter, *Walworth 1929–1939* (1985), 61. Cf. V. Berridge, 'Health and Medicine' in F. M. L. Thompson (ed.), *The Cambridge Social History of Britain 1750–1950*, 3 vols. (Cambridge, 1990), iii. 186–91.

[95] SCW, Int. 16.

[96] Llewellyn Smith, *The New Survey of London Life and Labour* (1934), ix. 252–3.

common activities, lays his personal cares aside and satisfies some of his social cravings.'[97]

As the period progressed the pub began to perform the same function for some women. For them the public house could act as an extension of the street. Lilian Tims described how her grandmother would go over to The World Turned Upside Down on the corner of Massinger Street and the Old Kent Road and shell her peas in her lap while having a pint with her friends, and thus avoid the crowded atmosphere of the house just before teatime.[98]

Many of the pubs of Southwark were squalid. They were enclosed by frosted glass, with sawdust on the floor and very basic furnishings. But for many they compared favourably with the home as a place of relaxation. The pattern of employment among the inhabitants of the area ensured that the pub remained predominantly a local institution in which men who travelled to work all over London could meet, drink, and talk on the basis of their common local identity rather than their economic or sectional interests.[99] As such the pubs were the main centres of the dissemination of local information: 'The public houses are recognised for exchanges of news, and a man who wishes to get in touch with another or find out what has happened to him naturally goes in, has a drink and asks, "seen so and so lately?"'.[100]

During weekday evenings pubs were mainly the domain of the men. The women were often sent a pint of beer at home. Lilian Tims's mother would receive her pot of stout from her husband at the pub which she would warm up with a poker and drink at home while watching the children.[101] This pattern of gender division did not necessarily diminish the familial character of the pubs at the weekends and on special occasions. A number of interviewees recorded how the entire family would visit the pub on a Saturday and Sunday and the children would play in the corridor or hide in the cellar if a policeman paid an unexpected visit.[102] Furthermore, they often formed the focus for an entire family and their entourage of friends and neighbours at weddings, births, and funerals. Lilian Tims described how, after any significant turning-point in family life, her family would step out of St Mary

[97] Ibid. 257.

[98] SCW, Int. 23.

[99] Cf. G. Stedman-Jones, 'Working-Class Culture and Working-Class Politics in London 1870–1900', *Journal of Social History*, 7 (1974), 460–508.

[100] Llewellyn Smith, *The New Survey*, 257.

[101] SCW, Int. 23.

[102] SCW, Int. 5.

Magdalene's Church in Massinger Street into The World Turned Upside Down on the opposite side of the road.[103]

The pubs also acted as determinants of local identity. Most of the public houses had their regular visitors. Elizabeth Merritt of Kinglake Street, Walworth, described how the inhabitants of the street would regularly spend their time at the Prince of Wales on the corner.[104] Bill Wardell of the Surrey Docks described in his interview with the Age Exchange how

Every guv'nor knew his customers. You see pubs had their regulars. If anybody came in who's been using the King and Queen and was coming in the Compass, they'd want to know why. The same people went in every time. They'd even be shelling their peas in there. You know the old aprons they used to wear, they'd chuck their peas in there. You'd always know what pub people belonged to, and the guv'nor knew his customers because of the sports teams attached to each pub.[105]

The failure of an individual to drink at the local pub on a consistent basis was seen as symptomatic of his separation from popular culture. Arthur Harding, for example, designated the family who lived at 15 Gibraltar Gardens in south-west Bethnal Green as peculiar, not only on the basis of their religious affiliation to the Red Church, St James the Great, but also because of the fact that the father did not drink with 'the herd' at the local pub. The pubs of Southwark exhibited none of the radical inclinations of their counterparts in north London or in the neighbouring borough of Bermondsey. There were few equivalents to the Goat Tavern in Tooley Street or the Horns Coffee Tavern in Bermondsey Square where the Dock, Wharf and Riverside, and General Labourers Union would meet to discuss business on a regular basis. The comparatively apolitical character of Southwark's pubs was symptomatic of a more deep-seated distinction between the Metropolitan Borough and its neighbour, Bermondsey. Frequent contrasts were made in the *Southwark Annual* between the political vitality of Bermondsey and the indifference of Southwark. In 1901 an article contrasted the response of the two areas to the Boer war. Where Southwark merely provided a quota of men to fight the Boers, Bermondsey held a patriotic carnival as well, and where Southwark gave a bare minimum to support the families of volunteers, Bermondsey went beyond granting half pay to the families during the absence of the wage earner, to raising special

---

[103] SCW, Int. 23.
[104] SCW, Int. 21.
[105] Age Exchange, *On the River: Memories of the River* (1989), 49–50.

funds for the relief of widows and orphans.[106] Political and radical leaders such as Dr Salter lived and worked in Bermondsey, while local branches of the Independent Labour Party and the Liberal Party operated in the area but made few inroads into Southwark.

In Southwark, therefore, the pub remained the centre of local recreation and tradition. Communal sports were organized in these places, as well as children's day trips and charabanc outings—'beanos' as they are called in a number of the oral testimonies.[107] E. J. Orford, for example, described in his *Book of Walworth* (1925) the charabanc outings arranged by local Walworth pubs for young ladies of the area.[108] The regulars of an entire public house would follow the fortunes of a particular football team playing at the Oval in Kennington or a boxer who fought at the Ring in Blackfriars Road, while the bookie's tout remained a familiar sight on the corner of the street by the pub. One of the complaints made by the Revd R. H. Duthy, the vicar of All Hallows parish church, Southwark from 1892 to 1912, was that the bookies used the fifteen public houses in his parish for the pursuit of their trade.[109] This blend of community and recreation in the local pubs of Southwark reinforced their role of providing practical and at times financial support within the neighbourhood. The informal network of mutual support which existed among neighbours was underpinned by the pubs which could act as unofficial headquarters where, as Llewellyn Smith remarked, 'someone passes the hat around for the relief of some particular hard case of misfortune, to, say the widow of a former habitué'.[110]

During the nineteenth century the music-hall began to emerge alongside the pub as another major institution of communal life. Gareth Stedman-Jones has argued that by the end of the century the music-hall was second only to the pub as a popular institution.[111] South London was the geographical focus of music-hall culture. The Upper Marsh, Lambeth was the home of Charles Morton's Canterbury Arms from 1848, which was rebuilt and opened specifically as a music-hall in 1852. The Grapes Tavern, later known as the Surrey Music Hall, was situated in Southwark Bridge Road. This was the first pub-based concert hall to

---

[106] The *Southwark Annual* (1901), 57.
[107] See e.g. Alice Iveson and Fred Woolenough in Age Exchange, *On the River*, 50.
[108] Orford, *The Book of Walworth*, 60.
[109] LSE, Booth Collection, B269, 89.
[110] Llewellyn Smith, *The New Survey*, 259.
[111] Stedman Jones, 'Working-Class Culture and Working-Class Politics', 478. See also P. Bailey, *Leisure and Class in Victorian England: 1830–1885* (1978) and *Music Hall: The Business of Pleasure* (Milton Keynes, 1986).

use the explicit title of music-hall. In addition, Borough Music Hall was situated in Union Street. This was renamed the Raglan Music Hall in 1884. The South London Palace of Varieties was built further south in the London Road near the Elephant and Castle in 1860. After it was rebuilt due to fire damage in 1869, this music-hall had a capacity to seat 4,000. It became particularly important under the management of the Poole family from 1873 to the end of the century. The 'Old Sahth', as it was known, attracted a local audience. Yet despite its infamous reputation, the fame of the 'Sahth' extended beyond the Elephant and Castle and George Leybourne, The Lion, Marie Lloyd, and Eugene Stratton were among the stars who graced its boards. The music-halls tailored their entertainment to the taste of the cockney working class. A succession of vividly contrasting acts in a single programme offered a distinct form of drama. The majority of pieces were melodramatic but were considered to be 'true to life'. Plays such as 'The Girls Who Knew Best' and 'The Bad Girl of the Family', for example, were said to be humorous but realistic portraits of working-class life.[112]

The oral interviews carried out in Southwark, however, downplayed the prominence of music-halls in the communal culture of the area. Individuals such as Stan Hall, who avidly followed the stars and spent all his surplus money on trips to the theatre, appear to have been exceptions among the inhabitants of Southwark. For most, the music-hall was an occasional place of entertainment rather than a regular feature of life. At the same time fashions and songs which emanated from the local music-hall were readily and widely assimilated in the locality. The pearl suit of Albert Chevalier (1851–1923), for example, became the hallmark of south London costermonger culture, while songs such as the 'Costers' Serenade' were regarded as expressions of local cockney life. Song sheets such as those published by W. S. Fortey were sold on the streets of Southwark. E. J. Orford specifically described the penny songsters which were sold at East Street Market, Walworth. The songs were played repetitively on a piano organ at the market to attract potential customers.[113] Lilian Tims described how family parties centred upon communal renderings of popular music-hall songs.[114] Similarly, Arthur Newton, a shoemaker from Hackney, described how

The songs sung were of the time, perhaps the songs sung by Harry Champion, Marie Kendall and many others. That period brought forth many popular songs

[112] The *Star*, 11 Nov. 1911.
[113] Orford, *The Book of Walworth*, 58.
[114] SCW, Int. 23.

tuneful, catchy and singable, songs that kept a party going. One had only to hear them a couple of times and the tune was soon remembered. The words were learned from the penny song sheets sold at almost any corner shop.[115]

Edith Anders described how every Saturday night after a few hours spent at the local pub it would be, as she said, 'a toss up' as to whose house the group should return to for a party.[116] These parties consisted of singing the 'old ones'. 'We'd go in one another's houses and have a party, 'cos we'd have a piano in doors, my aunt downstairs, 'cos we has cousins lived downstairs and we lived up stairs and we'd have like a family party.'[117]

E. J. Orford also described this local phenomenon:

In winter half of the year as one walks through the streets on Saturday and Sunday evenings, sounds of 'parties' can be heard enjoying a general sing-song. Someone will sit down at the piano and play off a whole string of popular choruses. Cheap music—the words and music of popular songs—has greatly extended the repertoire of the party on such occasions and given courage to those who find support in hiding behind a sheet or standing with their backs to the audience in order to read the piano copy. Gone are the days when to a large extent one-man one-song and the shy performer was rewarded with general cheers and shouts of 'All our side'.[118]

These songs vocalized many of the distinctive values of these communities during this period[119] and they were sung widely even among those who visited the music-hall on infrequent occasions only. Frederick Willis claimed that songs of these kinds were the folk songs of the people. Most of them had a foundation of truth and many had decency and common sense as their theme.[120]

Many of these songs were humorous portrayals of cockney life: courting, marriage, and gambling were common themes. Others gave a more melancholy portrayal of life and some quite realistic scenes of the squalor and misery of poverty. The thread which joined these songs was an appreciation of the communal dimension of life. Emphasis was placed on the shared experience of suffering. Many songs were light-hearted presentations of common woes which joined the singer and the listener in an embrace which either celebrated or commiserated over the

[115] A. Newton, *Years of Change: The Autobiography of a Hackney Shoemaker* (1974), 39.
[116] SCW, Int. 5.
[117] SCW, Int. 23.
[118] Orford, *The Book of Walworth*, 77.
[119] Cf. Stedman Jones, 'Working-Class Culture and Working-Class Politics', 460–508.
[120] F. Willis, *Peace and Dripping Toast* (1950), 159.

common lot of man. This is clearly illustrated in a song sung by George
Ripon in the late 1880s entitled *We've All Had 'em.*

> Misfortunes come to every man and woman in this life
> And all of us have had our share of trouble, woe and strife,
> We've all had 'em, we've all had 'em,
> And if we havn't had 'em we shall have 'em by and by.[121]

The communal life of the borough was composed not only of indigenous institutions such as the pub and the music hall, but also of a series
of religious institutions and agencies which were no less integrated within communal life. Woven within the streets and alleys of Southwark,
alongside the pubs and the theatres, were missions, Sunday schools,
soup kitchens, and parish churches. Like the East End, south London
witnessed a proliferation of social and religious movements in the last
two decades of the nineteenth century. The area was affected by the
settlement movement of the 1880s and 1890s, by the creation of missions,
the erection of mission halls, the provision of mission workers and
clergymen, by systematic visitation and by open-air services along with
the establishment of subsidiary church organizations of a social and
religious character. Many of these formed part of the mental and social
as well as the physical landscape of the local inhabitants. The medieval
church of St Saviour's dominated the skyline of the northern part of the
borough well into the twentieth century. Its presence overshadowed the
community which congregated around Borough Market. St Saviour's
became the pro-cathedral of south London in 1897 and the Cathedral
Church of the new diocese of Southwark in 1905. Its restoration during
the latter half of the nineteenth century was heralded as a sign of the
moral and spiritual improvement of the southern metropolis.[122] At the
turn of the century the church claimed to be in constant touch through
visitation with a large number of the 5,000 parishioners. The church was
also responsible for the work of a mission hall in Red Cross Street. Here,
'in the centre of low life',[123] there were bible classes, sewing meetings, a
penny bank, a library, a mothers' meeting, a Band of Hope, a children's
scripture union and a Girls' Friendly Lodge, as well as substantially
endowed parochial charities. In reality the church remained aloof from
the parishioners, functioning primarily as a trans-local centre for culture
and music. This was demonstrated powerfully by an article which
appeared in the *Daily Graphic* in February 1910, expressing the desire of

121 *The Aquarium Songster*, pub. W. S. Fortey (*c.*1888–90).
122 The *Quarterly Review, St. Saviour's Southwark*, 170 (Jan. and Apr. 1890), 413–14.
123 Booth, *Life and Labour* (1902), 'Religious Influences', iv. 12.

the congregation for the construction of a new and impressive entrance to the cathedral which would bypass the 'dustbins of Borough Market'.[124]

In the area to the south of Friar Street the costermonger community was closely associated during the 1870s and 1880s with the vibrant parish church of St Alphege situated in Lancaster Street under the oversight of the Revd A. B. Goulden. Goulden was known locally as 'the costers' bishop'.[125] St Alphege church started as a mission venture in a coster woman's stable in 1873. This mission then moved to a beer shop and a temporary church before a permanent building was erected in Lancaster Street in 1882. By this date it had established regular soup dinners for the children of the area; it had a Sunday school, a crèche, and a working men's club; and by 1886 it boasted a Sunday attendance of about 800 adults from the surrounding neighbourhood, many of whom were costermongers.

The coster community as a whole was renowned for its close affiliation with the church. The Parish Church of St Mary Magdalene, Southwark formed another costermonger focus, particularly after the death of Father Goulden in 1894. Lilian Tims described the arrival of the pearly kings and queens each year at St Mary Magdalene. The children of the surrounding courts would line the streets to watch them enter the church to celebrate harvest festival.[126] St Mary Magdalene soon came to be known as the 'Coster Cathedral'. The Pearly Association met in the hall of this church until the 1950s. The curate in charge, Revd V. R. D. Hellaby, acted as the chairman of these meetings during the 1940s and 1950s.[127] The parish church of St John's in Larcom Street, Walworth also had strong links with the costermonger community in the borough. By the turn of the century it had become the centre for christenings, weddings, and funeral services. North of Friar Street and the parish of St Alphege, in the riverside section of the borough, the local community also lived among a network of religious institutions. The parish church of All Hallows in Pepper Street and St Peter's in Sumner Street both had large Sunday schools which worked among the families of warehouse-men, dockers, and packers of the parishes.

In contrast to the inhabitants around Friar Street who were said to be 'too poor for dissent',[128] the area to the west, towards Westminster Bridge, was traditionally regarded as a stronghold of nonconformity.

[124] *Daily Graphic*, 4 Feb. 1910.
[125] LSE, Booth Collection, B269, 75.
[126] SCW, Int. 23.
[127] Brooks, *Pearly Kings and Queens*, 42.
[128] Booth, *Life and Labour* (1902), 'Religious Influences', iv. 14.

The Primitive Methodist Surrey Chapel in Blackfriars Road was particularly active during the last decades of the nineteenth century. This
drew to it the slightly more wealthy sections of the working class who
populated the area beyond Gravel Lane towards the Blackfriars Road.
They consisted of artisans, shopkeepers, clerks, and printers. It was to
the Sunday school and the Sunday services at this church that Miriam
Moore made her way each week from the Peabody Buildings on
Blackfriars Road where she lived with her grandmother.[129] The chapel
had a vibrant gospel service, a Pleasant Sunday Afternoon society, and a
men's brotherhood, while its social evenings, concerts, lectures, and
entertainments were well known in the area. Mrs Moore described how
during the week she would attend the Girls' Life Brigade and the Band of
Hope at the chapel.[130] Two Salvation Army Hostels also nestled in
among the lodging houses on the Blackfriars Road, yet the work here was
limited to social relief, as was the Fegan's Boys' Home and the Women's
University Settlement in nearby Nelson Square.

The Anglican churches in the area west and south of Great Suffolk
Street and Gravel Lane were not so well attended on a Sunday as the
Primitive Methodist chapel in Blackfriars Road; but St Paul's,
Westminster Bridge Road, St Jude's in St George's Road, and the parish
church of Christ Church, near Blackfriars Road, all had large Sunday
schools and active subsidiary organizations such as provident and
benefit clubs, maternity clubs, coal clubs and penny banks. One of these
may well have included the small mission building which both Miriam
Moore[131] and Rose Embelton, the daughter of a stableman, born in
Bower Street, Elephant and Castle in 1899,[132] were forbidden to attend on
the grounds that the free food distributed there was only for the poorer
children of the neighbourhood.[133]

THE ELEPHANT AND CASTLE

The area to the south of Borough High Street around the Elephant and
Castle formed a second major focus in the Metropolitan Borough of
Southwark. This area was both a commercial and an entertainment

---

[129] SCW, Int. 15.
[130] Ibid.
[131] SCW, Int. 15.
[132] EOHA, Int. 299.
[133] Both these women recall how they were severely beaten for going with the neighbour's children to the poor children's supper at the local mission on a Friday night in order
to get two thick slices of bread with jam.

focus for the borough as a whole. It features prominently in the reminiscence of local inhabitants such as Stan Hall.[134] Booth described it as the 'centre of centres',[135] yet the hub of communal life in the area seems to have been in the residential areas surrounding the Elephant and Castle such as those inhabited by Stan Hall's family. 'Here', Booth argued, 'we find a real stir of local life'.[136]

During the 1910s Stan Hall's family lived at the northern end of Newington Butts at the southern tip of the area described above, in one room that cost ten shillings a week. The Elephant and Castle was not only where his family shopped and washed in the public baths and laundry, but also formed the centre of recreation during his youth and after his family moved south to Camberwell. Stan Hall lived among the mixed population of mechanics, hawkers, and labourers which surrounded the Elephant and Castle in the block of land bounded on each side by Borough Road, London Road, and Newington Causeway. The social character of this area was generally higher throughout the period than those to the north but it was still punctuated by what Booth described as 'dirty little places',[137] narrow enough to allow clothes to be strung across the alley. These areas, like those to the north, remained strongly communal in character and they were marked by the presence of various church institutions. A large number of costermongers continued to inhabit the areas and form the kinds of communities described above. They tended to look south, however, to the parish of St John's Walworth and to the parish church in particular for their marriages, baptisms, and burials. The Elephant and Castle itself was overshadowed from 1861 by the famous Metropolitan Tabernacle, the home of the Baptist pastor Charles Haddon Spurgeon. The Tabernacle, however, tended to be physically prominent rather than socially active within the local community. Its Sunday congregation was drawn mainly from the suburbs.[138] The proof of this, remarked F. S. Forster, the Vicar of St Mark's Church, Walworth from 1896 to 1905, was to be seen when one observed the 'trams on a Sunday morning and you will find them full of people going to the Tabernacle from Brixton and Streatham'.[139]

Yet the Tabernacle had an enormous Sunday school which drew the

[134] SLSL, A. S. Hall, 'Reminiscences' (1988), esp. 5–14.
[135] Booth, *Life and Labour* (1902), 'Poverty', i. 276.
[136] Ibid.
[137] Ibid. See e.g. Tiverton Street, Tarn Street, and St Gabriel Street also described by Llewellyn Smith, *The New Survey of London Life and Labour* (1931), vi. 399.
[138] Booth, *Life and Labour* (1902), 'Religious Influences', iv. 76.
[139] LSE, Booth Collection, B276, 101.

children of local inhabitants from all over the borough, and its influence lay in a system of informal relationships with small mission halls in the surrounding area such as the Arthur Mission in Snowfields, which was run as a small independent mission in the Parish of St Olave's and which was associated with the Tabernacle through its superintendent Mr Hoyland. Similarly, a chapel was run by W. J. Mills just off Walworth Road in close association with the Tabernacle, as was a nearby mission in Richmond Street. Dora Bargate's reminiscence gives a vivid description of the Tabernacle Sunday school to which she travelled each Sunday from Rotherhithe.[140] Its mothers' meetings were also popular in the immediate geographical surrounding, while the Bible Carriage, sent out by the Metropolitan Tabernacle Colportage Association from 1875, became a prominent feature in the streets around the Elephant and Castle.

The inhabitants of Red Cross Street could not escape the presence of the Roman Catholic Church of the Most Precious Blood under the over-sight of the parish priest William Murnane from 1892 to 1911 and his assistant during the same period, George Newton. This drew to it much of the Roman Catholic population in the parishes of St Saviour's and St George-the-Martyr[141] and it provided an active boys' club, a Sunday school, and a League of the Cross. This church and its school, St Joseph's on Borough High Street, which opened in 1892, played a prominent part in Emma Reynolds's memories of the area.[142] In addition to the presence of these two major institutions in the community, the Church Army opened a station in the parish during the 1890s. The captain and his wife made their home in one of the blocks of artisan dwellings and they began visiting people in their homes, spending five to seven hours a day in this way. The parish church of St Michael's was situated in the heart of the borough in Lant Street under the high churchman the Revd W. H. Longsdon from 1893 to 1906. This church was said to draw 'a fair Sunday congregation of local people who are all poor'.[143]

St George-the-Martyr parish church stood in the most prominent position at the junction of Borough High Street, with its mission halls among the surrounding courts in the area known as 'The Triangle' and in Chapel Court. These mission rooms held Sunday services on a regular basis and catered for the poor who would not attend the church

---

[140] Brunel University, Burnett Collection, D. Bargate, 'Memories', n.d., n.p.

[141] The attendance at mass on a Sunday morning was set at 800 or 900 including 250 children.

[142] SCW, Int. 4.

[143] Booth, *Life and Labour* (1902), 'Religious Influences', iv. 17.

itself. Revd W. J. Somerville, vicar from 1898 to 1914, claimed in his interview with Booth that the church had an 'intimate knowledge of a large number of parishioners, particulars are entered in huge folios'.[144]

The church's most vigorous work among the local people was the Sunday school which boasted an attendance of 600 among a parochial population of 1300.

Further south of the parish church was the Borough Road Baptist Church. At the turn of the century the chapel drew its congregation from the immediate neighbourhood. The minister from 1898 to 1911, Poole Connor, ran a Sunday school, mothers' meetings, and a Band of Hope in the area as well as doing a considerable amount of open-air work under the railway arches during the summer months. London City Missioners were also active in Union Street and in the neighbouring parish of St Alphege, in Shaftesbury Hall,[145] in Lancaster Street, Park Street,[146] and in Friar Street.[147] W. Hitchcock, for example, held a Sunday school, a prayer meeting, an evangelistic service, a Monday penny bank, a mothers' meeting and a Saturday prayer and praise meeting in Park Street. The most successful aspect of the work of all these missions took place among the children. Sunday schools were a prominent and regular feature of local life. They were held in small mission halls which were hidden among the streets, such as the tiny Hope Mission run by Miss Martin in Friar Street and the Wesleyan Mission in Great Guildford Street, founded originally in 1838 for the employees of the Barclay and Perkins Brewery. Consequently, in this section of the borough a diverse network of religious facilities existed alongside the pub, alleys, and courts which housed the community.

WALWORTH

East Street Market in Walworth formed a third geographical focus for Southwark's working population. Former inhabitants of Walworth described East Street as the primary focus of the area. Its notoriety was such that Mrs Duncan's grandparents insisted that her parents move out of the street immediately after their daughter's birth in 1905 as they considered it an unsuitable environment in which to bring up a child.[148]

South of Great Dover Street, between Newington Causeway and the

[144] Ibid. 31.
[145] J. Coles, LSE, Booth Collection, B270, 45–6.
[146] W. Hitchcock, ibid. 59–67.
[147] J. Caine, ibid. 69–82.
[148] SCW, Int. 27.

New Kent Road, the expanse of poverty continued and the kinds of communal life described above were replicated as the population was forced south to Walworth through redevelopment in the north. By the turn of the century this part of Walworth consisted of old houses replaced in part by low-grade tenement blocks such as those in Lion Street which are described in detail by the 1929 Housing Surveyors. These consisted of six-storied blocks of self-contained flats; the front rooms on the upper floors were generally good but the back rooms were dark. The ground-floor flats were so dark that gas had to be burnt all day. The staircases were neglected and the tenants complained that tramps slept in them every night. Rooms were found to be dirty and verminous, and the courtyards strewn with refuse. Rents ranged from four pennies for a two-roomed flat to nineteen shillings for a four-roomed flat.[149]

The market provided the economic focus for this community and consisted of a large number of hawkers and street traders who also lived in the old and dilapidated cottages which remained clustered around East Street well into the 1920s. The cottages were ideal for the coster-mongers as they were punctuated by yard space sufficient for a donkey. It was here that J. H. Bennett grew up. He was born in 1902, the son of a Walworth cellarman, but, as he was careful to point out in his reminiscence, he lived at the 'Old Kent Road end' of East Street, away from the street market near the Walworth Road. Bennett described the difference between the two ends of the street as the difference between poverty and affluence.[150]

The communal character of Walworth was similar in kind to that of the Borough. Molly Layton described how she lived in a small two-up two-down cottage in South Street with her mother, her brothers, sisters, and her grandparents. Mrs Scott lived in a three-storied house in Villa Street, Southwark after she was married. She and her husband lived in the middle, her parents lived in the basement, with another set of close relatives above them.[151] Both Mrs Layton's and Mrs Scott's family knew everyone in the street. Similarly, when Elizabeth Merritt was asked if she knew many of the inhabitants of her native Kinglake Street, she began to list the names as if she still lived there: 'Mrs Richards, next door, Mrs Parsons, Mrs Gillingwater and Mrs Bruent and opposite was Mrs Carr . . .'[152]

[149] Barclay and Perry, *Report and Survey of Housing*, 8.
[150] SLSL, J. H. Bennett, 'I was a Walworth Boy' (1977), 1.
[151] SCW, Int. 19.
[152] SCW, Int. 21.

As in the northern part of the borough many of the inhabitants of Walworth were indigenous south Londoners. Sidney Barry of Merrow Street, Walworth was the son of Southwark people,[153] as was Elizabeth Merritt.[154] In the latter case the grandparents also came from Southwark.

The inhabitants of Walworth, like their equivalents in the north of the borough, were surrounded on every side by religious facilities, institutions, and houses of prayer. The South London Wesleyan Mission was formed in the area in 1889 from the rearrangement within a new circuit of two existing local churches: Southwark Chapel in Long Lane and Lockfields Chapel in Rodney Road. The South East London Mission also had two active bases in Trinity Street between 1876 and 1900 until it moved to St George's Hall in 1900. The Wellington College Mission in Etherden Street and Pembroke College Mission in Barlow Street were operated near East Street from the late 1880s, as did the Charterhouse Mission in Tabard Street which was established in 1885 and St John's College Mission in Chatham Place from 1889. Browning Hall was built in York Street and inaugurated in 1895, while St Mark's Church had what the vicar, the Revd F. S. Forster, described as the misfortune of being consecrated in 1874 right in the heart of the market itself. In addition, All Saints in Surrey Square was worked along strongly evangelical lines by the Revd R. B. Harrison, vicar from 1896 to 1901.

Many of these institutions were active in the area. Browning Hall, for example, held weekly mothers' meetings which attracted as many as 450 women, a Boys' Brigade, university lectures, French lessons, a thrift and goose club. It also had two poor man's lawyers, Mr O. Marsland and Mr W. C. Williams who together saw over 1,000 clients in 1900. A Pleasant Sunday Afternoon society for the men was also held which had enrolled over 300 members, along with a benevolent fund and an administrative committee. A weekly prayer and bible class, known as the fellowship of followers, provided a more directly devotional facility for local inhabitants, while regular open-air services were held in the area known as the 'waste' in the streets leading to the East Street Market. The college missions had mothers' meetings, Sunday schools and working mens' clubs which became popular institutions partly by virtue of their billiard tables.

In addition, two Particular Baptist churches were also situated in the East Street area, but these, like the Pilgrim Fathers' Church and Sutherland Congregational Chapel, appear to have had no involvement with the local area during this period and to have consisted mainly of the

[153] SCW, Int. 12.   [154] SCW, Int. 21.

tradesman class drawn from a wider geographical radius. On the New Kent Road there was the Murphy Memorial Hall which housed the Congregational Crossways Mission. Open-air services were also held regularly during the summer months in the 1890s prior to the transference of the Wesleyan missions to St George's Hall in Bermondsey. London City Missioners also worked in the area. E. Davies, for example, worked among the courts off Crosby Row such as Union Place and Porlock Place. Davies also ran a large Sunday school and one of the largest mothers' meetings in the area. Likewise, J. Coombs set up a cab drivers' mission in the cab yards of Walworth in 1894 alongside a working men's mission in the same area[155] and Mr R. H. Tomkins worked in Townley Street and Mr Starkey in Barlow Street.[156]

The popular and communal character of the parts of Walworth which surrounded East Street Market is in contrast to the area to the west towards Kennington Road and south towards the Camberwell Road. In these parts social conditions improved radically. Here one could find the homes of clergymen, schoolmasters, and clerks. Throughout the period, however, despite the overall aura of affluence, the area remained punctuated with tenements inhabited by costers, fish-curers, and casual labourers. Bertha Thornton, the daughter of a journeyman bricklayer, grew up in this area. The record of her childhood demonstrates the relative poverty of her family when compared to the inhabitants of the Kennington Road area. Her family were shunned by a more respectable social class: 'My sister told me never to let anyone know at school that Dad was out of work, if you do you will be looked down on and despised. I could not see this but soon learnt how right she was.'[157]

William Kent's family are an example of 'acceptable' inhabitants of this area. Kent was born in 1884 in Therose Street, Upper Kennington Lane; his father was a small private businessman who was well integrated among his immediate lower-middle-class neighbours who, like the Kent family, attended the local Methodist Church.[158]

It was in this more prosperous section of Walworth towards Kennington that a large number of religious institutions were situated. These included, to mention but a few, the Beresford Chapel which opened in 1818 as an Independent chapel, which Ruskin attended as a boy in the 1820s under Dr Edward Anders. This was later converted to an

[155] LSE, Booth Collection, B277, 195–204.
[156] Ibid. 205–15.
[157] SLSL, B. Thornton, 'Memories of Childhood' (1987), 7.
[158] W. Kent, *The Testament of a Victorian Youth* (1938).

open Brethren Assembly until the 1920s when it ceased to be used as a chapel. In addition, the Jewish synagogue was situated on the corner of Heygate Street and Vowler Street. The synagogue was built during the 1860s in order to accommodate the Jewish inhabitants of the Elephant and Castle after the original Borough Synagogue on St George's Road had become too small. The synagogue had an affiliated school and a friendly society for its members which continued to function until 1913. But by the 1910s, however, its influence lay mainly among the well-to-do Jewish tradesmen who were drawn to worship in the western part of Walworth but who lived elsewhere. By 1908 only 213 of its members resided in the area contiguous to Southwark.[159] The parish church of St John's lay in this area under the oversight of the Revd A. W. Jephson (vicar from 1893 to 1908). By the turn of the century Jephson claimed that the church in Larcom Street had become a centre for costers' rites of passage throughout the south of London. Yet Jephson's main energy was channelled into political activity. In 1885 he was elected a member of the London School Board; the following year he was elected to the Newington Vestry and then became part of the Southwark Borough Council from the time of its formation. His career was very similar in this respect to that of his fellow councillor, the Revd J. Horsley, the incumbent of St Peter's Church, Liverpool Street, Walworth from 1894 to 1911.

In the Borough, the Elephant and Castle, and the parts of Walworth which surrounded East Street Market, localized and indigenous communities retained a remarkable degree of continuity throughout the last decades of the nineteenth century until the Second World War. They remained to a considerable extent isolated from the gradual encroachment of modern housing, industrial, and commercial development and it took the devastation of the Blitz to usher in a new social era. Until then, these communities continued to exhibit local cockney identity, mutuality, and communality. Furthermore, they provided the context in which popular, social, recreational, and folk traditions were preserved and in which popular religious beliefs were expressed.

---

[159] M. Rosenbaum, *History of Borough Synagogue* (1917), 28.

3
Urban Folk Religion

An article published in *The Times* and reprinted in the *Folklore Journal* in 1917 claimed that 'faith in the supernatural still obtains in London'.[1] This comment summarized the conclusions drawn from the evidence presented in an exhibition in Southwark Central Library of the folklore material collected by Edward Lovett in the latter years of the nineteenth century. The article continued: 'It shows how widespread is the belief especially in East and South London that the fortunes of individuals can be affected by some inanimate object deemed to be lucky or potent against diseases'.[2]

The exhibition contained details of folk rituals and superstitious charms, amulets, dolls, cures, and mascots carried for the purpose of averting misfortune, ensuring good luck, and curing specific diseases. Folk wisdom and medical lore also combined with more overt expressions of folk superstition which sought to manipulate and control the super-empirical sphere and to bring order and predictability to the local human environment. This evidence represented only a small section of Edward Lovett's work which had begun in earnest in the 1880s and which continued into the 1920s. Numerous articles in the *Folklore Journal* and in other newspapers and periodicals summarized Lovett's findings and presented his tentative conclusions on the character of folk tradition in the south of England.

Lovett (1852–1933) ranked among the band of zealous folklorists who flourished in Britain in the late nineteenth century. He was the cashier of a large London bank who, from the age of 8, began an extensive collection of charms, legends, and superstitions which continued to occupy evenings and weekends throughout his working life. He was made president of the Croydon Natural History and Scientific Society in the late 1880s and by 1905 he was recognized as a national authority on folklore and superstition after a series of exhibitions of his findings in

---

[1] E. Lovett, 'The Belief in Charms', *Folklore*, 28 (1917), 99.
[2] Ibid.

England and Wales. He joined the Folklore Society in 1900 and submitted letters and articles to its journal. His first major exhibition
opened in 1914 in Cardiff. This was moved to Southwark Library where
it was reported on by *The Times* in 1917. He lectured at the Horniman
Museum and at Hove Natural History and Philosophical Society and
also at the Royal Society of Arts. After the war he concentrated on
London folklore. He made numerous excursions among street traders,
exchanging small toys for popular stories and superstitions. 'The people
from whom I gather these records belong to what is called the "hawker
class" whose business is carried on by means of a hand barrow.'[3]

The high concentration of street traders and costermongers in
south London ensured that the area featured prominently in both his
collection and his writings. Lovett did not have a specific theory as to the
persistence of magical beliefs in the modern urban environment; his
interest was in the collection and accumulation of evidence. In the
preface to his book *Magic in Modern London* printed privately by the
Croydon Advertiser in 1925, he wrote, 'I not only have no theory as to
the reason why these remarkable beliefs in magic still exist in modern
London, I simply say, I don't know'.[4]

The cumulative effect of his findings, however, demonstrates both
the prevalence and the diversity of folk customs, practices, and beliefs
within the urban environment. Far from having been extinguished within this context many aspects of folk custom and tradition remained part
of the popular religious repertoire. This is corroborated in a number of
ways by the written and oral reminiscences. The oral interviews provided
a particularly effective arena in which to explore folk customs, practices,
and beliefs, particularly as many of them existed in the form of proverbs,
sayings, and stories which were transmitted in oral form from neighbour
to neighbour and from generation to generation.

For some of the interviewees the practices described were nothing
other than trivial or habitual incidentals which appear to have had little
substance in terms of actual belief. Touching wood, throwing salt over
the shoulder, or not walking under ladders, for example, could emerge
in the course of interviewing as isolated and perhaps even humorous or
quaint quirks of custom and speech which mean little or nothing as an
expression of genuine sentiment.

In other cases, however, these same practices were described as
preludes to a discussion of a broader range of beliefs which extended

---

[3] E. Lovett, *Magic in Modern London* (1925), p. ii.
[4] Ibid.

into more overt and tangible practices involving a sustained ordering of activity in relation to the transcendental realm, such as the use of charms for the enactment of rituals. In such cases the description of what may appear to the observer as 'trivial superstition' must be treated seriously as part of an attempt to respond to existential questions. Such beliefs may well have been subject to various personal idiosyncrasies which could appear at one level to be random and independent of any commonly held system of belief. Yet, although eclectic, in some cases these contributed to a wider pattern of belief which extended beyond individual households to form part of a more extended narrative of meaning. The oral character of folk wisdom ensured that it remained closely bound to the personal associations of popular culture and to a concept of family, community, and popular heritage. These traditions were perpetuated primarily, although not exclusively, by women. They formed part of an explanatory framework of belief which placed the human world within a super-empirical and, on occasions, a supernatural frame of reference and it is as such that they are described here as a folk religious discourse.[5]

It is an assumption frequently made that folk beliefs of this kind were excluded from this sort of highly urbanized arena. If localized pockets of superstition are identified they are considered anomalies or treated as fossils of a previous pre-industrial age doomed to inevitable extinction in the course of socio-economic change. The persistence of a folk narrative in urban Southwark during this period qualifies the view that the kinds of folk beliefs traditionally associated with the countryside had either disappeared entirely or had degenerated into a mere residue of arbitrary and impersonal forms of luck. There was no straightforward process of decline from a traditional past to a modern present in which superstition and folk belief gradually fell by the social and religious wayside. The Lovett material and the oral evidence together call into question the assumption made by Jeffrey Cox, for example, that 'The spread of scientific ideas and the emergence of an urban working class culture finished the job begun by the Protestant Reformation and purged diffusive christianity of centuries-old non-Christian accretions'.[6]

Furthermore, it suggests that a number of the features of folk practice and belief identified by James Obelkevich in rural South Lindsey[7] were

[5] Robert Towler argues for the status of superstition as a form of common religion in *Homo Religiosus* (1974), 156, and David Martin includes superstition in his discussion of religion in *A Sociology of English Religion* (1968), 74.

[6] J. Cox, *The English Churches in a Secular Society: Lambeth 1870–1930* (Oxford, 1982), 95.

[7] J. Obelkevich, *Religion and Rural Society in South Lindsey 1825–1875* (Oxford, 1976).

also found in London at the end of the nineteenth century and in the early decades of the twentieth century.

The use of the term 'traditional' as a descriptive category for folk beliefs of this kind must bear at least some of the responsibility for their treatment as mere pagan, antiquarian, or pre-modern survivals. The term is often applied to particular forms of belief or behaviour at certain stages of social development. Yet custom and tradition are more profitably seen, as most folklorists now insist, as a dynamic process of social interaction rather than as a set of artefacts or as components in a canon of certain kinds of defined belief. Emphasis is placed, for example, on the process by which tradition is created and upon the conferment of customary or traditional status on recently acquired practices. The inhabitants of Southwark considered a particular remedy, such as the use of cat skin as a remedy for rheumatism and chest complaints,[8] as 'traditional' when it had in fact been newly introduced to the Borough of Southwark by Belgian refugees during the First World War. The status of such remedies as 'traditional cures' lies in a particular concept of the past with which the present claims continuity. The creation of an idea of popular heritage in which superstitious cures, remedies, rituals, and practices were central is in itself as significant as the persistence of particular traditions through time.[9] At the same time familiar folk customs like those found in rural areas and earlier periods were employed in different settings and invested with different meaning. The urban environment created new contexts in which anxiety and uncertainty were expressed and in which aspects of folk custom were employed. The so-called gap between certainty and uncertainty, anxiety and assurance did not inevitably diminish with social and economic change;[10] rather the points at which the controllable and the capricious met were located in different places and in different ways within the experience of the individual and in the culture as a whole. As the anthropologist Anthony Cohen has argued, aspects of culture from the past continue into the present,

. . . not because of inertia or conservatism but because they play important roles within contemporary social settings. Indeed some are revived from the past

---

[8] Original labels of the Lovett Collection.

[9] Both A. Gailey, 'The Nature of Tradition', *Folklore*, 100 (1989), 143–61 and P. Joyce, *Visions of the People: Industrial England and the Question of Class 1840–1914* (1991), 145–71, examine the idea of tradition as process.

[10] N. Abercrombie, J. Barker, S. Brett, and J. Foster, 'Superstition and Religion: The God of the Gaps', *Sociological Yearbook of Religion*, 3 (1970), 93–129.

to serve in the same way. Others are of recent origin and yet others are being continuously created for new or for old purposes.[11]

For a number of those interviewed in Southwark, and in much of the material amassed by Edward Lovett, seemingly trivial and incidental habits such as avoiding the spilling of salt, the crossing of knives, the opening of umbrellas indoors, and the placing of shoes on the table, were caught up in a more extensive expression of folk belief. This included a belief in portents and foreknowledge, the enactment of spells and rituals, and the employment of specific objects, charms, mascots, and amulets for particular purposes including the cure of diseases. Furthermore, the expression of these beliefs remained associated with certain figures within the community and embraced a more general fascination with the supernatural including a belief in the visible and personal manifestation of the spiritual realm in the form of ghosts. Mrs Cotton (the daughter of a compositor from Peckham, born in 1910), Barbara Luke (the daughter of a ladies' tailor from Peckham, born in 1921), Anna Telby (the daughter of a laundry woman from Colbar Square, Marylebone, born in 1905), and Elizabeth Merritt (the daughter of a carpenter from Walworth, born in 1912), all recalled how in their households and in their mothers' households particular activities were prohibited on the grounds of preventing the intervention of ill luck which threatened to strike the family at the slightest opportunity. For each of them, seemingly trivial or apparently incidental activities were diligently avoided as part of a broader system of belief in the presence and power of a supernatural realm to affect the course of everyday life. The placing of slippers on the table, for example, could induce a violent reaction in Mrs Cotton's household because of its unlucky associations: 'Wouldn't have slippers on table. They'd be slung flying . . . you might have got a wallop for that.'[12]

The same was true for Anna Telby and Elizabeth Merritt.

Never put a pair of shoes on the table or slippers that's bad luck, never, that's bad luck, right, that's bad luck . . . [13]

If I put some shoes on the table, take 'em off it's unlucky.[14]

A number of those interviewed recalled a similar reaction to the cross-

---

[11] A. Cohen, *Two Dimensional Man: An Essay on the Anthropology of Power and Symbolism in Complex Society* (1974), 3.
[12] SCW, Int. 22.
[13] SCW, Int. 13.
[14] SCW, Int. 21.

ing of knives and the upsetting of salt. Barbara Luke, for example, described how for her mother, '. . . you could never cross two knives together, or there'd be a row, you couldn't never do that and if you dropped salt you had to sling it over your shoulder for good luck . . .'[15] Similarly, Mrs Cotton recalled: 'Tell you what; my mum if she spilt the salt she'd throw a bit over her shoulder'.[16]

Such practices were commonplace and widespread not only in the interviews carried out in Southwark but throughout the country in rural and urban areas alike.[17] The journal *Notes and Queries*, for example, recorded the aversion to placing slippers on the table in Shropshire in 1869,[18] in Stromness and Orkney in 1909,[19] and in London in 1884.[20] Similarly, the crossing of knives was described as unlucky and liable to precipitate a quarrel by both E. M. Leather in Herefordshire in 1912[21] and by C. S. Burne in Shropshire in 1883,[22] while averting the ill effects of spilling salt by throwing a little over the shoulder was widely recorded.[23] The Primitive Methodist, Agnes Bowlin, who appears in Robert Roberts's recollections of Salford in the early years of the twentieth century, was said to be horrified at any of the above. 'You'll pay for that', she would say when any of them were transgressed.[24] In the recollections of these individuals, however, such practices emerge alongside a wide range of personal superstitions and practices. At least two of the women interviewed recalled avoiding certain colours for fear of incurring ill fortune. Mrs Cotton would not wear red. She described how she rejected a gift of some slippers as they had red rose buds on them which she believed were sufficient to attract bad luck. Elizabeth Merritt described in some detail how her mother would not have the colour green in her house.

I had a little black doll (only about as big as that), and the lady downstairs she knitted an outfit for it in green. I told mum, 'Oh', she said, 'unlucky colour'. I

---

[15] SCW, Int. 6.

[16] SCW, Int. 22.

[17] See e.g. I. Opie and M. Tatem, *A Dictionary of Superstitions* (Oxford, 1989), 350, 342–5, 219.

[18] *Notes and Queries: A Medium of Communication for Literary Men, Artists, Antiquarians, Genealogists*, 4th series, 4 (1869), 307.

[19] *Notes and Queries*, 10th series, 12 (1909), 484.

[20] *Notes and Queries*, 6th series, 9 (1884), 66.

[21] E. M. Leather, *The Folklore of Herefordshire* (1912), 87.

[22] C. S. Burne, *Shropshire Folklore: A sheaf of Gleanings*, edited from the collections of G. F. Jackson (1883), 279.

[23] Opie and Tatem, *A Dictionary of Superstitions*, 342–3.

[24] R. Roberts, *A Ragged Schooling: Growing up in a Classic Slum* (Manchester, 1976), 102.

said, 'It's only a doll' and put it away in my little toy cupboard 'cos I was pleased with it. The next day I went to look for it, I could find the doll but not the dress. 'Oh', I said 'Mum the dress has gone'. 'Yes I burnt it, put it on the fire . . .' Oh I was upset.[25]

Likewise, Philippa Ivy of Dulwich, born in 1904, described how her mother insisted, among other things, that lavender and lilac must never enter her house. 'Lavender, mustn't have lavender, my mother used to put her hands in her ears when the lavender people were crying and you couldn't take lilac into the house.'[26]

Although personal and idiosyncratic, the beliefs which lay behind these specific aversions were verbalized on the basis of a narrative in which the immanence of misfortune was stressed and the medium through which it could be averted described. For some, such practices were also associated with a belief in portents and foreknowledge. Mrs Cotton recalled how the behaviour of the household was restricted on the basis of certain portents of future evil or good fortune. These were discerned from reading the cinders which fell from the fire.

You know when you get a clinker, bit of cinder come out of the fire, leave it don't touch it, she'd wait and she'd pick it up. I know many a time . . . 'Oh my gawd', she'd say 'throw it back'. I know once it had a dent in it . . . oh yes in her mind she'd just touch it, shape of a coffin . . . she'd crush it and throw it back.[27]

Both Anna Telby and her mother insisted that the dropping of a knife was a sign of a surprise, and the dropping of a spoon an indication that a letter would soon be arriving and Anna Telby even argued that

If a sparrow comes in your place (and it's true . . .) If a sparrow comes in your place that's bad luck (and it does happen), someone dies in the family or they've been robbed or they've had an accident (that's true). The other one is . . . If I buy a loaf of bread (and I still do this today) if I buy a loaf of bread, a loaf of cut slice, and I take one and put it under the toaster and it's got a hole in it like that, I say that's someone died that I know and more or less that's always someone died that I know . . . [28]

Sayings which dictated behaviour surrounded not only the placing of cutlery but also fallen pictures and broken mirrors.[29] The latter were believed to presage a death in the family. As the folklorist E. M. Leather argued in the case of Hereford in 1912, little sayings about good and bad luck were found in almost everything that happened fortuitously.

[25] SCW, Int. 21.   [26] SCW, Int. 17.   [27] SCW, Int. 22.
[28] SCW, Int. 13.   [29] Ibid.

The crossing of a knife is the sign of a visitor; a coming stranger may also be announced by a smokey film hanging on the bar of the grate or by the lid of the tap being left open or by a bumble bee coming in through the window. If you go to see a neighbour and find that she is poking the fire as you enter it is a sign that you are not welcome. She may pretend to be glad to see you but that's no difference. If when dressing a woman put her stocking on the wrong side out it is for luck, but if she turns it the luck will change.[30]

Elizabeth Merritt recalled her belief in this last practice. She described how she would avoid turning her clothes the right way round if she accidentally put them on inside out, in order to preserve her luck.[31]

The active avoidance of bad luck was interwoven not only with portent and foreknowledge but also with the enactment of certain rituals and the specific use of charms, mascots, and amulets. Alf Westall of Rockingham Street, Southwark, born in 1910, recalled the commonplace ritual of turning round three times at the sight of a black cat,[32] while Jim Bower from Abbey Street, Bermondsey, born in 1919, described avoiding the cracks in the pavement, especially when one had had a bet,[33] and spitting on the ground at the sight of a white horse and saying 'first luck'.[34] Such commonplace rituals could be related more specifically to certain objects and to more elaborate spells and charms. Helen Westall, the daughter of a labourer from Deptford, born in 1915, recalled picking up pennies, keeping them, and rubbing them from time to time and saying '. . . that will bring me luck'.[35] Her recollection may explain the large number of old English copper coins which were found in the Lovett Collection and which he described as good luck charms. Lilian Tims from Massinger Street, Southwark, born in 1918, recalled how one old man in her street, who sent her to place his bets for him, would enact the ritual of tapping his rabbit's foot whenever a bet was made.[36]

The Lovett Collection also suggests that more elaborate rituals were used to secure specific forms of good fortune such as love, just as they had been in rural areas half a century before. Lovett recorded in *Magic in Modern London* (1925) how the root of a small yellow wild flower (*potentilla tormentilla*) was purchased by girls in the East End of London

[30] Leather, *The Folklore of Herefordshire*, 86.

[31] SCW, Int. 21.

[32] SCW, Int. 2.

[33] SCW, Int. 1.

[34] SCW, Int. 1. Cf. Iona Opie and Moira Tatem's description of this practice in Opie and Tatem, *A Dictionary of Superstitions*, 444–5. See also I. and P. Opie, *The Lore and Language of School Children* (Oxford, 1970), 208.

[35] SCW, Int. 2.

[36] SCW, Int. 23.

when they suffered in love.[37] Tormentil root was burnt at midnight on a Friday. The special efficacy of this ritual was believed to lie in its power to revive a dead or waning affection.[38] It was guaranteed so to torment and worry the offending male that he would soon return to his sweetheart. Lovett goes on to write that

Some years ago I was informed by one of my herbalist friends 'down east' that he often had visits to his shop by girls of the locality, chiefly factory hands, and that they came to buy penny packets of dragon's blood. His interest being aroused he asked them what they wanted it for and from the amused and sometimes confused appearance of the girls added to his own experience and knowledge he said there was no doubt the dragon's blood was used as a love philtre.[39]

Similar instances are recorded in Bromley-by-Bow and in Shoreditch.[40] These descriptions bear a marked similarity to incidents recorded by E. M. Leather in Herefordshire in the early 1900s. 'Dragon's blood' was used here as a love charm. It was thrown on the fire while the enquirer chanted,

> Tis this blood I mean to burn,
> Hoping ——'s heart to burn,
> That he (or she) can neither rest nor sleep
> Till he come to me to speak.[41]

The collection also suggests that in twentieth-century London evil could be avoided through spells and magical rituals. The ritual of piercing a heart with pins was not unheard of as a more elaborate measure used to avert the evil influence of a spell. A dairyman in Bethnal Green during the 1920s was convinced that a spell had been put on his cows after two of them had fallen ill and died. He took the heart of one of the dead cows, pierced it with pins, and hung it in his fireplace. It was not long before reparations were made to the dairyman by a neighbour who had poisoned the cows with yew.[42] Lovett's exhibition in 1917 also contained a sheep's heart pierced with pins to break the spell of a black witch. It was prepared by a woman who practised witchcraft in London in the 1910s. She both practised and recommended the remedy of piercing a heart with pins and hanging it in one's chimney as a means of protecting property against the machinations of an evil

---

[37] Lovett, *Magic in Modern London*, 9.
[38] Lovett, 'Belief in Charms', 99.
[39] Lovett, *Magic in Modern London*, 21.
[40] E. Lovett, 'Folk Medicine in London', *Folklore*, 24 (1913), 120–1.
[41] Leather, *The Folklore of Herefordshire*, 64.
[42] E. Lovett, 'Londoners still Believe in Superstitions', *The Evening News*, 1 Oct. 1926.

marauder.[43] These examples bear remarkable similarity to an incident recorded by Lovett in the *Folklore Journal* for 1909. A shepherd from the South Downs believed that his pigs had been 'overlooked' by a witch when a number of them began to sicken and die. His response, as in the cases cited in London, was to take the heart from one of the pigs and stick pins in it, thereby bringing various misfortunes upon the person with the evil eye and forcing him or her to renounce their malevolent influence.[44]

Both good and bad luck could be controlled not only though rituals of these kinds but also through a range of charms, amulets, and lucky objects. Lovett contended that most Londoners of the hawker class, by which he meant those who carried out their business by means of a hand barrow, carried some charm or mascot or performed some ritual which was believed to have magical efficacy.

It is a common idea that few traces of folk beliefs can be found in great cities but my experience is that, at any rate for the seeker after amulets, there is no better hunting ground than the hawkers' hand barrows in the poorest parts of our slums of such dense aggregations of people as London, Rome and Naples.[45]

The use of such mascots was to 'assist in bringing about the desires of the wearer or to ward off all that may be hurtful or unfortunate'.[46] The malevolent effects of 'overlooking', for example, could be averted not only through spells but also through the use of preventative mascots and charms. Lovett claimed that a fear of the evil eye was widespread in London during this period and that a number of charms were used to avert its influence.[47] It was the first piercing glance of the possessor of the evil eye which was believed to be formidable and which demanded a protective charm. Lovett attributed the practice among soldiers of pinning little golliwogs to their tunics to this particular fear of 'overlooking'.[48] He also cited the use of horse-shoe brasses by costermongers and hawkers as an example of an amulet used to effect the same purpose.[49] On occasions the wearing of a charm was accompanied by the ritual of crossing the fingers or raising the index and little fingers to achieve the same purpose

---

[43] Lovett, 'Belief in Charms', 100.

[44] E. Lovett, 'Superstitions and Survivals among Shepherds', *Folklore*, 20 (1909), 65.

[45] E. Lovett, 'Amulets and Coster Barrows in London, Rome and Naples', *Folklore*, 20 (1909), 70.

[46] E. Lovett, 'English Charms, Amulets and Mascots', *Croydon Guardian*, 17 Dec. 1910.

[47] Ibid.

[48] Lovett, *Magic in Modern London*, 83.

[49] Ibid.

or with the piercing of a pigeon's heart with pins in more extreme cases.[50] The former may be compared with the widespread custom in Rome and Naples during the same period of placing in shop windows a stuffed glove with the two middle fingers and thumb stitched to the palm so that the other fingers made the sign of horns. This device was also employed in these areas specifically to ward off the threat of the evil eye in conjunction with various amulets attached to horse brasses.[51]

Charms of various kinds were believed not only to avert bad luck but also to attract good luck. All abnormal forms of natural objects, such as the left-handed whelk, were considered lucky for the owner.[52] Examples were collected throughout London. Charms resembling the human heart were often worn in the early decades of the twentieth century for the specific purpose of charming love. Hawkers in Whitechapel sold these charms at the price of one penny in 1910. Lovett claimed that small copies of shoes were also found all over London. These were carried as lucky symbols to represent the path of life.[53] A patchwork pincushion in the shape of a boot was found by Lovett in Camberwell in 1919 and was used for the same purpose of attracting prosperity to the owners as they journeyed along the path of life. Similarly, Helen Westall, born in Camberwell in 1915 carried a small elephant charm in her bag to effect the same purpose: 'I've got my little elephant in my bag and ur . . . it been in there for years. If I change my bag that comes with me'.[54]

Both Barbara Luke[55] and Anna Telby[56] carried similar mascots in their bags. Philippa Ivy's mother also had a little silver brooch. Mrs Ivy recalled, 'When she lost it "Oh, we're not going to get any work, we shan't get any work" . . . and everybody had to search round for this little brooch'.[57]

The practice of carrying rabbits' feet was considered common by a number of those interviewed in the oral project. Sydney Barry of Merrow Street, Walworth, born in 1921, argued that it was widespread.[58] Small glass rolling pins were, likewise, a common feature in households in the

---

[50] Lovett, 'Londoners still Believe in Superstitions'.
[51] Lovett, 'Amulets and Coster Barrows in London, Rome and Naples', 71.
[52] Lovett, *Magic in Modern London*, 10.
[53] Ibid. 33.
[54] SCW, Int. 2. There are a number of suggestions elsewhere that elephants were considered lucky. D. Scannel, for example, in *Mother Knew Best* (1974), 53, described how everyone knew that an elephant's hair bracelet was lucky.
[55] SCW, Int. 6.
[56] SCW, Int. 13.
[57] SCW, Int. 17.
[58] SCW, Int. 12.

London docks. These were given to sailors filled with rum. When the rum had been consumed they were carried home filled with perfume and hung as lucky charms in the homes of sailors. The idea behind these charms bears a remarkable similarity to Mrs Cotton's practice of hanging a small bottle which used to contain French liqueur in her home for luck.[59] She described how she fixed coins or silver into the cork of this bottle and would never be without money because of it.

Lovett expressed surprise at the degree to which London street dealers could articulate the particular beliefs underpinning the practice of carrying amulets and charms of these kinds.[60] They were consciously employed as preventative guards against undesirable spiritual influences to which the individual was potentially subject. Moreover, a number of them derived particular efficacy from their association with the Deity or with overtly Christian symbolism. The Lovett material, for example, includes a small leather shoe found in Whitechapel in 1920. The intricate design of the Christian cross interwoven with the sun which covered the shoe was considered a particularly powerful charm and it was hung in the home for good luck. The collection also contained a charm against sudden illness in the form of a small sacred heart made of black silk containing ashes collected on Ash Wednesday. These were believed to be a potent preventative guard against illness because they had been blessed by the nuns at Donerville, Cork in 1845. In addition, Lovett's collection of charms and mascots contained a series of medals belonging to sailors of the London Docks area. These were worn to avert the specific danger of storms. On one side was the figure of St George and on the other was a design representing Christ directing the storm with the words, '*In tempestate Securitas*'. These were very similar to sacred heart charms collected by Lovett and carried by sailors in order to charm the demons of the storm.[61]

The connection of certain charms with Christian symbolism is borne out in the oral material. During the course of an interview with Anna Telby, for example, a number of objects were produced from her handbag. These included a rosary, a medallion which she claimed showed Christ in the garden of Eden, a set of keys which had formerly opened a money box, and a small piece of cork in a brown leather purse.[62] The set of keys was kept as a charm to bring prosperity alongside the medallion

[59] SCW, Int. 22.
[60] Lovett, 'Amulets and Coster Barrows', 70–1.
[61] Lovett, 'English Charms'.
[62] SCW, Int. 13.

and the rosary. Both of these had been worn on a string around her neck earlier in life and they had been kept subsequently in her bag for fifty years. She considered the rosary to have particular efficacy as it had been blessed: 'That rosary's been blessed, so I know that's alright. It's all been blessed.'[63]

The piece of cork was associated with a specific ritual through which Mrs Telby made wishes: 'You put that on the floor, go round it three times, say to yourself, I wish I could go, so and so . . . wish I could go so and so and it 'appens'.[64]

This practice of wishing by means of the cork was carried out in association with prayer. When Mrs Telby needed anything she would pray and wish and when she received the object of her desire both God and the cork would be thanked without any sense of incongruity in her mind.

For others the crucifix and the Bible were believed to be particularly potent lucky objects or charms. In her oral interview Elizabeth Merritt used the cross as an example of a lucky charm and she described how she was given it specifically to wear for luck.[65] Similarly, Jim Bower wore a crucifix during the war. When asked if he remembered soldiers carrying any charms during the war he replied immediately, 'Oh yeah, yeah, I used to wear a crucifix. Others had all sorts of things like sacred hearts pinned on the inside you know . . .'[66]

Copies of the Bible could be used in the same way. Possessing and carrying a Bible was also considered lucky. When asked if her family had a Bible, Mrs Ivy replied, 'Oh yes, you had to have a Bible otherwise you were unlucky if you didn't have a Bible'.[67] When asked why it was unlucky not to have a Bible she merely re-emphasised the point by saying, '. . . my mother used to say, yes, you won't have any luck if you don't have a Bible in the house'.[68]

Sid Venables, the son of a greengrocer, born in Camberwell in 1913, had little contact with church-based culture at any point in his life beyond attending Sunday school as a child, and yet he attached considerable importance to a Bible which he was given as he joined the Royal Air Force at the beginning of the Second World War: 'I had the Old Testament and the New Testament when I was in the RAF I always carried that wherever I went.'[69]

His concern to keep the Bible with him was an attachment similar to that displayed in Mrs Ivy's interview. He carried his Bible in the manner

---

[63] SCW, Int. 13.   [64] Ibid.   [65] SCW, Int. 21.   [66] SCW, Int. 1.
[67] SCW, Int. 17.   [68] Ibid.   [69] SCW, Int. 8.

of a preventative guard to secure good fortune and to prevent ill luck, in much the same way that Elizabeth Merritt and Jim Bower wore crucifixes. An article in *Cassell's Saturday Journal* for 1900 included a description of copies of the Bible in a more general list of charms carried by soldiers in times of war.

Numbers of men even among the volunteers do not depart from the front without a charm of some kind. One laid deeply to heart the old story about the bullet lodging in the Bible—a providential escape that really happened two or three times during the last Egyptian campaign. The 'Tommy' in question purchased a copy of the scriptures that was partly perforated at Omdurman, deeming it a 'lucky object' that would preserve him against harm at the enemy's hands. But to make doubly sure, he brought a copy of the Bible to which no history out of the usual was attached and thus became, as he thought quite bullet proof.[70]

The Bible and the crucifix were part of a more extensive range of mascots and amulets carried in wartime. The same article went on to describe other 'curious mementos of the battle field'.[71] These were all brought at a high price as 'luck bringers'. They included a bent and battered penny which had been struck twice by a bullet. Other military mascots were carried which had been handed down in fighting families from one generation to the next. The same article described how one soldier

. . . now at the front, for instance, is carrying about with him a 'lucky' wallet which an ancestor bore through the peninsula war and which has since been in the thick of many a bloody fight. There is said to be a strange tradition associated with the article which is supposed to render its owner invulnerable.[72]

Lovett also described how most soldiers carried mascots into action during the First World War both to attract luck and to prevent mis-fortune.[73] A number of lucky boots were found in the Lovett collection which were carried as a charm by soldiers in the Great War. In addition, Lovett reported that 'During the Great War many men had a farthing sewn on the left brace just above the position of the heart'.[74]

These acted as lucky charms in much the same way as those described by Jim Bower. In July 1917, Lovett also found pincushions carried widely by sailors from the London docks as a charm against drowning, and 'Old

[70] *Cassell's Saturday Journal*, 4 Apr. 1900, 620.
[71] Ibid.
[72] Ibid.
[73] Lovett, *Magic in Modern London*, 10.
[74] Ibid. 70.

Charlie', who kept an oyster and whelk stall in Whitechapel, is recorded as having given left-handed whelk shells to soldiers returning from action.[75]

Such descriptions of the use of amulets and charms during war-time conditions is strongly supported elsewhere. Samuel Stouffer, for example, in his extensive study of soldiers in the wake of the Second World War, recorded many magical or semi-magical practices among combat men. These included the carrying of a protective amulet or good luck charm such as a rabbit's foot. In addition, certain supposedly unlucky actions, such as three men lighting their cigarettes on a single match,[76] were carefully avoided. Pre-battle preparations were carried out in a fixed 'ritual order'. Articles of clothing and equipment which were associated with some past experience of escape from danger were kept jealously.[77] Similarly, Geoffrey Gorer estimated that during the Second World War one serving man or woman in three had his or her own 'piece of solid magic'.[78] Many of these charms and practices were also associated with the act of prayer. Most men prayed before going into action. Stouffer argued that 'the Lord's Prayer is on men's lips all the time'.[79] He described this kind of prayer as expressive of a 'quasi-magical act'[80] which was born out of a deep-seated belief in an 'unseen power who they feel is there'.[81] This was closely identified with a more general and wide-ranging resurgence in the belief in luck, fate, and fortune which emerged during the war and which persisted into the interwar period.

The uncertainty of wartime conditions was seen to precipitate a revival of fatalistic beliefs. The Army and Religion Survey which recorded the attitudes of soldiers during the First World War, carried out by a committee chaired by the Bishop of Winchester, noted common sentiments such as 'If there is one for you [a shell] you'll get it if your number is on it', 'I'm not for it until one comes for me . . . If I've got to go, I've got to go it's no good worrying. I'm what you'd call a fatalist I am'.[82] Jay Winter has argued on the basis of this kind of material that

[75] Lovett, *Magic in Modern London*, 10.
[76] This practice was common in Walworth in the interwar period. See, for example, E. J. Orford, *The Book of Walworth* (1925), 61.
[77] S. A. Stouffer, *The American Soldier; Combat and Its Aftermath* (Princeton, 1949), 188.
[78] G. Gorer, *Exploring English Character* (1955), 265.
[79] Stouffer, *op.cit.*, p. 186.
[80] Ibid.
[81] Ibid. 167.
[82] D. S. Cairns (ed.), *The Army and Religion, An Enquiry and its Bearing upon the Religious Life of the Nation* (1919) 159.

The sense of the uncanny, the over-determined nature of survivals in combat can be found in many memoirs and letters written by service men. Many maintained the paradox between belief in personal invulnerability and belief in the power of fate determining whether a sniper's bullet or the shell had 'their number on it'.[83]

Moreover, Hubert Llewellyn Smith associated the explosion of popular gambling during and after the war with the same kinds of belief and with a social climate in which chance predominated.[84]

Recourse to these kinds of beliefs and activities was not limited to the front line. Llewellyn Smith was careful to point out that popular gambling and its associated mentality were also prevalent at home.

If there was a great temptation to gamble amongst soldiers and sailors there was not much less amongst the civilian population. With them too a profound sense of instability was the prevailing emotion. The only certain thing was the uncertainty of the morrow.[85]

He estimated that four out of every five families in poorer London undertook some form of gambling from time to time.[86] Similarly, in his study of Walworth, E. J. Orford associated gambling with the uncertainties of the interwar period: 'Life is so full of hazards that the first voluntary plunge that leads to the habit is almost inevitable'.[87] At home as well as the front, prayers were associated with these kinds of fatalistic beliefs. Mrs Croft, born in 1908, the daughter of a soldier from Dulwich, described how her mother would often pray and teach her children to do so whilst at the same time avoiding certain practices on certain days and adhering to an active philosophy of 'whatever shall be shall be'.[88]

During the war and interwar period when uncertainty and change were felt to be key characteristics of the period, a familiar folk theodicy took on a new significance, whereby suffering was placed within a wider explanatory and mitigatory framework on the basis of notions of good and bad luck.[89] The forms which various responses to the super-empirical sphere took, both during and after the war, were determined by already familiar folk responses. Lovett, for example, identified how certain superstitions took on a renewed significance during the upheaval

---

[83] J. M. Winter, 'Spiritualism and the First World War', in R. W. Davis and R. J. Helmstadter (eds.), *Religion and Irreligion in Victorian Society* (1992) 191.

[84] H. Llewellyn Smith, *The New Survey of London Life and Labour* (1931), x. 273–4.

[85] Ibid. 274.

[86] Ibid. 281.

[87] E. J. Orford, *The Book of Walworth* (1925), 61.

[88] SCW, Int. 18.

[89] David Clark uses this definition of a folk theodicy in *Between Pulpit and Pew: Folk Religion in a North Yorkshire Fishing Village* (1982), 8.

of the war. At the time of the Napoleonic wars there was a limited trade in cauls as a popular charm against death at sea. A single specimen would fetch as much as twenty pounds. For most of the nineteenth century, however, there was less demand for these objects and in 1910 they sold for as little as twenty-five shillings a piece. Lovett argued in 1917, however, that, 'Now thanks to the activities of the German underwater craft they are being sold at the London Docks for two pounds ten shillings'.[90]

Furthermore, practices which were in themselves specific to the early twentieth century such as the practice of avoiding 'three on a match', resembled many earlier forms of prescriptive behaviour. Moreover, various folk artefacts and customs were employed in adapted and novel forms as a means of bridging the gap between the old and the new, the familiar and the unfamiliar. In much the same way new urban phenomena of various kinds were accompanied by charms and folk rituals. Notable among these were certain kinds of modern house decoration and motor car mascots. In 1926 Edward Lovett wrote an article for the *Daily Mail* in which he described the common practice of incorporating 'old-fashioned' witch balls into modern house decoration. Coloured glass balls suspended in a part of the room where they attracted the most light were becoming a frequent accessory of modern dwellings. Lovett identified these witch balls as revivals of some made in Bristol in the latter part of the eighteenth century. They were supposed to bring good luck to the owner as they gradually accumulated dust. Modern copies of witch balls were being manufactured for this purpose during the 1920s in various colours to blend with a choice of decor.[91]

Similarly, there was a great demand for the new motor mascot during the same period. These included metal dogs or cats, tigers, teddy bears, and other toys and wooden effigies of motor cars. These were often advertised as part of the package one received when purchasing a motor car and as an additional means of ensuring the reliability of the vehicle. These new or 'commercial' charms were frequently used in conjunction with older types of travelling mascot in the form of representations of St Christopher. In addition, Lovett noted that chauffeurs often carried a nail which had caused a puncture or a holed stone as a charm to prevent the repetition of such difficulties. Other items included effigies of policemen with hands outstretched to stop the traffic bearing the words, 'propitiate the fate'.[92]

[90] Lovett, 'Belief in Charms', 99.

[91] E. Lovett, 'Old-Fashioned Witchballs in Modern House Decoration', *Daily Mail*, 29 Dec. 1926.   [92] Ibid.

Both the witch balls and the motor car charms were subject to a degree of commercialization which was accompanied by a change in the language used to describe charms and amulets from the 1880s onwards. Lovett argued that the word 'mascot' was replacing earlier words such as amulet or charm. He traced the currency of mascot to the popularity of the comic opera *La Mascotte* which made its debut in 1880. This change in nomenclature is borne out in an article in *Cassell's Saturday Journal* in 1899 entitled, 'Do You Possess a Mascot?' Here the writer defines a 'mascotte' as an object carried widely to bring good luck and to ensure the possession of a 'good eye' rather than an 'evil eye' for the owner. The writer also describes how the shorter term 'mascot' was more frequently used in recent years.[93] These mascots were part of wider exploitation for commercial advantage of the various beliefs in luck. During this period numerous advertisements harnessed the notion of obtaining luck by things worn or carried as an effective medium through which to appeal to the consumer. Newspaper and periodical advertisements of this kind were designed to appeal particularly to women of all ranks of society. Lovett described articles which used as their opening line the question, 'Do you want to know what are the lucky days, months, numbers, colours or the Christian name of the person you should marry?'[94] He argued that while the servant girl studied her *Dream Book,* her mistress had *Planets of the Month, Consult the Oracle,* and many other books telling her what to do and what to avoid for luck.[95] A language of luck and popular superstition was interwoven with popular advertising. Dr Tibbe's Cocoa, for example, was advertised with the slogan: 'Never despair. A silver Six-pence may be your mascot ... but just straight away invest it in a packet of cocoa.'[96]

Lovett did not believe that the upsurge in commercial exploitation undermined genuine beliefs of this kind; rather he saw it as an indication of the expansion of a belief in luck which he argued had taken place during the later decades of the nineteenth century and into the twentieth century.[97] Furthermore, there was continuity both in form and function between the modern mascots and earlier types of charms. Newly imported green stone or lucky jade mascots from New Zealand, for example, continue to resemble earlier charms designed to hang in the

---

[93] *Cassell's Saturday Journal,* 5 Oct. 1899, 85.
[94] Lovett, 'Belief in Charms', 99–100.
[95] Ibid.
[96] Ibid.
[97] E. Lovett, 'Specimens of Modern Mascots and Ancient Amulets in the British Isles', *Folklore,* 19 (1908), 288.

home. Similarly, although large department stores such as Spiers and Ponds and Hamleys were in this period selling 'Nelro's cup of fortune', the same modern teacup was used widely for the traditional practice of tea-leaf fortune-telling.

The possession of various types of charm and the enactment of certain rituals described above were believed not only to secure luck and avert misfortune but also to cure specific diseases. Lovett found that whooping cough was treated in late-nineteenth- and early-twentieth-century London by an ancient witchcraft custom. The hair from the head of the suffering child was taken and placed between two pieces of bread. This was then given to a passing dog who, it was hoped, would carry the disease away: 'Put a hair of the patient's head between two slices of buttered bread and give it to a dog. The dog will get the cough and the patient lose it.'[98]

William Henderson recorded the use of a similar ritual in the 1860s in the northern counties of England. Here the crown of the head was shaved and the hair hung on a bush or tree in the belief that the birds would carry the cough away.[99] Similarly, a common cure for warts was to touch each wart with a different small stone and to place the stones in a parcel which was then left in the road or footpath. The warts were thus transferred to the person finding the parcel.[100] John Harland and T. T. Wilkinson, recording Lancashire legends in the 1870s, described the same practice.

In order to cure warts we are told to put the same number of small pebbles into a bag as there are warts, then to drop the bag where three or four roads meet and the person who picks it up will obtain the warts in addition.[101]

A similar practice was found by William Henderson a decade earlier in the northern counties and the Borders,[102] by Robert Hunt in Devon at the same date,[103] by Richard Blakeborough at the end of the nineteenth century in North Yorkshire,[104] and by E. M. Leather in the early years of the twentieth century in Herefordshire.[105] Like the other writers, Leather records how a packet was made up, in this case of grains of wheat or

---

[98] Lovett, *Magic in Modern London*, 33.
[99] W. Henderson, *Notes on the Folklore of the Northern Counties of England* (1879), 111.
[100] Lovett, 'Folk Medicine in London', 120–1.
[101] J. Harland and T. T. Wilkinson, *Lancashire Legends* (1873), 226.
[102] Henderson, *Notes on the Folklore of the Northern Counties*, 108.
[103] R. Hunt, *Popular Romances of the West of England* (1865), 210–11.
[104] R. Blakeborough, *Wit, Character, Folklore and Customs in the North Riding of Yorkshire* (1898), 146.
[105] Leather, *The Folklore of Herefordshire*, 83.

notches in a stick of elder wood, and was thrown over the shoulder of the sufferer at a place where four roads met, in the hope of transferring the warts to the one who discovered the packet.[106]

Teething children were also treated in London in much the same way as they had been elsewhere. The parents' teeth were preserved and placed in a small bag around the baby's neck.[107] Where the parents' teeth were unavailable it seems that some Londoners were not averse to placing a calf's tooth in the bag instead. Lovett found one market-stall keeper selling calves' teeth for this purpose in south London in 1905.[108] Small bags containing preventative or curative objects for the same purpose were used elsewhere during the same period. In King's Pyon in Herefordshire, for example, seven or nine woodlice were placed in a bag around the baby's neck.[109]

The enactment of rituals to cure specific diseases was also found in the oral testimonies of Anna Telby. In the event of an accident involving bleeding, Mrs Telby's mother would adopt the folk practice of stopping the cut with a cobweb.

And if she cut her finger . . . she wouldn't bandage it up. She'd go right round the room looking for cobwebs. She'd stick it in the cobweb like that and that's it healed up. My mum used to do that . . . She never believed in bandaging up her fingers she used to put it in the cob web (go like that . . .). If she cut her finger she'd be looking for the cobweb.[110]

In addition, if her daughter had either toothache or mumps, she would adopt a ritual which she had learnt from the 'old woman' who brought her up.

If I'd been wearing socks, she used to take the sock off what I wear every day and every night I went to bed with a sock round me throat pinned with a safety pin. To stop me mumps and it stopped me mumps . . . my mum cured me . . .[111]

Certain specific objects were also used alongside the performance of various rituals as a means of preventing or curing diseases. Many Londoners, for example, adhered to the practice of wearing blue beads in infancy and maturity as a preventative guard or cure for bronchitis.[112]

[106] Ibid.

[107] Lovett, 'Londoners still Believe in Superstitions'. These bags were also found in the Lovett Collection and his original labels suggest they were collected in south London.

[108] Lovett, *Magic in Modern London*, 23.

[109] Leather, *The Folklore of Herefordshire*, 81.

[110] SCW, Int. 13. Iona Opie and Moira Tatem record the use of spiders' webs as cures for ague. Opie and Tatem, *A Dictionary of Superstitions*, 370–1.

[111] SCW, Int. 13.

[112] Lovett, 'Londoners still Believe in Superstitions'.

This was particularly the case among women. At Islington Market during the early 1920s, Edward Lovett was informed by one old woman that 'everyone wears them . . . I do myself'.[113] When Lovett protested that they were not in evidence she explained that they had to be worn next to the skin and when he raised the delicate question of what happened to them when she had a bath the same woman replied that 'they were never taken off or she would catch cold. If the string broke she would at once thread them again but they must be worn throughout life and be buried with her'.[114]

In order to verify such statements Lovett visited 130 small shops throughout London.[115] In every one of these shops he found that blue beads were sold to be worn by children to prevent and cure bronchitis. The special efficacy of these beads was ensured by their colour. As blue was the colour of the sky, it was believed to put the wearer in sympathy with heaven.[116]

Blue beads were only one example among many of the use of lucky necklaces in the medical lore of London in this period. Coral and oak-apple necklaces were both used against sore throats in children. Amber fragments were worn for general good health, 'fairy' or 'adder' beads[117] were worn to prevent nightmares and acorns were worn for diarrhoea. Both Anna Telby and Philippa Ivy possessed coral necklaces when they were young. Mrs Ivy recalled how 'I had some coral beads. They were round. They were put on tape and I didn't dare take them off. If I did I'd catch cold.'[118]

Molly Layton also recalled how she placed amethyst under her pillow to aid in sleeping.[119] Lovett claimed that potatoes were also used as a less elaborate charm in east London in this period in order to guard the carrier from rheumatism, as they had been used in Lancashire in the 1860s. John Harland and T. T. Wilkinson wrote that 'Those who suffer from rheumatic pains are to carry a potato in their pocket . . .'.[120]

Lovett found that the bone of a sheep was also carried by some for the same purpose in 1916. Cramp was similarly prevented by the possession

[113] Lovett, *Magic in Modern London*, 81.

[114] Ibid.

[115] He described these shops as small establishments usually presided over by an aged woman selling cheap toys and sweets.

[116] Lovett, 'Londoners still Believe in Superstitions'.

[117] A fossil organism found naturally perforated.

[118] SCW, Int. 17.

[119] SCW, Int. 20.

[120] Harland and Wilkinson, *Lancashire Legends*, 226.

of various charmed objects. These included a mole's front paw, a dried frog, and dried skins of various kinds. A number of other writers record the use of dried skins as preventative cures. Eel skin was particularly popular. It was tied round the ankle when swimming as a charm against developing cramp while in the water.[121] Lovett also observed the widespread use of the acorn in London as an amulet against being struck by lightning.[122] Likewise, donkeys' shoes covered in cloth were found hanging over the beds of a number of south Londoners as a charm to drive away nightmares.[123]

Many of the charms, rituals, and remedies described above were associated with the person of the wise-man or woman who, Lovett claimed, was trusted in London as well as in many parts of the countryside.[124] The dairyman from Bethnal Green, for example, on suspecting a spell, visited a 'local wise-woman' who recommended the procedure of piercing the heart of a dead cow.[125] In this example the wise-woman was clearly employed to provide an antidote for the malignant power associated with either a spell or the witch, as individuals had been in rural South Lindsey in the middle of the nineteenth century.[126] Similarly, the *potentilla tormentilla* was recommended by an East End wise-woman,[127] as were the use of a snake skin worn in the hat as a cure for sunstroke,[128] the supplying of a dried frog as a cure for croup and whooping cough, the root of black briony for pains in the limbs, oak-apples for throat troubles, stems of nightshade for cutting teeth, a knuckle bone and sealed bottles of mercury as cures for rheumatism.

The term wise-woman was not used in any of the oral interviews, autobiographies, or reminiscences, but memories about local fortune-tellers do suggest that these women may well have fulfilled the same function and that the distinction was perhaps in some cases simply a matter of terminology. Mrs Cotton, for example, described how she regularly accompanied her mother to visit Mrs Rose, the local fortune-teller who lived in the Old Kent Road.

Yeah her name was Mrs Rose. She lived in the Old Kent Road and then she

---

[121] Henderson, *Notes on the Folklore of the Northern Counties*, 17.

[122] Lovett, *Magic in Modern London*, 65.

[123] Cuming Museum, Original Lovett Collection.

[124] E. Lovett, 'London Witch Doctors', The *Star*, 23 Apr. 1927.

[125] Ibid.

[126] J. Obelkevich, *Religion and Rural Society in South Lindsey 1825–1875* (Oxford, 1976), 286.

[127] Lovett, *Magic in Modern London*, 9.

[128] Lovett, 'London Witch Doctors'.

moved to a turning down here . . . She was very good . . . She'd sit there and go into a kind of trance but she was true. My mum sat one side she used to have her fortune told. What she told us did happen.[129]

Jim Bower also described the existence of local fortune-tellers in Bermondsey who could be consulted for the fee of a penny.[130] Like the wise-women consulted in Cleveland in the 1890s, these women were sought in their homes. They were believed to possess extraordinary power in remedying diseases and in foretelling the future,[131] while their position remained based on local trust as it had been elsewhere.[132]

Such activities appear to have possessed some heritage in urban south London. An interesting example of belief in the power of the wise-woman is given by the case of a girl of 20 who was brought before Bermondsey police court in 1869 charged with fortune-telling. One man had paid her many shillings to turn the heart of his sweetheart towards him. Eventually in desperation he paid the 'wise-woman' a gold ring to cast a spell to cause the girl to turn and love him. After seeing no results he took the woman to court.[133] She was eventually charged with obtaining money under false pretences and was sentenced to twelve months imprisonment.[134] The failure of her spell is, however, perhaps less significant than the fact that a 'wise-woman' was sought to intervene through magic in the arena of love. Examples of local consultations of this kind are similar to those given by Robert Roberts in his autobiography *A Ragged Schooling* (1976). Roberts described a Mr Carley who appears to have performed a balance of magic, occult ritual, and the dissemination of medical lore in urban Manchester in the early twentieth century. Mr Carley was widely consulted for his powers and his wisdom. He could 'fetch up' poltergeists. He ran seances and as a sideline he could treat 'female bad legs' (varicose veins) through various herbs and magical ceremonies.[135] Like the south London fortune-tellers described in the oral reminiscences, Mr Carley lived on the gratuities handed out by satisfied clients.

In south London, fortune-tellers were not averse to visiting the clients in their homes or workplaces. Philippa Ivy described in detail how a

[129] SCW, Int. 22.
[130] SCW, Int. 1.
[131] J. C. Atkinson, *Forty Years in A Moorland Parish* (1891), 111.
[132] P. Rushton, 'A Note on the Survival of Popular Christian Magic', *Folklore*, 191 (1980), 118.
[133] *Bermondsey and Rotherhithe Advertiser*, 24 Oct. 1868.
[134] Ibid.
[135] Roberts, *A Ragged Schooling*, 151–2.

fortune-teller would come each Thursday to her parents' clothes work-shop in order to read the employees' fortunes.

She used to come every Thursday, one of the workers told my Mum about it . . . We used to give her six pence. She used to go upstairs and the workers used to go up there one by one and she used to tell them their future. She told a lot true she did.[136]

Similarly, Rose Embleton recalled how

An old girl used to come round, to read tea cups, she used to come and see my old granny and she said 'all right Tops', she said, 'my mum's come in this after-noon, all right Tops' she said 'I'll tell you your fortune', she said. 'Oh' she said, 'you a bit hard up now', she said 'in time you'll come round, you'll never be hard up, you'll be able to build up', she said, 'so don't worry'. And it's funny my mother like after a time, she always got a few bob, she was never, never without, know what I mean?[137]

The presence of such figures in the community appears to have been firmly linked to female culture in particular. No examples of wise-men have been found in London and even Mr Carley in Manchester appears to have specialized in a female clientele. Both Mrs Cotton and Mrs Ivy were insistent that the practice of consulting a local fortune-teller was strictly a matter for the grandmother, the mother, the daughter, and, in the case of Philippa Ivy, the female workforce. The fortune-teller was admitted to her father's on Thursdays only, when he had gone to deliver coats in the City. Mrs Ivy emphasized the female character of these meetings by pointing out, 'mustn't let Father know . . . '.[138] Later in the interview she returned to the subject and described her father's opposition to the practice; 'Oh no he wouldn't have had that . . . '.[139] In much the same way, Ivy Cotton described how she and her mother would say they had been to visit the 'King and Edward's' in order to hide their visit to Mrs Rose from the male members of the family.

My sisters don't mind, but one of my brothers, 'You bin to that fortune-teller?', 'No we bin round to Farmers or King and Edward's'.
Q: Your brother didn't hold with that then?
A: No, but my Mum did see.
Q: What about your Dad?
A: Oh no, he wouldn't have that but we did.[140]

Jim Bower's description of local Bermondsey fortune-tellers was

[136] SCW, Int. 17. [137] EOHA, Int. 299, 11. [138] SCW, Int. 17
[139] Ibid. [140] SCW, Int. 22.

couched in language which reflected his opposition to the practice. This
opposition was not the product of disbelief, however, but it was based
rather on a strong belief in fate. He considered it wrong to interfere with
the process or force of fate through foretelling the future because, as he
argued, 'If it's going to happen it will happen . . . '.[141] In contrast to the
women, he appears to have held a belief that fate was non-negotiable. He
seems to have believed that it was not open to manipulation or to the
control exerted through foretelling the future.

A large number of the oral interviews also describe specific local
women within the community who were consulted in the event of illness, accident, birth, and death. Although it is impossible to state a clear
connection between these women and those who acted as fully fledged
'wise-women', they were undoubtedly consulted for their wisdom and
their advice. They were the chief propagators of 'old wives' tales', as one
Walworth churchman called their specific brand of advice,[142] and the
respect which they commanded in the community suggests that the
values which they represented continued to hold explanatory authority
within the community. Emma Reynolds of Red Cross Street off the
Borough High Street described how everyone in her court knew her
mother, Mrs Reynolds. She was called upon in moments of anxiety within the community and particularly in the event of a death.

If anyone died (say in the flats) they used to come and say Mrs Reynolds (say Mrs
Jones died) would you come and wash and lay her out. My Mum used to do that,
she used to go round with a collection for the flowers and she used to have the
job of getting tea ready when they got back from the funeral.[143]

Dora Bargate also recorded how her mother was respected throughout the tenement block as a woman of particular wisdom on whom
others relied. Although Bargate does not specifically mention any
magical powers or the recommendation of specific charms or cures, it is
clear that her mother fulfilled a remarkably similar position of trust to
that which appears to have belonged to the wise-woman: 'She would be
called upon to act as midwife or to perform the office of laying out of the
dead or perhaps supply a cure for a cough, or sore throat, a cold or a sore
knee'.[144]

In her autobiography, D. L. Ash describes a similar role for her
mother, as did a number of those interviewed for an Age Exchange

[141] SCW, Int. 1.
[142] L. J. Carter, *Walworth 1929–1939* (1985), 61.
[143] SCW, Int. 4.
[144] Brunel University, Burnett Collection, D. Bargate, 'Memories', n.d., n.p.

project on attitudes towards medicine and health care in the early part of the century.[145] This survey revealed the extent of traditional remedies and beliefs in 'old wives' tales'. In place of the doctor there was a wide range of home cures passed down from one generation to the next. These were propagated in the community by certain women who were believed to have a particular knowledge of the subject.

I know I was climbing a brick wall and they had all glass sticking in the top and I gashed my leg and there was a lot of blood and when I got home my mother took me across to Mrs. Dixon, she wasn't a nurse or anything but she knew a bit about surgery and I'd lost a lot of blood like, you know. But she looked after me and done me well. And every time we had any other accident we were over there, she only lived across the road.[146]

A personal connection was thus maintained between certain individuals within the community and particular kinds of communal practice and wisdom. In these examples the help given is apparently straightforward and practical, yet the evidence also suggests that it may well have overlapped with various kinds of superstitions, as Mary Chamberlain and Ruth Richardson have argued.[147] The practice of laying out the dead, for example, appears to have retained a spiritual colouring. One of Mrs Reynolds's responsibilities was to say a prayer over the dead body. Similarly in other cases the administration of practical help operated alongside the expression of prayer. Louise Codd, for example, born in 1899, the daughter of a carman from Jamaica Road, Bermondsey, described how her mother would attend to sick neighbours.

Yes anyone ill, she would go in. . . . Mrs Panning was dying next door to us and she went in, she said, 'Oh I didn't like her pillow cases, I thought they looked grey'. So she took her in—took her in a couple of her pillow cases, and when she took them in she said, 'would you like me to say a prayer for you?' And she knelt down, said the Lord's Prayer.[148]

In these ways, therefore, many of the customs and beliefs described in this chapter maintained a link with the community in a manner which had not become entirely diffuse or impersonalized. The female community in particular was still able to rally together on the basis of these beliefs against what was considered to be an outside threat. L. J. Carter, for instance, described the deep-seated influence of 'wives' tales' in

[145] Age Exchange, *Can We Afford the Doctor?* (1985).
[146] Ibid. 20.
[147] M. Chamberlain and R. Richardson, 'Life and Death', *Oral History Journal*, 11 (1983), 31–44.
[148] EOHA, Int. 235, 235.

Walworth which united the population in common opposition to the introduction of modern medicine and hygiene during the 1920s and 1930s.[149]

The customs and beliefs, rituals and charms described in the early part of this chapter were not only linked to a personal figure within the community but were also enacted within the context of a more wide-ranging fascination with the supernatural and the corporate perpetuation of legends and stories concerning the visible manifestation of the spiritual realm. A striking aspect of this preoccupation was the belief in ghosts. One notable incident which occurred in Bermondsey during the 1860s became part of the lore of the community. The calendar of notable events published in the *Southwark Annual* continued to record the appearance of the Bermondsey ghost each year until 1895. The ghost became a legendary figure after crowds had been seen nightly surrounding the churchyard in Abbey Street, Bermondsey in July 1868. Their intention was to take a look at the ghost of a man who had drowned in the Thames some days earlier and had been conveyed in a coffin to the dead house adjoining the church in order to await the coroner's inquest.[150] The ghost appeared first on Sunday evening after divine service. This drew crowds, which, according to the police constable on duty in the area, were numbered in hundreds. They congregated by the church walls and waited. One man, James Jones, was remanded in custody for assaulting a police officer while trying to catch a glimpse of the apparition. He had left his employment at a local tan-yard at twilight to see the ghost. The judge overseeing the case, Mr Bucham, expressed his surprise that in the nineteenth century, when education was making such rapid progress, the people ' . . . should be so superstitious as to surround Bermondsey Churchyard for hours in the chance of seeing a ghost'.[151]

The judge went on to add 'That in the year of our Lord 1868 such a tale should be so easily credited does not say much for our boasted civilisation or the alleged superiority of the cockney over the country bumkin'.[152]

Like the ghosts of Lancashire recorded by John Harland and T. T. Wilkinson,[153] the Bermondsey ghost was believed to be most likely to reveal himself at the hours of twilight and midnight and, like the ghosts

---

149 Carter, *Walworth 1929–1939*, 61.
150 *Bermondsey and Rotherhithe Advertiser*, 6 Aug. 1868.
151 Ibid.
152 *Bermondsey and Rotherhithe Advertiser*, 30 Jul. 1868.
153 Harland and Wilkinson, *Lancashire Legends*, 226.

in South Lindsey, his existence was largely dependent upon the socially created expectation within the community.[154] In his work on authority and social structure in three Black Country towns between 1840 and 1890, R .H. Trainor notes a similar instance. A West Bromwich newspaper recorded with dismay the widespread belief in ghosts in the area during the 1880s.[155] Furthermore, the evidence presented by Geoffrey Gorer in his book *Exploring English Character* (1955) suggests that this may have been a feature of urban life which persisted through to the 1950s. He writes of his surprise on discovering that the belief in ghosts was most evident in London and the South East, followed by the Midlands.

I had thought that the belief in ghosts would be most common in the west country and in small towns and villages. In point of fact it is nearly as frequent in the metropolis as in the villages and somewhat less in the middle sized towns.[156]

Furthermore, the work of Gillian Bennett has shown an extensive belief in ghosts among the inhabitants of the Manchester suburb of Gaitley during the second half of the twentieth century. During the course of 120 oral interviews with elderly people in the area, she collected a wide range of stories describing the intervention of ghosts in domestic crises and in the regulation of family affairs. The ghost frequently appears in recollections as the embodiment of a deceased member of the family who returns to make his or her presence felt at decisive moments in family history. Bennett locates these beliefs within a wider system of belief which extended to concepts of premonition, omens, second sight, and telepathy which she argues were widely diffused within the modern environment.[157] Moreover, the recollection of ghosts was structured and narrated on the basis of a common pattern or discourse. Personal stories of the supernatural which circulated within the community thus provided the material from which a consensual view of the supernatural was built. Personal experiences and beliefs were narrated as part of a wider cultural tradition. They both appealed to and were subject to local opinion which shaped, interpreted, and adapted them on the basis of a social folk discourse as well as a personal or individual rationale.

[154] Obelkevich, *Religion and Rural Society*, 282.
[155] R. H. Trainor, *Black Country Elites* (Oxford, 1993), 190.
[156] G. Gorer, *Exploring English Character* (1955), 263.
[157] G. Bennett, 'Aspects of Supernatural Belief, Memorate and Legend in a Contemporary Urban Environment' (Sheffield University Ph.D. thesis, 1985); see also, G. Bennett and P. S. Smith, *Contemporary Legend* (Sheffield, 1990).

The visible manifestation of the supernatural in the form of ghosts or spirits was also connected with the person of the wise-woman or the fortune-teller in the community. These figures could act as popular spiritualists. Southwark's local fortune-teller Mrs Rose, for example, also performed the role of a medium.[158] A resurgence of spiritualism has been attributed to the closing decades of the nineteenth century[159] and to the period of the First World War in particular.[160] Contemporary observers described an increase in the number of those consulting mediums both at the front and at home. An officer in a highland regiment claimed that a very dangerous belief in spiritualism was gaining ground[161] both in the army and especially among the bereaved at home.[162] Alan Wilkinson argued that

The pressures of bereavement drove some mourners to spiritualism and seances were reported to be increasing in number. At one stage of the war there were said to be one-hundred and eighteen mediums in the Kensington area alone.[163]

The experiences of the trenches and of bereavement drove many to spiritualism. Tales of the return of the fallen were common in the popular literature of the war and interwar period, while numerous stories circulated about the experience of supernatural phenomena on the battlefield.[164] John Morley associated this expansion with a general fascination with the supernatural which predominated from the closing decades of the nineteenth century to the interwar period.[165]

This association is supported in Southwark at this time by the resurgence of Southcottism in Walworth during the 1920s. The prophecies and foretellings of the Devonshire woman by the name of Joanna Southcott, who made her home in Walworth in 1802, were treated with a new fascination at this time. Parades and petitions were organized in the early 1930s to insist that the sealed boxes containing her prophecies should be opened once more for the people of Walworth.

In 1934 a strange event occurred. Sandwichmen paraded through London, enormous placards appeared in the underground stations, churches were flooded with pamphlets and papers and up to ten thousand signatures appeared

[158] SCW, Int. 22.
[159] L. Barrow, *Independent Spirits: Spiritualism and the English Plebeians 1850–1910* (1986).
[160] Winter, 'Spiritualism and the First World War', 187.
[161] Cairns, *The Army and Religion*, 20.
[162] Ibid. 19.
[163] A. Wilkinson, *The Church of England and the First World War* (1978), 179.
[164] Winter, 'Spiritualism and the First World War', 191.
[165] J. Morley, *Death, Heaven and the Victorians* (1971), 104–6.

on a petition left at Lambeth Palace asking the bishop to open Joanna Southcott's Box.[166]

Southcott was originally a domestic servant born in Devonshire in 1750. At the age of 42 she claimed that voices had spoken to her calling her the 'Bridge of Christ' and commanding her to give prophecies and write books. Her first book, *The Strange Effects of Faith*, appeared in 1801. It was a forty-eight page pamphlet which sold all over England at the price of nine pence. In 1802 Joanna Southcott took a coach to London and made her home in Walworth. There she achieved renown. L. J. Carter claims in his study of Walworth that 'thousands of lay folk became her disciples'.[167] In one mission alone 14,000 people became her adherents. A chapel was set up in Amelia Street, Walworth to act as her headquarters. Handbills issued at the time claimed that the chapel had been opened by the express command of God. Southcott remained a popular figure in the local lore of Walworth. Yet this sentiment was revived particularly in the incident outlined above. During the 1920s a short book entitled *The Southcott Despatch* was published. This claimed that the prophesies of Southcott had been fulfilled in the events of the First World War while her prophetic message of peace, which was eventually re-published in 1936 due to the popular demand, was considered particularly appropriate to the interwar period.

The material considered in this chapter suggests a widespread belief in the possibility that one's fortunes could be affected through certain actions, practices, or rituals. These included seemingly 'trivial' practices and the enactment of commonplace rituals but also extended on occasions to the weaving of spells and to more elaborate rituals. In addition, they involved the employment of specific charms, mascots, and amulets and a body of folk wisdom in the form of medical lore. The latter involved strategies for controlling, allaying, or transferring the adverse effects of illness through the enactment of rituals or the use of charmed objects. A continuity is thus suggested between the kinds of beliefs found in the English villages during and before the early nineteenth century and those found in urban Southwark at the end of the nineteenth century and in the early decades of the twentieth century. The concept of the cosmos which James Obelkevich identified in South Lindsey between 1825 and 1875 had not disappeared by the end of the century nor had it been entirely depersonalized. In Southwark the super-empirical realm continued to act 'as a treasury of separate and specific

---

[166] Carter, *Walworth 1929–1939*, 60.   [167] Ibid.

resources to be used and applied in concrete situations'.[168] Like the South
Lindsey villager, the south London costermonger used charms and
enacted rituals to harness the super-empirical realm in order to serve the
present and to assist, as Lovett argued, 'in bringing about the desires of
the wearer or to ward off all that may be hurtful or unfortunate'.[169] Lovett
specifically pointed out that the costermongers' avid use of charms and
mascots was in contrast with his lack of interest in contemplating the
constellations of the stars.[170] In Southwark, no less than in South Lindsey,
absorption in daily toil and the drudgery of the home did not necessarily
mean indifference or disbelief in the super-empirical realm, as some
contemporary commentators suggested. It was exactly when next week's
rent had to be found that a lucky boot hanging above the fireplace was
believed to have particular efficacy. The 'well-nigh universal tendency to
cling to the visible and concrete and to ignore all else'[171] which Paterson
ascribed to the south London working man, did not necessarily preclude
an appeal to the 'treasury of resources' to affect 'concrete situations'.
Similarly, the relative prosperity which many members of the working
class enjoyed from the 1890s and which was accompanied by what
Paterson called the 'flash material order of life' did not prevent an individual from tapping his rabbit's foot when placing a bet, or turning and
rubbing a copper coin to increase the family's material prosperity. An
interest in the cosmos to affect one's fortunes within the context of daily
life was not, however, the only interest which individuals displayed in
the super-empirical sphere. Obelkevich juxtaposed the concept of the
cosmos as 'a treasury of resources' with the idea of the cosmos as a realm
to be 'contemplated and worshipped'.[172] The material considered in this
and the following chapter suggests that to divide these concepts of the
cosmos into two exclusive categories misrepresents the complexity of
contemporary perceptions of the non-rational and super-empirical
sphere. To use it to enhance one's present material or physical standing
did not always preclude a desire to worship or contemplate the Deity.

The perpetuation of this kind of concept of the cosmos, as well as a
'mass of low grade magic and superstition',[173] also continued to encom-
pass personalized superhuman forces and in some cases could extend, as
it did in South Lindsey, to the notion of the witch, the wise-woman, the

---

[168] Obelkevich, *Religion and Rural Society*, 281.
[169] Lovett, 'English Charms, Amulets and Mascots'.
[170] Lovett, *Magic in Modern London*, 65.
[171] Alexander Paterson, *Across the Bridges* (1911), 46.
[172] Obelkevich, *Religion and Rural Society*, 281.
[173] Ibid.

evil eye, and the ghost. In the case of the dairyman from Bethnal Green, for example, the cows were 'overlooked' by a personal figure whose contact with the dairyman was direct. Furthermore, the antidote used to reverse the effects of the spell was personal and recommended by a specific figure within the community. This example is in contrast, however, with the more general fear of 'overlooking' which drove soldiers during the First World War to pin 'tiny golliwogs' to the inside of their tunics as a general guard against the first piercing glance of the evil eye. The range of examples suggests that a general and diffuse fear of the evil eye or of ill luck did not necessarily preclude more elaborate, defined, and personified confrontations with superhuman forces. Moreover, it qualifies a straightforward and oversimplistic portrayal of the process of 'impersonalization' which Obelkevich envisaged as a linear decline from earlier and 'higher' forms of popular belief associated with the country-side towards 'lower' and more diffuse remnants of belief in the city. These kinds of belief continued to operate within the context of local communities and as part of the fabric of family life. Certain local women were still regarded as fountains of folk wisdom and many of the practices and beliefs considered in this chapter were passed down from one generation of women to the next. Furthermore, these kinds of belief were considered part of a notion of communal and familial heritage. They were talked about as that which was 'always done' or as the 'way things were'. They were thus incorporated within the community's, or within a family's sense of past and present identity.

The kinds of continuities between the rural and urban environment which are suggested by the material considered in this chapter also qualify some of the comments made by Jeffrey Cox in his discussion of diffusive Christianity. The evidence suggests the persistence of 'semi-pagan magic' of the kinds described by Obelkevich, for the survival of which in London Cox claimed there was 'not much evidence'.[174] It challenges the notion that these beliefs had simply 'subsided into a belief in luck'.[175] Furthermore, the material also leads to a questioning of Cox's terminology: first, it qualifies the treatment of these beliefs as mere 'survivals'; and secondly, it raises a number of questions concerning the validity of categorizing these beliefs as 'semi-pagan' or in direct contrast to Christian or orthodox beliefs. Many of the practices and ideas considered were invested with new meaning in the urban context. They were not subject to inertia but were adapted in form and character to play important roles in different social settings. Moreover, a number of the

---

[174] Cox, *The English Churches*, 95.   [175] Ibid.

charms and amulets which were described incorporated Christian imagery and language. Anna Telby, for example, considered the items which she carried in her bag to be part of her devotion to God. Although most of the elements of folk custom and tradition examined in this chapter have been considered without reference to the institutional church or to orthodoxy, they did not exist in isolation from other elements of the popular religious repertoire and they cannot simply be labelled as 'pagan'. The following chapter will broaden this discussion by considering in more detail the intermingling of folk dimensions of the popular religious repertoire with church-based customs, values, ideas, and practices.

4
Occasional and Conditional Conformity

Participation in the religious rites of passage at key transitional moments was a prominent feature of life in late nineteenth and early twentieth-century Southwark. The community was in this sense typical of its time and location.[1] Hugh McLeod has recently pointed to the figures for the years 1902–14 which reveal that the proportion of Anglican baptisms to live births ranged from between 66 to 70 per cent, with a further 5 per cent of children baptized as Catholics.[2] Alan Bartlett's study of baptismal registers in Bermondsey, likewise, suggests that there was a significant rise in the number of children brought forward for baptism from the late 1880s, which continued until 1914, indicating a shift in popular attitudes towards the ritual.[3] Jeffrey Cox identified the same pattern in Lambeth, where Anglican baptisms increased until the 1920s[4] and where the number of marriages solemnized in church rose to 80 per cent during the 1880s.[5]

This high level of participation was regarded by many contemporaries as something of an anomaly when compared with the failure of the majority of the working class to attend church on a regular basis. The Revd W. Thompson, the Rector of St Saviour's, Southwark, expressed the sentiments of many of his peers when, during his interview for the Booth survey, he contrasted the absence of these groups from church each Sunday with their selective commitment to the enactment of ortho-dox rituals at certain turning-points in life: 'The poor think it proper to

---

[1] O. Chadwick, *The Victorian Church*, 2 vols (1972), ii. 221–2; J. Kent, 'Feelings and Festivals: An Interpretation of some Working-Class Religious Attitudes', in H. J. Dyos and M. Wolff (eds.), *The Victorian City*, 2 vols. (1973), ii. 855–72.

[2] *Facts and Figures about the Church of England*, 3 (1965), 54, as cited by H. McLeod, *Religion and Society in England 1850–1914* (1996), 73.

[3] A. B. Bartlett, 'The Churches in Bermondsey 1880–1939' (Birmingham University Ph.D. thesis, 1987), 182–4.

[4] Cox, *The English Churches in a Secular Society: Lambeth 1870–1930* (Oxford, 1982), 87.

[5] Cox, *The English Churches*, 99.

have their children baptised, marriages solemnised and burial services read in church but anything more is generally conspicuous by its absence'.[6]

Similarly, the Revd W. J. Somerville, the Rector of St George-the-Martyr parish church, said that, for the poor,

The church is the place for baptisms, churchings, weddings and funerals and for attendance on the last night of the year and the harvest festival, on both of which occasions St George's presents a wonderful spectacle being crowded from floor to ceiling, but to attend the ordinary Sunday Service never seems to enter the mind of the ordinary parishioner.[7]

This anomaly was generally interpreted as a symptom of the religious indifference of the people. Historians have been quick to follow this line of argument and have explained these patterns of observance on the basis of ecclesiastical, institutional, and orthodox criteria or in relation to factors external to the beliefs or religious persuasions of the participants, such as a desire for social status, recognition, and respectability.[8] They have tended to oversimplify the values, concerns, and goals of which participation in these rituals was a part and to overlook the way in which orthodox meaning was renegotiated within a popular cultural context. In urban Southwark church-based religious idioms and Christian rituals were part of a more complex and wide-ranging pattern of urban popular belief which extended beyond the institutional church to the kinds of folk beliefs considered in the previous chapter. This did not mean that these rituals were entirely subverted towards 'folk' purposes as though 'folk' and Christian or orthodox ends were mutually exclusive categories. Church-based rituals were enacted alongside various folk responses to the super-empirical sphere without necessarily diminishing the importance which the participant attached to the orthodox content of the rite or to the overtly Christian elements of belief associated with it. Some individuals interpreted their occasional participation in these rituals as a response of duty or devotion to the Deity. Churching, baptism, marriage, and watch-night services could thus provide a context in which two religious idioms operated at once and in association with one another. It was this combination of types of religious language which constituted a distinct and characteristic feature of what may be described as popular religion and which forms the focus of this present chapter.

[6] C. Booth, *Life and Labour* (1902), 'Religious Influences', iv. 20.

[7] St George-the-Martyr, *Annual Report* (1902), 14.

[8] E. Ross, *Love and Toil: Motherhood in Outcast London 1870–1918* (Oxford, 1993), 132–3.

Individuals such as Mrs Cotton and Philippa Ivy were among those who held strong and clearly articulated folk beliefs and who at the same time insisted vehemently on the necessity of observing various orthodox rites. For them, participation in the rites of passage formed part of a response to the super-empirical realm which embraced and extended beyond orthodox images and ideals. This realm was not far off but immanent and formative as good or ill luck mediated one's daily life. Nor was this realm beyond the manipulation of individuals through certain actions, practices, or rituals ranging from the seemingly trivial to more elaborate rituals involving charms, mascots, or amulets or strategies for controlling, allaying, or transferring illness. The charms used for this purpose drew on overtly Christian symbolism and imagery to increase their power or efficacy and the church-based rituals of churching, baptism, marriage, and watch-night services to celebrate New Year were associated with these responses to the super-empirical sphere. Mrs Cotton, for example, recalled during one oral interview how her mother ensured that her daughters were churched after giving birth, that her children and grandchildren were baptized, and that members of her family were married in church:

She wasn't and nor was my Dad, they never punched that in to 'y, the church, church, church . . . but say when you had a child, oh before you went out to have that baby christened you had to go to church, oh yes and she wouldn't let you in her house if you hadn't been churched . . . no, she believed all that, but . . . no we were all been married in a church, because she didn't hold in with registry office. If you, anybody said . . . in her mind you wasn't married and ur . . . you only had to mention going up to town hall and she'd do her nut.[9]

Mrs Cotton's oral testimony does not explicitly state that her mother's refusal to admit an unchurched person to her house was connected to specific superstitions but the connection is strongly implied: 'She was very superstitious. I don't know what she thought you was if you didn't go to be churched . . . '[10] Mrs Cotton's description of churching was given in the context of a discussion about folk practices and it was a pre-lude to a description of other superstitions. These included the prescription of behaviour within the household to ensure that various kinds of ill luck would not befall the family and that specific forms of good fortune would be attracted in their place. In much the same way the behav-iour and actions of a woman who had just given birth were restricted until such time as she underwent the churching ceremony. Mrs Cotton

[9] SCW, Int. 22.   [10] Ibid.

recalled how she and her sister were prohibited from entering her mother's house until they had 'been to church', even if this meant, as the extended quotation demonstrates, walking for miles through the fog to find a church which would conduct the ceremonies of churching and baptism at the same time.

I know one of my sisters, it was November, thick fog, that was her second child. We started out early . . . well where we'd been all the churches were closed and she said, 'Ivy we'll come this way round'. We walked everywhere to be churched and um . . . (never knew it, you don't never have a church shut really), no every one we tried . . . closed . . . 'We'll go over Surrey Square . . . '. Where we walked . . . all closed but I knew I couldn't take her back home and she knew we daren't go to my mum's house but we ended up at St George's Church (thick fog), 'Oh look', I said, 'there's a light on in the church.' I had her other little girl with me, up the steps we went. They used to have a kind of nurse there. I spoke to her, she said, 'Oh yes straight away, Come in where is she?' I stood for that babe as well 'cos in them days you had to get another witness and anyway . . . I stood outside the church I could hear . . . (the fog was so thick), I could hear this little kid and I could hear the mother speaking so I said 'Excuse me' (you couldn't see a hand before 'y.) 'What's the matter love?' the woman said, 'don't be offended by what I am going to ask but could you come in the church and stand by my sister? the baby's being christened and we've got to get somebody else where we've been.' 'Oh yeah', but whoever that woman was I don't know . . . My mum once you'd had a baby if you hadn't been to be churched she wouldn't have 'y in her house and we knew it . . .[11]

The dramatic structuring of the narrative underlines the meaning of the experience. In other cases the connection between ill luck and the failure to be churched was made more directly. Barbara Luke specifically associated the ritual with the avoidance of bad luck.

It was really bad luck if you didn't go.
Q: It was bad luck was it?
A: Very . . . my mother made me go.[12]

David Clark has highlighted a similar pattern of the social 'liminality' of the mother after childbirth in his study of late nineteenth-century Staithes. Here a mother's actions were also limited and she was prevented from engaging in normal day-to-day activity until she had been churched.[13] These kinds of restriction were associated with the belief that

11 SCW, Int. 22.
12 SCW, Int. 6.
13 D. Clark, *Between Pulpit and Pew: Folk Religion in a North Yorkshire Fishing Village* (1982), 115.

bad luck would follow the appearance of an unchurched woman in the community. They form a common theme in the writings of folklorists describing rural communities of the late nineteenth century. William Henderson wrote:

As to the mother's churching, it is very uncanny for her to enter any house before she goes to church and she carries ill luck with her. It is believed also that if she appears out-of-doors under these circumstances and receiving any insult or blow from her neighbours she has no remedy at law.[14]

Similarly, Richard Blackborough described how 'No woman ever dreamed of crossing any threshold but her own until after she had been churched as doing so she carried ill luck into every home she entered'.[15]

Such associations were made in early-twentieth-century Southwark. The Revd T. P. Stevens, the rector of Southwark Cathedral from 1917 to 1924 and vicar of St Matthew's, New Kent Road from then until 1930, described in his memoirs of clerical life in London how

In the poorer parishes churching is a matter of very great importance. The mother must be churched at the earliest possible moment. There is superstition that something will happen if there is delay. I discovered a poor woman waiting for the church door to open one bitterly cold night. She told me she had been there half an hour, having made a mistake in the hour, she said she did not like to return home because she might meet an acquaintance on the stairs and that was unlucky.[16]

Similarly, in Southwark getting married in church was, in some cases, associated with a range of folk beliefs and practices. Certain churches were believed to be particularly lucky: St Paul's Church in Kipling Street, Bermondsey, for example, was a very popular church for weddings as it was considered to be highly efficacious in this respect.[17] The marriage ceremony itself was surrounded by a number of superstitions. *Cassell's Saturday Journal* for 1906 described how

Superstition played its part at another wedding solemnised at the same church (St George-the-Martyr). It is a belief with many people, not exceeding the coster and the labouring element of the London community, that an interrupted marriage ceremony is a bad omen. The crowd rushing into the church could not

[14] W. Henderson, *Notes on the Folklore of the Northern Counties of England and the Borders* (1866), 8.
[15] R. Blakeborough, *Wit, Character, Folklore and Customs in the North Riding of Yorkshire* (1898), 115.
[16] T. P. Stevens, *Cassock and Surplice: Incidents in Clerical Life* (1947), 49.
[17] Bartlett, 'The Churches in Bermondsey', Int. 6.

be kept back whereupon the clergyman left his place at the altar and gave orders for a padlock to be put on the door. The married couple and their friends felt sure that bad luck would follow this interruption and made smothered protests in the church. The next day the sister of the bride lost a baby girl and shortly afterwards the father of the bridegroom died.[18]

The Journal claimed that in a certain part of the borough this marriage was talked about for months afterwards. Whenever a member of the family was married, Mrs Cotton's mother would take a bit of salt, a bit of bread, a few 'odd coppers', and a bit of coal and place them in a box to ensure the lasting prosperity and good fortune of the new family,[19] just as her rural counterparts had done and were still doing at this date.[20]

Yeah, take a bit of salt (any of us got married), bit of salt bit of bread a few odd coppers and a bit of coal and it's all be covered up. You don't touch that box . . . you'll never be without money, course you wouldn't, 'cos that couple of coppers would be up there . . . [21]

The watch-night service was also associated with the prevention of bad luck and the ensuring of good fortune. For many individuals, their absence from a religious service on New Year's Eve was sufficient to generate anxiety about their fortunes in the New Year. Henry Bradley, born in 1903, the son of a carman from Cromer Road, London, described in his interview with the Essex Oral History Project how his parents would only ever attend church for the watch-night,[22] and Rose Embleton of Bonner Street, Elephant and Castle, insisted that she attended the midnight service each year without fail.[23] Similarly, when F. A. Kent, born in 1901, the son of a crane-slinger from Canning Town, was asked if his parents attended church, he replied; 'Oh yes—they were inclined to be that way; they would go on—nearly always go on—nearly always go on—Old Year's Night'.[24] There are vivid descriptions which highlight the crowded nature of these services. They were often filled to over-flowing with those who had left a nearby pub just before the stroke of

[18] *Cassell's Saturday Journal*, 11 Apr. 1906, 725.
[19] SCW, Int. 22.
[20] The ritual of placing a deposit of material necessities in a new house was a practice described by J. Harland and T. T. Wilkinson, *Lancashire Legends*, (1873), 236. 'Those moving to a new house are advised to place a bible, some oatmeal and some salt in the cupboard of the new home in order that they may have prosperity during their stay. '
[21] SCW, Int. 22.
[22] EOHA, Int. 214, 27.
[23] EOHA, Int. 299, 71.
[24] EOHA, Int. 334, 46.

midnight in order to see in the New Year inside the church, chapel, or mission hall: 'In many cases they rush out of the public house to get into the watchnight service just before the stroke of midnight'.[25]

Some would even bring their fish and chips in with them,[26] while others were clearly the worse for drink. Yet, it was none the less important to 'spend the closing minutes of the old year in a religious service',[27] whatever may have preceded those moments. The desire of participants to 'start the year right', by undergoing a public act of worship, was associated with a belief that to do otherwise was unlucky.[28] The notion of spiritual cleansing which formed a prominent part of these services may have closely paralleled the practice of cleaning and tidying the house, washing the crockery, and cleaning the hearth before the new year as a symbol implying starting time over again at its beginning, or, as David Clark puts it, 'scourging the passing year's accumulated dirt'.[29] Clark describes such cleansing rituals in the North Yorkshire fishing village as both a physical and a moral act whereby past actions, misdemeanours, and failings were ritually expelled: 'The slate thus wiped clean is prepared once more for the imprint of "New Year's resolutions" '.[30]

In much the same way, during the First World War, the Army and Religion Survey attributed a superstitious attachment to the ritual of communion. It noted that for a number of people participation in the communion service before going into combat was believed to be sufficient to ensure divine protection, just as the enactment of a folk ritual or carrying a lucky charm was held to enhance one's chances of safety in battle. One respondent noted that 'They believe that having taken communion they will be safe'.[31]

These associations of orthodox rituals with luck were thus made on many fronts. They tend, however, to be made exclusively in the observations of most contemporary observers, as though the association with luck prevented other types of meaning being ascribed to the rituals. A. W. Jephson, the vicar of St John's, Walworth, for instance argued baldly that,

[25] The *Christian World*, 4 Jan. 1900.
[26] Bartlett, 'The Churches in Bermondsey', Int. 7.
[27] The *Christian World*, 4 Jan. 1900.
[28] Ibid.
[29] Clark, *Between Pulpit and Pew*, 92.
[30] Ibid. 92–3.
[31] D. S. Cairns (ed.), *The Army and Religion: An Enquiry and its Bearing upon the Religious Life of the Nation* (1919), 172.

At present the people come to church to this extent; for marriage, churchings and baptism, for the last night of the old year and for Harvest thanksgiving but all this is mainly from superstition; they do it to keep or change their luck.[32]

His slightly derogatory comments implied that the church rituals were carried out mainly or merely from superstition with little or no additional significance for the participants. A similar exclusivity is found in the comments of Jeffrey Cox when he argued that, 'In the popular mind the Christian sacraments were associated with luck more than anything resembling Christian devotion'.[33] The range of evidence considered in Southwark suggests that to state the connection between the enactment of a ritual and the maintenance of good fortune did not necessarily diminish the sincerity attached to the orthodox meaning of the ritual. Indeed the rituals themselves communicated on a variety of levels. In V. W. Turner's words they were 'multi-referential' and 'multi vocal'.[34] In many cases what the actor saw as the Christian Deity was not excluded from the ritual; rather, attributing thanks to Him or receiving His blessing through the enactment of the ritual, became the agent by which bad luck was averted. 'Luck' and 'Christian devotion' were too intimately associated with one another to be distinguished in these terms.

At the watch-night service, for example, a belief in the importance of 'starting the year right' in order to ensure good luck, did not preclude a sincere belief in the importance of repentance and reaffirming a commitment to an ideal of Christian living. Those who performed the ritual of attending church in the closing minutes of the old year were exposed to what was often a highly charged emotional atmosphere, into which many of them appear to have entered with reverence and sincerity, even when they were, in some cases, the worse for drink. The service consisted of prayer, hymn singing, and a short address and it was not infrequently accompanied by great shows of emotion on the part of the congregation. A watch-night service held at the Surrey Gardens Memorial Hall in Penrose Street, Walworth in 1913 included a rousing address illustrated by limelight slides: 'There was an attendance of nearly two hundred and fifty and perfect and reverent silence was maintained throughout a most earnest appeal to those who still remained in the broad way that leads to destruction'.[35]

[32] LSE, Booth Collection, B270, 27.
[33] Cox, *The English Churches*, 97.
[34] V. W. Turner, *The Ritual Process* (1969).
[35] Surrey Gardens Memorial Hall, *Annual Report* (1913), 11.

Similarly, on the last night of the old year a congregation of about 7,000 gathered at the Metropolitan Tabernacle in order to see in the New Year. This congregation consisted of 'persons of every class':

It would be impossible to imagine a more affecting spectacle than that which met the eye at the hour of midnight when, at Mr. Spurgeon's suggestion, apparently every member of this vast multitude engaged in silent prayer. Every voice was hushed, not a sound was heard. After the lapse of a few minutes the silence was broken by a reverent gentleman giving one verse of a hymn with almost dramatic effect on the vast assembly.[36]

On such occasions it was common for a large number of the congregation to stand and testify to a dramatic conversion experience or to go forward at the close of a meeting and sign the pledge. Mr Rounsfell noted that at a similar service in the Old Vic a large number of the audience rose to their feet in order to express their desire to lead a new life in the new year and specifically to sign the pledge.[37] Similarly, John Harper, the minister at Walworth Road Baptist Church from 1910, claimed that, 'We have never held a watchnight service at which less than half a dozen people accepted Christ as saviour . . . '.[38]

Participation in the service could include a reaffirmation of an ideal of 'right living' drawn in part from church-based culture. It aroused a wave of nostalgia which was signified in the response to prayer, preaching, and hymn singing and it involved an emotional link with the church which formed a powerful, if intangible bond with church-based culture even among those who only attended very infrequently. Participating in these services cannot simply be dismissed as a desire for good luck in the New Year, when the vehicle by which this good luck was obtained involved a complex interweaving of various kinds of religious language and experience, much of which drew on overtly Christian symbolism and sentiment.

Similarly, getting married in church was not only considered lucky, but was often inseparable from a belief in the importance of securing divine blessing on the couple. Ivy Cotton's mother could make a deliberate effort to ensure the luck of the couple by making a package of bread and coppers, but at the same time she believed that if they failed to get married in church they were not blessed. Enacting these rituals within the context of the church was bound up with the image or notion

---

[36] Brunel University, Burnett Collection, J. Ashley, 'Autobiography' (1908), n.p.

[37] *Christian World*, 4 Jan. 1900.

[38] SLSL, from the manuscript notes donated to the library by Miss Doris Worthy (1980), 2.

of the church as a special and somehow holy place which formed the correct arena in which to ask for and to receive the divine blessing. Mrs Cotton recalled the alarm and contempt with which her mother viewed any couple who had not been married in church: 'and if you got married not in a church you might as well not be married—didn't hold with it. For one thing you're not blessed and you're not gone to God Almighty'.[39]

To go to church to enact these rituals was not only considered lucky but was also associated specifically with 'going to the Almighty', both to thank Him and to receive His blessing.

In the same way, at the churching service, the desire for good luck was inseparable from the belief that it was inappropriate to omit a visit to church to thank the Almighty for a safe delivery. Edith Anders, the daughter of a costermonger, born in Decimer Street, Bermondsey in 1919, described in her oral interview how 'after you'd been in bed for ten days you had to go to church . . . you went to church to thank the Almighty for getting you over it'.[40]

She re-emphasized this point later in her interview by repeating it. She insisted that to be churched was to thank God: 'we all went to church to thank the Almighty for getting us over our delivery'.[41]

Indeed, in the case of churching, the act of going to church to thank the Almighty was in itself considered a vital responsibility as well as a morally or religiously appropriate act. It is described in a number of cases as one's duty after a safe delivery. Molly Layton, for example, described churching, along with baptism, as an imperative: 'You had to be christened and to thank God for getting you over your confinement in those days, you know'.[42]

Moreover, Ivy Cotton's mother considered it wholly inappropriate, even immoral, to leave the Almighty unthanked for a safe delivery.

She'd say if you haven't been to thank God see, for the pain of hell you've gone through, oh no don't know what she wouldn't call'y. But she let you go in then, as soon as we got home after all that, 'oh' she said, 'aint'y been a long time out in all this fog?'. Then she said, 'Was she churched', and I said 'Oh yes' but otherwise . . . [43]

It was necessary to go to church in order to enact such rituals which had to be carried out not only to ensure good fortune but also to discharge a responsibility towards the Deity.

Just as the church was endowed with a sacred quality as a place in

[39] SCW, Int. 22.   [40] SCW, Int. 5.   [41] Ibid.
[42] SCW, Int. 20.   [43] SCW, Int. 22.

which to meet with God, so the vicar, the priest, or the nonconformist
minister who conducted these ceremonies was believed to have particular powers of prayer and benediction. By the end of the century
churches were not chosen randomly as places in which to enact these
rituals, but individual families and communities had formed strong links
with certain local churches and through them with the representative
religious figure. The rites of passage were generally carried out in a local
church which the inhabitants of surrounding courts and alleys viewed as
'our church'. Lilian Tims described St Mary Magdalene church which lay
at the end of Massinger Street,[44] Southwark as 'our church'.

We had a church, St Mary Magdalene, that was our church, we was all christened
there, my Mum was married there, we was all christened and we all went to
church. I was in the brownies, then in the guides and my brothers in the Band of
Hope.[45]

Similarly, Molly Layton's family, who lived in South Street, Walworth
were all married at St Peter's parish church; as she recalled, 'I was
married in 1935 in St Peter's church on the Walworth Road and all my
family's been married there, me nieces, sisters and all relatives, at that
church . . . '[46]
A similar pattern was found in the case of the Croft and Ivy families.
Both families considered Emmanuel Church, Dulwich to be 'their
church'.
In some cases a particular group or community could identify itself
with specific churches independently of local geography, as was the case
with the pearlies and St Alphege church, St Mary Magdalene, and St
John's Church, Walworth. These became known as Coster churches and
the vicar of St Alphege, A. B. Goulden, as the Costers' Bishop. Furthermore, the connection of a family with an Anglican church did not
necessarily preclude an equally strong affinity with a local mission hall or
nonconformist chapel; these too might be described as 'our church'. In
addition to St Peter's Walworth, for example, Molly Layton commented
that, 'We also had another church in Wellington College at the other end
of the street'.[47]
Similarly, the Croft and Ivy families not only viewed Emmanuel

[44] St Mary Magdalene's was situated at the end of Massinger Street and it overshadowed
the houses. The World Turned Upside Down lay at the other end of the street on the
corner of the Old Kent Road.
[45] SCW, Int. 23.
[46] SCW, Int. 20.
[47] Ibid.

Church, Dulwich as their church but also included in this category Barry Road Baptist chapel where the children attended Sunday school and where the women attended the mothers' meeting. It is noteworthy that the maintenance of such loyalty was from one generation of women to the next, just as women were the primary agents whereby this pattern of participation was integrated within popular folk culture and tradition.

The association of these families with the local church, chapel, or mission extended to an identification with the representative religious figure of these institutions. Mrs Duckes, born in 1892, the daughter of a chimney sweep from King Street, is reflective of a number of those interviewed in Southwark when she specifically identified the mission chapel, in which all her family were christened and married, with the person of the clergyman.

We was all christened in a chapel at Wolfendale down in Somers Town, the Rev [interviewer speaking at the same time] yes, yes and he was a lovely man. I had him afterwards when I got married he lived to a good old age . . . [48]

Her narrative concerning the local church continued with an extended description of the local vicar who visited and cared for the community. In her mind the place of ritual benediction was connected with the person who gave the benediction. The religious figure was considered part of the fabric of communal life and in some senses as 'belonging' to the community. The Revd J. Mackrell, A. B. Goulden's successor at St Alphege, for example, described the argument which broke out among a group of local children in the parish of St Alphege over the identification of Goulden with their communities.

I shall never forget the battle royal which raged one day between the kiddies of St Alphege and those of the neighbouring parish of All Hallows. Both laid claim to the present vicar of St Alphege who was previously assistant priest at All Hallows, "e's our father' cried the All Hallowites 'no 'e ain't', volleyed back the Alphegians, "e's our father.'[49]

It was expected that the community could lay a special claim upon the representative of the local religious establishment by virtue of its identification with that church. This special claim consisted not merely of the demand for references for jobs or clothing and food for the distressed, though it could and often did involve these things as well, but it was also associated with his representative role as a holy man.[50] The

[48] EOHA, Int. 3, 16.
[49] St Alphege Mission, *Annual Report* (1897), 35.
[50] Cf. G. P. Connolly, 'Little Brother be at Peace: The Priest as Holy Man in the Nineteenth-Century Ghetto', *Studies in Church History*, 19 (1982), 202.

administration of charity, for example, was often connected with requests for prayer—a connection which was strengthened by the direct and personal role which many churchmen in the area appear to have played in the distribution of material relief. At St Stephen's church in Boyson Road, Walworth, for example, relief was given through the vicar or specifically reported to the vicar from the visitors,[51] while at St George's Cathedral it was said that,

The total amount spent in relief the canon put down at about £200. Of this £40 is raised from outside, including, I think, the £12 or so raised by the service of St Vincent de Paul and certainly including the amount taken in the collection on Good Friday. The rest is given by the priests privately and at the expense of their own pockets. There is no 'fund' and no committee and thus no 'administration'.[52]

A similar personal association is suggested in the description given of Mr R. A. Halls, a London City missionary in the Old Kent Road area. Mr Halls used to give from ten to two hundred dinners to children each winter. These dinners were initiated and organized by him and the local population appears to have identified the receipt of them specifically with Mr Halls himself: 'He knows everybody and young grown-up people will not infrequently say "many a good dinner that Mr Halls has given me"'.[53]

A number of the autobiographies also suggest that the receipt of relief was often inseparable in people's minds from a direct relationship with a specific religious figure in the community and with his kindness.[54] These kinds of relations created a context in which the religious figure was far more than the 'philanthropic policeman'[55] and where prayers were believed to have particular potency at times of benediction as well as in times of sickness and distress. During the early years of the First World War, the South London Mission was inundated not only with requests to relieve the material conditions of struggling families but also with requests for prayer. Week-night prayer meetings were filled to overflowing and the bereaved came to places such as St George's Hall, Bermondsey in large numbers to receive prayer and comfort. It was the upsurge in practices of this kind which led many to make extravagant claims concerning spiritual revival during the early years of the war.

51 LSE, Booth Collection, B276, 189.
52 LSE, Booth Collection, B278, 9–11.
53 Ibid. 135–7.
54 Brunel University, Burnett Collection, A. T. Collinson, 'One Way Only' (1966), n.p.
55 Connolly, 'Little Brother be at Peace', 206.

Their significance lay, not so much in the kinds of religious revival anticipated by contemporary churchmen, but in the sense of the accessibility of the church and its representative role as a haven of support, both physical and spiritual. These attitudes had a heritage which pre-dates the extremity of wartime conditions. The annual report of the Pembroke College Mission for 1895 suggests similar connections between the mission as a 'house of prayer', the community, and the religious figure as the bearer and offerer of prayers on behalf of the people.

Our people always know that the prayers are being offered for them morning by morning and evening by evening. Mothers told me that even when it was impossible to leave their children and come they have been comforted again and again when they hear the bell ring and know that they are remembered. I am now visiting daily a dying woman whose last words each time I see her are 'please remember me in the church when the time for service comes'.[56]

Such material qualifies the assumption which is still repeated that the communal role of the churches was entirely dissolved by the industrial revolution.[57]

As well as providing prayer and relief for the suffering, the presence of the religious figure was also sufficient to quell bad language and to stop a fight,[58] while the religious man was also believed by some to provide an extra degree of divine protection. The son of a local Bermondsey missioner, who was interviewed by Alan Bartlett, recorded how during the Zeppelin raids on London during the First World War, the people of the area believed that they would be safer in the missioner's house than in their own houses, owing to his association with God: 'So we had a long passage and a staircase and we used to have about twenty to thirty people in there you see, because it was with Dad you see and I suppose something to do with God'.[59]

These glimpses of the attitudes of the community towards the religious man strengthen the suggestion that the enactment of these rituals may well have involved a notion of the holy and a desire for specific benediction and blessing within the context of the church and under the auspices of the local religious figure whose position was related to particular ideals and definitions of morality and spirituality.

The desire for the kind of benediction described above did not, how-

[56] Pembroke College Mission, *Annual Report* (1898), 5–6.
[57] See e.g. J. Stevenson, *British Society 1914–45* (1985), ch. 13.
[58] LSE, Booth Collection, B270, 273–5.
[59] Bartlett, 'The Churches in Bermondsey', Int. 7.

ever, preclude a desire to ensure good luck for the participant. Receiving the protection afforded by taking shelter in the missioner's house, for example, may not have precluded the use of a lucky charm to effect the same purpose, nor may getting married in certain churches have precluded the belief that they were, like St Paul's Church, Bermondsey, in some sense lucky. The notion of blessing and the notion of luck were bound up with one another in a way which did not necessarily nullify, preclude, or diminish the sincerity attached to either dimension of belief.

In addition to stressing the various sentiments attached to the context in which these rituals were enacted, the oral evidence also highlights the importance attached to the orthodox content of the ritual itself. It suggests that orthodox elements should not be played down as a motivating factor in participation in these rituals. Baptism, for example, was believed to have efficacy from a Christian point of view. Undergoing the ritual was believed to make a child a 'Christian' while it allowed him or her to enter both the earthly fold of the church and the eternal fold of Heaven. Helen Westall, of Camberwell, asserted confidently that she had always believed that 'if you're not christened you're not in the fold'.[60] The view was widely held that an association with the church in infancy was sufficient to entitle an individual to claim the various privileges of that community, without fulfilling what the church itself saw as the obligations. The nominal membership of the church which was conferred through the baptismal ritual was believed to be sufficient to ensure that an individual would be 'all right' when it came to the final judgement, as his or her identification with the sacred community was ensured.

A number of the interviews also suggest that an individual's insistence on the importance of participating in church rituals was interpreted and seen within popular culture as an indication of genuine religious belief. When asked if her mother went to church, Miriam Moore, for example, replied, 'no but . . . ' and provided the qualification that her mother none the less believed, by implication in the teaching and values which that institution was seen to represent, because she participated in various church rituals.

Q: Did your mother go to church?
A: She believed and I mean when any of us children were born she'd go to the church before she went out anywhere to be blessed and she'd make sure we was all christened.[61]

[60] SCW, Int. 2.   [61] SCW, Int. 15.

Mrs Cotton also considered that the act of having her children baptized provided evidence of her commitment to both the Deity and the church. She even criticized the local vicar when he failed to recognize this action as sufficient evidence of the sincerity of her belief. She went into considerable detail when describing the local vicar at All Saints Church, Dulwich, in order to point out that the Revd W. J. J. Cornelius, unlike his successor, Mr Riddle,[62] had been a 'good vicar'. He was good, she argued, because he understood and accepted that for the infrequent church attender, to have a child baptized and churched was proof enough of both commitment to and belief in the Deity and of support of the church.

Cornelius was our vicar round All Saints. Cornelius was a good man but the other man wasn't . . . Mr Riddle . . . .'Cos he knew that we was all working-class people and he knew that there was all families and he knew what the families was like didn't he? They'd go there round there straight away up out of confinement to be churched. Had their children christened.[63]

Unlike his successor Mr Riddle, Mr Cornelius did not seek to impose an additional standard of regular attendance on his parishioners, but would continue to visit them in their homes when they were sick and would happily baptize their children.

The examples considered so far, while stressing church-based elements alongside folk beliefs, also suggest a further strand in the meaning which these rituals held within the community. Participation was seen as fulfilling one's duty not only to the Deity but also to the wider community, and as such it could be employed as evidence not only of the sincerity of religious commitment but also of social respectability. Speaking of Limehouse in the 1910s and 1920s, Annie Foley recalled that,

When I had my Billy I got out of bed to change his napkins they came and caught me and said I was flying in the face of the Lord. You couldn't come out of the door into the open air unless you went straight to the church after you had children and the child wasn't allowed out until it was christened. If you did not you was treated like dirt.[64]

Her description suggests that to omit the religious ritual was to displease the Deity; it was 'to fly in the face of the Lord'; to do so was, at the same time, to make oneself socially unacceptable. These two emphases

---

[62] Reference to Mr Riddle is not found in the diocesan directories and it is possible that Ivy Cotton confused the name.

[63] SCW, Int. 22.

[64] Age Exchange, *On the River: Memories of the River* (1989), 34.

exist together within a range of meanings associated with the enactment of the ritual. To be churched and to have one's baby christened was to be socially as well as spiritually cleansed. Thus, as Alan Smith has argued,

Such was the fear of ritual uncleanliness that to undergo the 'churching' ceremony—for all its official name the thanksgiving of women after childbirth—was a social necessity for a new mother wishing to resume her place, however humble, in the community.[65]

The social dimension of the ritual, just like the superstitious elements encompassed by it, did not necessarily preclude a desire to please the Deity. One cannot explain participation in the rituals simply as a desire for social status without reference to the wider range of meanings which combined in the motivation to act in this way. A concern with social propriety and even conformity as a result of pure habit or communal pressure did not necessarily exclude a respect for the orthodox meaning of the ritual. Pearly christenings and weddings, for example, were occasions during which the church ceremony was used as a stage on which to display the grandeur of the local pearly king and queen and thus to celebrate the lifestyle and status of the London costermonger. Alfred Ireson, the London City Missioner for the New Cut area of Lambeth between 1882 and 1911, described the show made by pearlies at public events:

They generally made a great show at public events: When a babe was christened its dress would be covered with pearl buttons. Weddings produced a gorgeous display. Their funerals were made splendid with flowers and pearls.[66]

It would be easy to focus solely upon the social function of such ceremonies within the pearly community, but the social meaning attached to life-cycle rituals by the pearlies did not nullify the sincerity with which the participants sought to identify their community and lifestyle with God, the church, and the representative religious figure in the area. The ritual was carefully associated with specific churches in Southwark. St Mary Magdalene's, for example, was known as the 'pearly cathedral' from the turn of the century, because of the frequency with which the coster community sought ecclesiastical benediction there on their familial and communal events. Even the business meetings of the pearly association were held in St Mary's church hall with the curate presiding as chairman over the gathering. Each meeting was solemnly

---

[65] A. Smith, *The Established Church and Popular Religion 1750–1850* (1971), 19.
[66] Brunel University Library, Burnett Collection, A. Ireson, 'Reminiscences' (1930), n.p.

closed by the entire gathering joining in The Lord's Prayer before adjourning to The World Turned Upside Down.[67]

A commitment to the Christian efficacy of an orthodox ritual was, therefore, often inseparable from a web of folk superstition, from the customary expectations of communal society, and from an assertion of communal identity. As Anthony Cohen points out, rituals have an

offical form and rationale, but their participants may well find in them quite different meaning and experience. Indeed it is probably the very opportunity they afford to their participants to assimilate the symbolic forms of their individual and idiosyncratic experience and social and emotional needs that makes them so compelling and attractive.[68]

Apparently incompatible narratives of religious belief formed one rationale for action, in which many dimensions of belief were present. The eclectic character of popular attitudes tends to be overlooked when the actions of participants are interpreted with reference to factors external to the meanings and interpretations which the actors themselves brought to bear upon their practices. Thus while orthodox rituals were enacted by south Londoners as part of a wide range of belief which sought to extract good luck or remove ill luck by manipulating the super-empirical realm, they were at the same time part of a desire to seek and gain the blessing of a personal God via the medium of the representative religious figure within the community. They were in this way bound up with a sense of communal or familial heritage, memory, and nostalgia which included a belief in the Christian efficacy of the ritual and a sense of its social propriety, as well as a belief in the attendant benefits it bestowed in terms of securing good luck. Orthodox elements of belief were not excluded by the diffusion of folk beliefs and neither of these elements of the popular religious repertoire was excluded by the presence of social pressures. Consequently, good luck could be secured by reaffirming one's commitment to a church-based ideal at the watch-night service and through the blessing received or the gratitude given to God at the churching, baptism, or wedding without any apparent incongruity from the perspective of the observer.

[67] P. F. Brooks, *The Pearly Kings and Queens of England* (1975), 42.
[68] A. Cohen, *The Symbolic Construction of Community* (1992), 53.

5

The Ideal of the True Believer

The previous chapter described what may be regarded as one defining characteristic of popular religion, by emphasizing the coalescence of religious idioms within popular culture. This chapter considers a second and closely related feature of the popular religious repertoire, notably the selective incorporation and transformation of certain church-based ideals, images, and symbols within popular culture on the basis of particular definitions of religious duty and of genuine religiosity. Although the rituals considered in the previous chapter involved an incorporation of certain aspects of church-based religious language, they were enacted and orthodox sentiments were expressed, within clearly defined parameters. These involved not only the incorporation of folk expressions of religiosity but the assertion of a code of practice and a value system which remained distinct from those of church-based culture. The benediction of the church was sought through the rituals considered in the previous chapter on the basis of a distinctly popular framework of belief. Thus the costermongers of south London insisted on ensuring the blessing of the church on their marriages and births and on undergoing a ritual ceremony in specific churches but at the same time they did not allow the church to dictate fully the manner in which major family turning-points were celebrated. They continued to smuggle whisky into St John's parish church, despite the regulations of the clergy, in order to celebrate family weddings and births in a traditional manner.[1] As one popular song put it,

> The babe's praised right down to the ground,
> Pronounced by all quite safe and sound,
> Then once again the glass goes round,
> And the booze is there.[2]

The church was esteemed but it was not regarded as a final arbiter of public truth within popular culture. Likewise, although, as the previous

[1] 'London's Easter Marriage Rush', *Cassell's Saturday Journal*, 11 Jun. 1906, 752.
[2] 'Booze is there', *The Paragon Songster*, published by W. S. Fortey (c.1890–2).

chapter suggested, the religious figure was considered holy, he only lived up to the expectations inherent within this image when he fulfilled certain popular criteria regarding what a holy man should be and do. Thus, as Mrs Cotton pointed out, Mr Riddle of All Saints Church, Dulwich, was rejected as a local vicar while Mr Cornelius was esteemed on the basis of a particular concept of religiosity. It is these concepts of religiosity and ideals of genuine Christianity which are examined in this chapter. These definitions formed part of the system of values, norms, and moral codes which furnished the symbolic construction of popular culture and provided a sense of identity for members of the community. The boundaries of these definitions are not always easy to reconstruct. They did not exist obviously and unambiguously in a fixed, clearly articulated shared rationale; rather they emerged in practice when they were contravened by a deviant or an outsider. Definitions of spirituality, holiness, goodness, and badness became coherent and distinctive as popular and church-based culture confronted one another. They became apparent in the context of oral narratives as individuals defined themselves indirectly by extended descriptions of local hypocrites, 'sinning vicars', and inadequate husbands or neighbours. The boundaries of these definitions emerge in the material as distinctive meanings were threatened within the community's social discourse. At such times they provided individuals with referents for their personal and corporate identity. These definitions were then expressed and reinforced through the evidence of spirituality, morality, and goodness in everyday life.

The annual report of All Saints Surrey Square for 1899 observed that in the minds of many who lived in the mission districts and who appeared to many churchmen to be quite uninfluenced by religion 'there lurks still an ideal of what the truly Christian life should be'.[3] This ideal of the true believer as it emerged within popular culture had two primary dimensions: the ideal of religiosity as it applied to those who were perceived to be outside popular culture and who professed a formal allegiance to the church whether by regular church attendance, conversion, confirmation, or church membership; and the ideal as it applied within popular culture to those who attended church infrequently and who did not necessarily profess a formal allegiance to church-based religion. The distinction between these two dimensions rested upon certain kinds of expectation. Specific things were expected of the pro-

---

[3] All Saints Surrey Square, *Annual Report* (1899), 7–8.

fessing believer and the regular church attender which individuals did not necessarily expect of themselves and of their immediate communal or cultural group. Having chosen to identify themselves with the churches in a formal and direct sense, believers were seen to have submitted themselves to a high standard involving both a code of conduct, a particular kind of ethical and moral goodness, and a particular form of belief or world-view: 'there still remains an ideal and a strict one for others, which would be the same for themselves of what the life and behaviour of the professing Christian should be'.[4]

It was assumed that the formal profession of belief would be accompanied by distinctive patterns of behaviour, lifestyle, and leisure, signified in written and oral autobiographies by recurrent images such as the frock-coat, the top hat, and the Bible on the table in the parlour, abstention from gambling, excessive drinking and swearing. As Alexander Paterson pointed out, for the working boy, one image of the average Christian was a person who

. . . does not drink or swear or gamble, and goes to concerts but never to a music hall. On the more positive side little more is demanded than that he should dress better and go to his Sunday service. Virtue has become abstention from vice and the line between the two is the rigid line that divides the positive and the negative.[5]

The Army and Religion Survey also described this sentiment among soldiers: 'Their idea is that a Christian man must not drink, swear, must not smoke, must not gamble and must not amuse himself—as to positive duties he must go to church'.[6]

It was widely recognized within popular culture that once individuals had identified themselves with the church, they had to conform to a range of expectations which would necessarily demand a change in lifestyle and behaviour as well as in outlook and belief. In his book *Days and Nights in London* (1880), J. E. Ritchie recorded a conversation between a city missioner and a lodger of Flower and Dean Street, a notorious haunt of pickpockets in Soho. The lodger remarked to another fellow engaged in conversation with the evangelist,

'You will never get to heaven that way. You must believe in the Lord Jesus Christ and then you will be saved.' 'Ah,' said the Evangelist 'You know that do you, I

---

[4] Ibid. 8.

[5] A. Paterson, *Across the Bridges* (1911), 175.

[6] D. S. Cairns (ed.), *The Army and Religion: An Enquiry and its Bearing upon the Religious Life of the Nation* (1919), 65.

hope you live accordingly.' 'Oh yes I know it well enough' was the reply, 'but I can't practise it. I am one of the light fingered gentry. I live in Flower and Dean street.'[7]

This account highlights the absorption of church-based religious language by the lodger of Flower and Dean Street to the extent that he had a clear understanding even of the nuance of the language used by the evangelist. At the same time this description illustrates the lodger's recognition of the gulf which existed between his own lifestyle and demands which were perceived to be inherent within the teaching propagated by the evangelist. There is little doubt that these demands acted as a barrier to involvement for many and as a prime source of working-class alienation from formal religion, as writers such as Hugh McLeod[8] and Gillian Rose[9] point out. The churches' association with middle-class values and the administration of charity might have produced a tendency among the working classes to regard religion as a symbol of 'servile status' and with the desire for free hand-outs and the 'appearance' of respectability, as social historians such as Gareth Stedman Jones[10] and Joanna Bourke argue.[11] However, traditional images of middle-class churchgoing respectability formed only one element of the descriptions of religiosity found within popular culture. The ideal did not stop at respectability alone. 'Middle-class' symbols of right living were held in tension with images of ethical and humanitarian goodness which were fiercely defended as the common territory of all people and as the true foundation of 'Christianity'. Mere abstention from vice, the wearing of a frock-coat, possession of a bible, discipline in work, and attendance at church services on the part of those who formally allied themselves with the church were seen as worthless in so far as they were substitutes for 'genuine belief' expressed through acts of humanitarian kindness. Stan Hall, born near the Elephant and Castle in 1901, the son of a bus conductor, was typical in this respect. He established in his reminiscence a definite contrast between the mere church-attender who might exhibit an abstemious and disciplined lifestyle and even use respectable religious images to bolster his individual social

[7] J. E. Ritchie, *Days and Nights in London* (1880), 135.

[8] H. McLeod, *Piety and Poverty* (New York, 1996), 35–9.

[9] G. Rose, 'Locality, Politics and Culture: Poplar in the 1920's' (London University Ph.D. thesis, 1989), 287.

[10] G. Stedman-Jones, 'Working-Class Culture and Working-Class Politics in London 1870–1900', *Journal of Social History*, 7 (1974), 471.

[11] J. Bourke, *Working-Class Cultures in Britain 1890–1960* (1994), 146.

reputation, and the 'genuine believer' or the true Christian like Miss Webber, his Sunday school teacher. He described, for example, how

It seemed the right thing to do to have a Bible on the table in one of the rooms, if you were fortunate to have more than one room. But it was hardly ever read although the larger it was the greater the impression of the holiness of the family.[12]

The use of images of religiosity such as the Bible to reinforce social respectability are clearly differentiated from true belief, while attendance at church from social or material motives is differentiated from the sincerity of the true believer: 'At church you met the best people, although they were not all true believers . . .'[13]

Stan Hall retained an essential distinction between the 'true believers' and the equivalent of the 'cant participator'.[14] The 'cant participator' or hypocrite failed to combine the first set of images of respectable religiosity with the image of simple goodness. The genuine believer on the other hand combined an adherence to the standards of moral and social respectability expected of the regular churchgoer with an over-riding humanitarianism. Such was the picture which Stan Hall gave of his beloved Miss Webber.

Miss Webber was a single woman who had lost her fiancé in the First World War and had devoted her life to the care of the community. As Stan Hall put it, 'I think Miss Webber had settled that . . . she would give love to those who had not suffered as she had and be with the young children in place of those she would never now have'.[15]

Her devotion was proved by her kindness and the way in which she invited the children in her Sunday school class to her one-roomed home and spent her weekly allowance on providing them with food.

She would in turn invite us in two's or three's in groups of boys and girls to her flat for tea. Her flat was in fact one room in which she had a bed, a table, three chairs and a piano . . . Miss Webber would serve tea with bread and butter (if butter could be had), some cake and after that we would gather around the piano and sing hymns and songs and then a simple game and we would always leave with a few sweets. How she must have gone without to give these little tea parties . . . [16]

---

[12] SLSL, A. S. Hall, 'Reminiscences' (1988), 24.
[13] Ibid.
[14] Booth uses this phrase in *Life and Labour* (1902), 'Religious Influences', vii, 152.
[15] SLSL, A. S. Hall, 'Reminiscences' (1988), 25.
[16] Ibid.

Her kindness did not stop there; if any children were in trouble she would visit them and attempt to help in any way she could, and she would send each child a birthday card every year. Stan Hall pointed out that these cards were 'not just ordinary cards that could be purchased at that time for a 1d or 2d but a hand-painted card of flowers, these being a better card must have cost about 4d, even with a postcard she was setting an example to follow'.[17]

Figures such as Miss Webber were not merely a mythical ideal but had a substance in reality among the ranks of devout working-class believers who are frequently ignored in studies of religion in this period and who existed in far greater numbers than was appreciated by observers such as Charles Booth. The descriptions given of local vicars in the recollective material also illustrate not only the alienating effect of Oxbridge educations, comfortable homes, and expensive vacations[18] but the same kinds of distinction between mere church-attenders or middle-class religious professionals and genuine believers. A good or holy vicar, for example, was described in language which combined the two strands of respectability and simple humanitarian goodness in much the same way as Hall described Miss Webber. Mr F. A. Kent, born in 1901, the son of a crane-slinger from Canning Town, claimed that Mr Barney, a local church worker, was a 'great old chap' who was respected by everyone, even the 'roughest of the rough', because he had the 'right ideas'; that is, he visited the poor and was charitable to them: 'he'd help waif and stray and all the children; he used to spend his money and give 'em sweets'.[19]

Mrs Duckes, born in 1892, the daughter of a chimney sweep from King Street London, described her local vicar as 'ever so nice' because he would always raise his hat to acknowledge the people in the street and he would visit them when they were sick: 'don't matter where you was, anywhere, he'd acknowledge you, come across ask you how you were. Mother used to like him.'[20]

Mrs Hallam, born in 1890, the daughter of a tram-worker of Upper Holloway, described in the same terms a couple at the local mission: 'And they must have had the right ideas because they called on the poorer class'.[21]

The goodness or holiness of the religious man was determined above all by his care of the poor and his neighbourliness and friendliness with-

[17] SLSL, A. S. Hall, 'Reminiscences' (1988), 25.
[18] McLeod, *Piety and Poverty*, 36.
[19] EOHA, Int. 334, 77.
[20] EOHA, Int. 3, 17.
[21] EOHA, Int. 317, 67.

in the community. One such figure was Father Cadman of the Pembroke College Mission, Walworth—'the fish' as he was known locally (due to his sweaty hands). L. J. Carter described how:

The missioner, Father Cadman walked the streets in flowing black robes, keeping always to the centre of the street and barely slowing his pace as he chatted to adults and children alike at doorways and windows or acting as a sanctuary against avenging blows from erstwhile friends or being pleaded with to be allowed to go on the next treat.[22]

The religiosity of the professing believer was not straightforwardly equivalent to middle-class respectability. It involved an ideal of spirituality which remained, in part, independent of class. Social respectability alone could not fulfil the ideal, while to ape the manners and customs of the true believer without embracing an understanding of humanitarian goodness was to open oneself to the charge of hypocrisy. Thus the opposition to churchgoing respectability was not simply an opposition to a social code; it was an opposition on the basis of an ideal which also involved a concept of morality and spirituality. The role of these ideals and their operation within the culture of non-church attenders can easily be overlooked when the interpretative categories used rely too heavily upon the concept of class and pay insufficient attention to the ways in which contemporaries talked about different members of the community and ascribed to them moral and religious status. During the Essex Oral History Survey, respondents were specifically asked to comment on the kinds of people who went to church and chapel. Some were indeed adamant that church attenders were merely middle-class or concerned to 'show off their Sunday best'.[23] This dimension should not be lost, as Hugh McLeod points out when he challenges the new generation of historians working in this area not to neglect class differences and antagonisms as sources of working-class alienation;[24] yet one cannot neglect the indication that some respondents believed that there was no difference between attenders and non-attenders in terms of class, and some even went so far as specifically to exclude the clergy from these kinds of categorization. James Tomkins, for example, born in Bromley-by-Bow in 1879, the son of a building labourer, argued that 'all classes' went to church and that the clergy were in a class of their own because ' . . . well they had to mix with the lot'.[25] Similarly, when asked

[22] L. J. Carter, *Walworth 1929–1939* (1985), 57–8.
[23] See e.g. EOHA, Int. 58, 19.
[24] McLeod, *Piety and Poverty*, 207.
[25] EOHA, Int. 124, 29.

what kinds of people attended chapel, James Mahoney answered: 'We didn't class them different at all. They were—they were in the same working position as ourselves irrespective of their religion.'[26]

The oral evidence suggests a more subtle dimension which must also be drawn out of the material available. It was not the social respectability of the church-attender or minister which was rejected *per se*. Rather, a patronizing, condescending, or aloof attitude towards the community appears to have been a far more frequent source of complaint among those interviewed in the Essex survey. This is borne out in other kinds of material. The Pembroke College Mission, for example, specifically warned its members that: 'To approach in a patronising way or to take up a sort of fashionable "slumming" aggravates the evil. The contact must be simple, natural and heartily welcomed and then it can work wonders.'[27]

As has been seen, those who displayed this natural affinity for the community were classified as good, while those who were patronizing were rejected, often being accused of manifesting mere respectability without genuine religiosity. Vicars were rejected not simply for their Oxbridge associations[28] but for their success or failure in upholding a definition of goodness, morality, and holiness which included and extended beyond social criteria. There are very few cases in which churchgoing respectability was rejected on the principle of the opposition of one class to another. Mrs Rose Underwood, for example, was dismissive of the concept of class as a form of social categorization.

Q: Some people say that there's upper and lower working class.
A: Lower—I see class—well, I don't believe in that. I believe we're all as good as each other. They're people I looked up to.
Q: Why was that?
A: Oh I don't know—It's a feeling, only if they're—they're good. I wouldn't look up to them if they—if it wasn't right.
Q Its not just because they're rich?
A: No, no it's kindness, it's the feeling and you can have that feeling from these people.[29]

[26] EOHA, Int. 70, 31.
[27] Pembroke College Mission, *Annual Report* (1898), 3.
[28] Alan Bartlett has shown how until 1935 the majority of clergymen working in the Bermondsey area had had an Oxbridge education. He also highlights other symbols of class differentiation in terms of housing and the public attention which the clergy received, but his oral material suggests that it was patronizing attitudes which were disliked rather than their social class in and of itself. Bartlett, 'The Churches in Bermondsey 1880–1939' (Birmingham University Ph.D. thesis, 1987), 116–29.
[29] EOHA, Int. 92, 36.

Rose Underwood classified people on the basis of their fulfilment of an ideal of goodness which she identified with the feeling they communicated within the community.

This less tangible ideal of the true believer was respected and admired and even aspired to within popular culture. Its validity was defended through such customs as a respect for the sabbath and through the conscious effort to identify succeeding generations with the main tenets of this ideal through sending them to Sunday school, both of which will be considered in the following chapter. Furthermore, the ideal was defended in a more direct sense through the strong denunciations of hypocrisy which frequently emerge in discussions of religiosity among those who did not regularly attend church. The ideal itself provided the foundation for a critical reappraisal of contemporary churches and churchgoers and it formed the basis of the rationale for a second series of images of the true believer as they applied within popular culture. Those who brought disgrace upon the ideal by formally allying themselves with it and then failing to live up to it were a specific target of attack within the community, and the integrity of those who adhered to the ideal but did not profess to live up to it was upheld. The annual report of All Saints Surrey Square pointed out that:

To be a churchgoer will not square with certain habits and practices which as yet they do not feel equal to giving up; to be confirmed undoubtedly means a much stricter life. They do not feel equal to it. They could not live up to what the definite practice of religion means. They have their ideal; they respect even admire it but doubt their ability to at all realise it. So any outward profession of religion is not for them.[30]

Similarly the Revd W. Thompson argued that: 'Church going implies a much higher standard of consent among the lower class. They will not be hypocrites. If they go to church they must go the whole way and they are not prepared to do this.'[31]

The integrity of this position was upheld within popular culture by the assertion that on some kind of religious scale the irregular church-attender who made no pretence to fulfil these ideals was at least superior to the hypocrite: 'At least he won't be like them, at least they won't bring disgrace upon religion'.[32]

Denunciations of hypocrisy which fill many of the oral testimonies were rooted in this high ideal and in the assertion that the non-church-

[30] All Saints Surrey Square, *Annual Report* (1899), 8.
[31] LSE, Booth Collection, B269, 107–9.
[32] All Saints Surrey Square, *Annual Report* (1899), 8.

attender could in fact live more closely to an ideal of true Christianity than a regular attender.

The standard by which church-attenders were judged and hypocrisy denounced rested on an appeal to an ideal which the participants believed was enshrined within a pure form of the churches' teaching and in the Bible itself. The Army and Religion Survey claimed that it was the soldiers' strong ideal of what the church should be which provoked both the abundance and the nature of the criticism offered:[33] 'Today the very standards by which the men are criticising the churches are ones . . . derived from its labours and witness through the centuries'.[34]

The Revd Conrad Noel argued in 1912 that the working man was 'cynical in his attitude towards the Anglican Church' because he considered it to be the corruption of an earlier and purer ideal:[35] 'The fact for him remains that Peter and Paul might have been his mates and dined at his table and slept under his roof and by no stretch of imagination can he conceive of the Anglican Bishops doing the same'.[36]

Individual church-attenders were likewise criticized on the basis of a standard of simple goodness which was epitomized in the life of Christ and in the gospels. Those who failed to live up to the ideal of true Christian living were held in considerable contempt among the people. *Life and Labour* is full of comments such as the following: 'Moreover the working men feel very strongly about pious employers who sweat their work people . . .'[37]

One chaplain questioned for the Army and Religion Inquiry noted that: 'Constant reference is made to the inconsistency of the lives of professing Christians with the faith which they say they believe'.[38]

Walter Southgate described an employer in great detail in his autobiography *That's the Way it Was* (1982). Mr Dale was hated, not for his pious displays of religious fervour *per se*, but for the combination of these with what was seen as a flagrant abuse of real Christian values in his exploitation of the workforce. Similarly, W. H. Longsdon, the vicar of St Michael's Lant Street, described in his interview with Booth the outrage that was provoked when a man was penalized by his employer for stopping away from his work in order to look after his father who was

---

[33] Cairns, *The Army and Religion*, 194.

[34] Ibid. 193.

[35] C. Noel, 'The Working Classes', in W. K. Lowther Clarke (ed.), *Facing the Facts* (1912), 99–100.

[36] Ibid.

[37] Booth, *Life and Labour* (1902), 'Religious Influences', vii. 36.

[38] Cairns, *The Army and Religion*, 203.

ill. The employer refused to grant his day's pay of five shillings and six-pence on the grounds that the company was a limited one and there was a danger of setting a precedent. The indignation which spread through-out the courts around Lant Street centred in part on the fact that the employer was a churchwarden and Sunday school teacher at Hornsey and that such action was a corruption of good Christian practice.[39]

This denunciation of hypocrisy formed the basis for a vindication of personal disassociation from the church without rejecting what was considered to be a higher and purer Christian ideal. One of Booth's interviewees claimed that the poor justified irregular or non-church attendance on the grounds that 'What was the good of church-going if churchgoers are no better than so and so . . .'[40]

As they saw the 'churchgoing class spending large sums on all kinds of luxury they look upon their religion as humbug, while with regard to charity, the administration of relief and the insisting on churchgoing in return disgust the self-respecting'.[41]

The existence of such hypocrisy justified disassociation from the church and even permitted some individuals to avoid church on the basis of the principle of personal religious integrity. Thus Mrs Cotton argued:

I always say you don't have to go to church, cos a lot of 'em when they go to this service and that what are they? . . . When they say about going to church. I've seen so much of it and the next moment they're in the boozer and there's a few of them, I know they're hard-working ladies, they think they're God's saints but they're not. That's when I say as long as I am a clean living person who cares? . . . As I say when the Lord calls me there's nothing wrong I've done all my life. But no, no, I've brought my children up decent and respectable and they bring their children up the same.[42]

By adhering to the integrity of non-involvement it was possible for individuals such as Ivy Cotton to disassociate themselves from the particular standards which formal profession entailed while still pleasing God, being moral, and ensuring their salvation in the life to come. The essential element of the ideal of genuine Christianity in the form of goodness could be upheld within popular culture without 'going the whole way' as self-professed believers were expected to do. An occasional and conditional adherence to orthodox rituals was seen as sufficient to fulfil one's duty towards God, while simple humanitarian goodness was sufficient to make a person 'truly Christian' despite his neglect of the strictures of the institutional church.

This notion of the 'true Christian' as it applied within popular culture appeared to many contemporary observers to be an excuse to avoid the rigours of the Christian life. It was regarded as a licence to extract the palatable aspects of the Christian gospel but to neglect the elements which involved duty, responsibility, and obedience. In particular, it was believed to relegate the notion of sin and to negate the doctrine of the atonement. Some churchmen argued that the people had no sense of sin: 'They have never done anything wrong.They positively bask in the sense of the approbation of their indulgent deity'.[43] Or, as it appeared to another churchman, 'Most men believe in God to whom they ascribe their vague humanitarian impulses but he is a God who makes small demands upon them in terms of worship and right conduct and with whom they are consequently on the best of terms . . . '[44]

A respondent to the Army and Religion Survey expressed this view in more specific terms when he argued that:

The whole deeper side of the churches' teaching about Jesus Christ seems to have little or no hold upon them, except of the loosest kind. Of Jesus as the Son of God and as the atoning sacrifice for the world, they have little or no knowledge at all.[45]

Similarly, in his description of working-class sailors, F. T. Bullen pointed out that

As to the plan of salvation they knew next to nothing. Dim and hazy ideas of the vicarious sacrifice of Christ for man were somewhat timidly hazarded but of the great fundamental truth of Christianity summed up in the words 'God was in Christ reconciling the world to himself', they had not the shadow of an idea.[46]

The concomitant of these kinds of attitudes was believed to be an inadequate grasp of the concept of judgement and of the afterlife. Although it was recognized that the defenders of this kind of image of Christianity often had an idea of Heaven, this was dismissed as having: 'hardly the shadow of a semblance to any Christian doctrine because there is no hint of the condition of sin or of life as a tainted thing, crying for purification'.[47]

---

43 Booth, *Life and Labour* (1902), 'Religious Influences', vii. 103.
44 Ibid.
45 Cairns, *The Army and Religion*, 33.
46 F. T. Bullen, *With Christ at Sea* (1901), 27.
47 Cairns, *The Army and Religion*, 16.

While the comments of these churchmen highlight the contemporary perception of a distinction between concepts of morality and religiosity, they tend to suggest that a concept of the atonement had been entirely dismissed and to overlook the complexity of popular reinterpretations of church-based religiosity. However, the notion of religiosity as it applied within popular culture was not entirely arbitrary or completely divorced from church-based religion. It too encompassed a clear set of expectations. Certain kinds of behaviour were acceptable and other forms unacceptable both to the community and to God. Certain kinds of behaviour would lead to salvation, to the assurance of future reward and admittance to the afterlife, while other kinds of behaviour invoked the judgement and disapproval of the Deity. A notion of punishment and reward was retained, but individuals were acquitted or atoned for on the basis of a different definition of morality. Moreover, this concept of sin formed the basis for a concept of the hereafter and of punishment and reward. The fulfilment of a distinct set of moral and ethical criteria was seen as sufficient to give the irregular church-attender the right of access to the hereafter and the award of the title of the true believer. These concepts remained linked to language drawn from both New Testament and church-based imagery. The actors continued to regard their definitions as orthodox and their morality as specifically Christian. The ethics of popular culture were associated, for example, with a concept of God and with the notion of an absolute moral standard of which a transcendent Deity was the arbiter. Both these concepts were related to a notion of a hereafter which would involve some kind of final reckoning for both the righteous and the unrighteous and in some cases to the specific strictures of New Testament teaching. God was believed to reward goodness and to punish wickedness beyond death. The perspective of the socio-religious commentators must again, therefore, be brought alongside the interpretations and ideals of the participants.

The ideal of genuine religiosity as it applied to the infrequent church-attender involved a distinct definition of morality and of 'sin'. It was above all neighbourliness and brotherliness which defined the point at which sin and goodness met. This was often deliberately contrasted with upholding a moral law in an orthodox sense or subscribing to a particular code of practice defined by the church-based community. In particular, it was contrasted with an absolute association between morality and church attendance and between immorality and non-church attendance. Many of those interviewed exhibited a belief in the concept of 'sin', but sinning did not include the absence of individuals from regular church involvement or various misdemeanours when they were carried out without a malicious intent towards one's fellow man. This concept of morality was given a biblical legitimacy and it was regarded as 'Christian' by the participants. Moreover, fulfilling its criteria ensured their favourable reception by God and their reward in terms of entitlement to Heaven. Mrs Graig, for example, born in Marylebone in 1900, the daughter of a hairdresser, described her mother as a great Christian on the grounds of her honesty and care for her fellow men.

The chief aim was to do your best in life, to be honest of course, was the great principle in life. My mother was a great Christian, in any case. And of course the great thing was to do your best in life and the best to your fellow creatures.[48]

Similarly, Louise Codd, the daughter of a carman from Jamaica Road, Bermondsey, describes how her mother, although she did not attend church, practised religion with her neighbours: 'I wouldn't say she was religious but she practised religion—she does—she did give us a lead in helping people'.[49]

Likewise, Edith Anders, the daughter of a costermonger from Decimer Street off Tower Bridge Road, expressed her opinion of her mother's goodness and morality in terms of her relationship with the neighbours in their street.

I mean I remember my mother, she'd go in the person's next door who was having a baby and help the doctor out, come running in our house and sort out all the baby's clothes and take them in and lend them to the next door neighbour 'cos she had none.[50]

To be 'good' in a 'truly Christian' sense it was sufficient to do good to one's neighbour independently of one's attachment to the institutional church. Sydney Barry of Merrow Street, Walworth stressed that 'treating people kindly this is my religion, to make a big show of it, I don't believe in all that show and that kind of thing in front of people'.[51]

The ethical criterion of the ideal as it applied within popular culture was distinguished from the idea of the church as the moral arbiter. Admission to heaven and the fulfilment of the essentials of Christianity were determined by a criterion of goodness which made little or no reference to the institutional church or its claims. 'One is met everywhere with the question (put in such a way as to imply an assertion)

---

[48] EOHA, Int. 6, 13. [49] EOHA, Int. 235, 45.
[50] SCW, Int. 5. [51] SCW, Int. 12.

whether a decent respectable life is not enough to recommend one to God and to ensure that it will be alright with one in the hereafter'.[52]

One respondent to the Army and Religion Survey claimed that the average soldier had an ideal of the true believer but that this was divorced in their understanding from the church.[53] The moral teachings of Jesus, for example, were separated from the teachings of the church: 'They distinguish him from the churches, which they criticise without stint'.[54]

Jesus was seen as the model for a pattern of morality which was determined above all by the practicalities of communal relationship. The attainment of heaven or the 'hereafter' and the definition of sin were subject to what was regarded as the quintessence of religion, notably 'doing good to one's fellow man'.[55] Thus Arthur Harding's Mrs Casey, the Irish laundry woman of Gibraltar Gardens, is said to have had nothing to fear from 'death or the hereafter' as she had done no wrong to those around her.[56] In the same way a match-seller in the parish of St Alphege was upheld as genuinely good when she kept a neighbour's family for three weeks while the parent was in hospital. 'She will deny herself simple necessities of life sooner than see her friend in want.'[57]

One woman in Friar Street lent her clothes to her lodger so that she could go out to work, even though she was forced to stay in bed herself until her friend returned. If a neighbour was sick, a hard-working woman who had stood all day at the washtub would think nothing of watching her bedside night after night for a whole week together.[58] When Lucy McLelland, the daughter of a waterman from Blackheath, born in 1900, was asked whether her mother went to church on Sunday, she interjected strongly, 'no,no,no, she never got to church, 'cos she was a Christian woman you know, in her way'.[59] This position was summarized by one of the Essex Oral History Project interviewees who remarked in response to the question of whether his parents were churchgoers: 'one hundred percent Christians but not church-goers'.[60] Similarly, Miriam Moore, the daughter of a sailor and a laundry woman,

[52] Cairns, *The Army and Religion*, 117.
[53] Ibid. 62–3.
[54] Ibid. 33.
[55] Booth, *Life and Labour* (1902), 'Religious Influences', vii. 224.
[56] R. Samuel, *East End Underworld: Chapters in the Life of Arthur Harding* (Oxford, 1986), 240.
[57] St Alphege Church, *Annual Report* (1883), 52.
[58] Ibid.
[59] EOHA, Int. 391, 45.
[60] EOHA, Int. 70, 16.

insisted that her mother, although she did not regularly attend the church 'believed in Christ, she believed in God, and she was . . . well to me she was a Christian, cause you didn't have to go to church to be a Christian'.[61]

The qualification which merited that title so far as Mrs Moore was concerned was her hard work, her careful effort in the upbringing of her children, and her concern for her neighbours: 'It didn't matter if the neighbour was out of work ur . . . Mum would make, if she had it, she'd make extra food and give over to them and say, "I wasn't thinking, I made too much" and give it to the kids'.[62] Mrs Moore went on to emphasize this point later in her interview: 'as I said to you a little while ago, my mother to me and I am sure to God, she was a true Christian'.[63] She described how the children in the local area loved her and gave her the honorary title of Nanny Roberts because of her kindness in the community.

In addition to these standards of moral goodness, God was also believed to tolerate both pleasures and moral laxity and even breaches in what most churchmen would have considered as the moral law when these were made for ethical reasons or from mere human error and weakness. Upholding what one churchman, interviewed by Booth, described as, 'the most prevalent gospel, a vague bias towards that which is believed to be good to one's fellow man',[64] was considered morally sufficient to vindicate an individual and to cover over what was seen as a multitude of minor wrongs. Arthur Harding, for example, did not regard theft as immoral when it was undertaken for the purposes of personal and communal survival. He describes how his mother used to steal clothes at jumble sales. She justified such action as morally acceptable by arguing that the vicar had no right to charge for the clothes in order to raise money to buy himself another bottle of whisky while she and her family had to eke out a bare subsistence.[65] Such a consideration may also account for the fact that many prostitutes refused to regard their means of subsistence as a sin, much to the exasperation of the Charing Cross Rescue and Vigilance Committee.[66] Anna Telby described how she was prepared to steal buns from the tea at the local mission in Penton Place, Islington with a clear conscience when she did so for her

---

[61] SCW, Int. 15.
[62] Ibid.
[63] Ibid.
[64] Booth, *Life and Labour* (1902), 'Religious Influences', vii. 37.
[65] Samuel, *East End Underworld*, 25.
[66] Booth, *Life and Labour* (1902), 'Religious Influences', vii. 361.

mother who was struggling to make ends meet after the death of Anna's father.[67]

I used to go all under the stalls sorting out for my mum. Sundays I used to go down Kings Cross coal halls, where they bag up the coal and coke, I used to take a bag down there and get coal and coke for nothing, get chased by the blooming man all the way.
Q: Didn't you think that was naughty?
A: No, I was helping my mum, I wasn't thinking that what I was doing wasn't right, I was thinking more about helping my mum. That was naughty. That was thieving but I didn't know that.[68]

This form of 'social crime' was not only linked to a customary code of honour, loyalty, and obligation within the community,[69] but was also bound up with a particular kind of moral and ethical value system which was regarded as a form of religion within popular culture. This code of moral acceptability, although broad and inclusive, had clearly defined boundaries which were enforced through the medium of local public opinion and ultimately by the threat of the punishment of the Deity. The community, for example, would turn a blind eye to pre-marital sexual relations,[70] and yet those who were unfaithful once their marriage vows had been taken were subject to various kinds of social and even physical censure in the community. Joyce Milan, of a street community around the docks in Woolwich, described how 'If a docker's wife was found carrying on with someone else well she was absolutely ostracised by the whole street'.[71]

Similarly, Annie Foley described how the dockers would throw bags of flour over a man who was 'carrying on' in the same manner.[72] Popular religion was in this way both distinguished as a pattern of belief and enforced as a code of conduct. It was overarched by a notion of a personal God who not only rewarded goodness but also punished evil. Gipsy Smith's description of the gipsy community of which he was a part before his conversion to evangelical Christianity, is reminiscent of the general sentiment found in Southwark during this period: 'We believe in God, we believe he is good and great, that he will reward the good and punish the wicked'.[73]

[67] SCW, Int. 7.
[68] Ibid.
[69] S. Humphries, 'Steal to Survive: The Social Crime of Working-Class Children, 1890–1940', *Oral History Journal*, 9.1 (1981), 24–32.
[70] Booth, *Life and Labour* (1902), 'Religious Influences', 'Conclusion', 44.
[71] Age Exchange, *On the River*, 36.
[72] Ibid. 35.
[73] Gipsy Smith, *From Gipsy Tent to Pulpit: The Story of My Life* (1901), 1–2.

It was considered inappropriate, even ethically suspect, when an individual who was held to be 'good' and 'moral' by the standards outlined above was accused of sin on the basis of moral criteria defined by the church-based community. A number of churchmen record the offence taken by their parishioners when they remonstrated with them about sin and urged them to uphold the regular religious duty of attending church.[74] Such remonstration was tantamount to accusing individuals of moral deficiency when by their own standards and by those of the family and the community they were considered morally righteous. Mrs Blackhall of Queen's Park, for example, born in 1895, described her indignation when a local vicar spoke to her mother of sin during an illness. She considered such standards inappropriate to apply to her mother who was such a 'good person' in terms of her care for her family and her fellow man.[75]

During the First World War aspects of this ideal of genuine religiosity were believed to be vindicated as the soldiers became popular sainted heroes. They exhibited fellowship and brotherly kindness during active service in a context which bypassed the mainstream churches. The war supported the notion that a man could be good in these senses without the aid of the church. The war was believed to have produced a wealth of unselfishness and heroism in the men[76] which was disconnected from institutional Christianity. One chaplain serving in France wrote:

They say that they see no difference as regards this positive energy of goodness between the people who go to church and profess themselves to be Christians and those who do not. The only distinguishing marks for them are the negative marks that the churchgoing public keeps the ten commandments and has as its outstanding virtue the fact that it goes to church.[77]

Although immorality, gambling, and drunkenness all increased during the war, they did not preclude great acts of benevolence: 'To see a badly wounded man barely able to limp out of battle, stop under fire to help another man to his feet and support him along the road is a sight as common as it is unforgettable'.[78]

Such acts lent support to the criticism of an absolute association of one vice such as gambling with all vices. They appeared to enhance the popular assertion of the fundamentals of human kindness while

74 Booth, *Life and Labour* (1902), 'Religious Influences', vii. 77.
75 EOHA, Int. 76, 25.
76 Cairns, *The Army and Religion*, 8–9.
77 Ibid. 71.
78 T. W. Pym and G. Gordon, *Papers from Picardy* (1917), 49.

diminishing the significance of various misdemeanours which the church considered morally serious. The Revd T. W. Pym and Revd G. Gordon claimed that the war had produced a widespread appreciation of the 'inarticulate Christianity' of the ordinary working man.[79] Such actions also emphasized the relative heroism of the men as compared with the vicars who sat on recruiting platforms and stayed behind the front lines preaching from a position of inactivity. Robert Graves, for example, deliberately contrasted the courage of the men with the weakness of Protestant chaplains at the front.[80]

The tone of annual church reports after the war suggests that the local churches may have shared a similar appreciation of 'inarticulate Christianity' which led some to go so far as to compare their own churches unfavourably with the army as an institution for good among the working classes. Where the church was lacking in communal life, the army was seen to supply both fellowship and brotherliness. The annual report of the South London Mission for 1919 argued that

The only world 'fit for heroes' to live in is a world where brotherhood prevails. The Army was a brotherhood, a blood red fellowship of pain and endurance and courage. We must rejoin hands to make individual and social and indeed church life too, more brotherly.[81]

The kinds of brotherliness and humanitarianism exhibited in the army were, in this way, held up as models. Roger Lloyd describes how an article in *John Bull* questioned the right of the churchmen to fault England's splendid men and to speak to them of repentance: 'They don't need repentance; they are all saints everyone of them. To preach repentance to them is an insult.'[82]

Within popular culture, therefore, the approbation of the Deity was induced by a value system which was considered deficient if not entirely erroneous by many contemporary churchmen and observers. The definition of sin was subject to a different set of moral and ethical criteria which was often overlooked by observers but which the participants considered sufficient to give the irregular church-attender the right of access to the hereafter and to warrant the title of the true believer. The material considered in this chapter thus supports, on the one hand, the conclusions presented by Elizabeth Roberts in her study of working-class

---

[79] Ibid. 223.
[80] R. Graves, *Goodbye to All That* (New York, 1930), 230–2.
[81] South London Mission, *Annual Report* (1919), 19.
[82] R. Lloyd, *The Church of England in the Twentieth Century 1900–1965*, 2 vols. (1946), i. 43.

women in central and northern Lancashire between 1890 and 1940 concerning the deep-rooted influence of Christian teaching within popular culture,[83] but on the other hand it challenges the notion that these were drawn 'directly from the Church's teaching', as Roberts argues.[84]

The form which popular beliefs took cannot be simply equated with Christian teaching without appreciating the process of reinterpretation which took place within popular culture. Although there was an appeal to the language of 'loving thy neighbour', doctrinal criteria were subservient to the expedients of communal life and survival, while breaches in the moral law from an orthodox point of view were not seen as inconsistent with maintaining the core of the second ideal of the 'true believer'. A tacit agreement as to the validity and the truth of the Christian gospel, therefore, combined with a rejection of the claim of the church to act as the moral arbiter, which was strengthened by the experience of international conflict. At the same time, these concepts and the ideals of religiosity of which they were a part, drew on specifically orthodox language. Such qualities as neighbourliness were considered to be universal standards of behaviour which appealed to a transcendental absolute communicated through specific church-based terminology. It mattered, for example, that people who never attended churches, and who may even have resented the suggestion that they should, called themselves and believed themselves to be Christians, as Jeffrey Cox argues in his consideration of diffusive Christianity in Lambeth. Church-based religious language and orthodox rituals were not seen simply as the territory of a social élite. They were deeply ingrained and incorporated within popular culture and it is in this sense perhaps that Don Lewis is right in the observation that popular religion was closer to Christianity at the end of the nineteenth century than it had been for the last two centuries.[85] Aspects of the church-based religious discourse had become part of a religious repertoire which was distinctly popular in its emphasis and form. In this way orthodox images and ideals had, through a process of assimilation and reinterpretation become the territory of popular religion. Working-class aloofness from the church should not neccessarily be regarded as indifference but as an outcome of a different definition of what it meant to be a 'true believer' and a 'genuine Christian'. It is on the grounds of non-church attendance

---

[83] E. Roberts, *A Woman's Place: An Oral History of Working-Class Women 1890–1940* (Oxford, 1984).

[84] Ibid. 5.

[85] D. Lewis, *Lighten Their Darkness* (1986), 274.

that the working class were often stigmatized by contemporaries and have been judged by historians as irreligious, yet when a wide range of material is considered these institutional criteria appear subsidiary within popular culture to the fulfilment of a popular ideal of the 'genuine Christian'.[86]

[86] E. J. Orford, *The Book of Walworth* (1925), 70.

6

Religion by Deputy: The Church and the Community

The popular ideal of the 'true believer' considered in the previous chapter not only involved a notion of religious duty towards one's family, neighbours, and friends but also a certain relationship with local churches which extended further than participation in the rites of passage. This included the practice of sending one's children to Sunday school, teaching them to pray, maintaining the personal habit of private prayer within the context of the home, respecting the sabbath as a different and somehow holy day, along with a willingness to uphold the place of the church within the community without necessarily demanding attendance at church services on a regular basis. These practices were surrounded by and enacted within a context of nostalgia, loyalty, and tradition as well as personal and communal identity. They were part of a complex process of interaction between church-based and popular culture which cannot be fully appreciated when relying solely upon formal indicators of practice or behaviour. Many of these customs are familiar to studies of this period,[1] yet they are considered here as part of a distinct repertoire of popular belief expressed within clear limits and distinguished from an indiscriminate incorporation of fragments of church-based culture.

The practice of sending one's children to Sunday school is among the most frequently cited of these customs. This common pattern of observance has been interpreted in various ways from an assertion of familial respectability to the product of mere convention or the desire for an hour's peace on a Sunday afternoon. The material considered in Southwark, however, suggests that the practice was also a conscious effort of parents to identify the family with the teachings of the church

[1] See, in particular, J. Cox, *The English Churches in a Secular Society: Lambeth 1870–1930* (Oxford, 1982), 90–105; A. B. Bartlett, 'The Churches in Bermondsey 1880–1939' (Birmingham University Ph.D. thesis, 1987); H. McLeod, *Religion and Society in England 1850–1914* (1996), 71–133 and *Piety and Poverty* (New York, 1996).

through the medium of their offspring. The Revd W. J. Somerville, the vicar of St George-the-Martyr parish church, considered this phenomenon sufficiently well defined to warrant the title of 'religion by deputy'.[2] Exposure to the teachings of Christianity was seen as necessary and appropriate to the formation of individual character within popular culture and the practice could even be regarded by the participants as symptomatic of their belief in the importance of certain church-based values within the popular religious repertoire.

Contemporary observers and historians alike stressed the regularity with which children attended Sunday school in this period. Charles Booth described the importance of Sunday schooling in the area in his section on parish institutions in the summary volume of the 'Religious Influences'. By 1897, the Wesleyan Methodist Southwark Sunday School Society alone had fifteen schools in the northern part of the borough in the area round the Mint, Borough High Street, Tower Street, and Waterloo Road. It employed over 400 teachers, and provided for approximately 5,080 scholars. This represented an increase on the provisions made by the same Society during the 1850s. In 1859 the Society oversaw twelve schools, 400 teachers, and 4,000 scholars. Owen Chadwick claimed that, by 1883, three out of every four children in England and Wales attended Sunday school[3] and Alan Bartlett likewise argued that in Bermondsey in the period from 1880 to 1939 very few children escaped the attentions of the Sunday school at some point in their childhood,[4] while Jeffrey Cox in his study of Lambeth called its influence 'virtually universal'.[5]

The significance of Sunday schools does not appear to have diminished during the inter-war period. Llewellyn Smith remarked that 'children are still sent in large numbers to Sunday School',[6] and E. J. Orford made a striking comparison in 1936 between the regularity of junior attendance at Sunday school in Walworth and the infrequent appearance of adults at church during the later 1920s and 1930s.[7] Where the majority of adult Walworthians stayed in bed on a Sunday morning, its children were diligent in their regular visit to the church.

The picture given by these writers is in marked contrast to the pessimistic estimation made by the philanthropist Alexander Paterson in

---

[2] St George-the-Martyr, *Annual Report* (1902), 14.
[3] O. Chadwick, *The Victorian Church*, 2 vols. (1970), i. 257.
[4] Bartlett, 'The Churches of Bermondsey', 195.
[5] Cox, *The English Churches*, 95.
[6] H. Llewellyn Smith, *The New Survey of London Life and Labour* (1931), iii. 75.
[7] E. J. Orford, *The Book of Walworth* (1925), 55.

his book *Across the Bridges* (1911). He argued that only one-fifth of the
children of south London attended Sunday school. The oral evidence,
however, suggests that this figure may well have been unduly low and
supports the impression given by Booth, Llewellyn Smith, and Orford.
Each of those interviewed by the Essex Oral History Project recorded
attendance at Sunday school, and these institutions formed a significant
part of the recollections of early life in all of the interviews carried out in
Southwark. Only one respondent did not attend Sunday school regularly
as a child.[8]

The decision to send one's children to Sunday school had both a
social and a religious element. By the end of the century the Sunday
schools were associated not only with general juvenile education but
also with more overt Christian teaching. The values of punctuality,
order, and cleanliness, which Thomas Laqueur has associated with
the Sunday schools[9] constituted merely one strand of education which
many parents considered important but which was not the sole factor
motivating the widespread practice of sending one's children to Sunday
school.

Thomas Laqueur challenged the view of the Sunday schools as agents
of social control and manipulation[10] and in contrast presented them as
indigenous working-class institutions which arose out of the values of
working-class respectability. He highlights the role of associations
between cleanliness, punctuality, secular education and instruction in
establishing a congruence between the Sunday schools and working-
class respectability. Yet although he is concerned to argue that the
Sunday school sustained a Christian culture among working-class
children and that these institutions 'played a central part in the spiritual
lives of its students',[11] he does not examine in any detail the religious
sentiment and teaching bound up in the popular notion of 'religion by
deputy'.

As the century progressed, many of the educational and social oppor-
tunities which Laqueur argued were the monopoly of the Sunday schools
were transferred to elementary schools. In 1851 half the children of school
age in Southwark attended school. In 1871 this increased to about 69 per
cent as the Education Act of 1870 came into effect. In 1881 this had risen

[8] SCW, Int. 11.
[9] T. W. Laqueur, *Religion and Respectability: Sunday Schools and Working-Class Culture
1780–1950* (1976).
[10] E. P. Thompson, *The Making of the English Working Class* (1963); S. S. Tamke, *Make
a Joyful Noise unto the Lord: Hymns as a Reflection of Victorian Social Attitudes* (Ohio, 1978).
[11] Ibid. 160.

to 73 per cent, in 1891 it was 80 per cent or more, and by 1901, 85 per cent. By 1930 all were provided for in schools. In the early years of the Booth survey, where more than 90 per cent of children of school age had been brought into day schools, less than seven in ten of their parents had themselves passed through day school, while nearly half of parents would have received no school education at all. It was estimated that, for persons between the ages of 25 and 55, the percentage of such persons without elementary school education was about 48 per cent in 1891, 35 per cent in 1901, 22 per cent in 1911, 10 per cent in 1921 and 5 per cent in 1929.[12] By 1931 all the children of Southwark were provided for in 31,500 places in the forty-five elementary schools in the area.

The kind of education offered by the Sunday schools thus became more directly associated with religious instruction as secular agencies took over many other aspects of juvenile instruction. The provision of elementary education did not necessarily displace local Sunday schools; rather the schools appear to have acted as a goad towards the increased efficiency and specialization of the Sunday schools. Organizations such as the Southwark Sunday School Teachers' Association were galvanized by the development of board schools in the area. L. E. Trousdale, the vicar of St Andrew's, gave a paper at the Newington Sunday School Teachers' Association in April 1885 entitled, 'How May Sunday Schools Keep Pace with the Growing Efficiency of the Day Schools?'.[13] Two years later, the Revd G. Palmer, Rector of Newington, speaking to the same group argued that 'The importance of their [the Sunday schools] being efficient has been enormously increased by the excellency of the Board School education in secular subjects and the imperfection in religious subjects'.[14]

During these years the Sunday School Teachers' Association provided detailed training in various kinds of management and teaching skills. At a meeting in April 1888 the Revd W. A. Corbett of St Peter's parish church, Sumner Street, gave advice on preparing lessons, presenting material, and ensuring the comprehension of pupils.[15] A series of meetings was also held by the same society at Holy Trinity Girls' School in Swan Street, Newington Butts to train teachers to communicate more effectively. The lectures given at these gatherings included a series of model lessons by the Revd Father Cadman of St Matthew's, New Kent

[12] Llewellyn Smith, *The New Survey of London Life and Labour*, i. 246–8.
[13] *South London Press*, 4 Apr. 1885.
[14] *South London Chronicle*, 18 June 1887.
[15] Ibid. 21 Apr. 1888.

Road and C. H. Grundy, the organizing secretary to the bishop of the diocese.[16]

The effect of this impetus was not only an increase in efficiency but the clarification of the aims and focus of Sunday schools in a manner which distinguished them from the teaching received in the board schools. In talks such as those given by Corbett, emphasis was placed on religious instruction, the fostering of a 'Christian atmosphere' in the Sunday schools, and particularly on the dimension of Christian love in the relationship between the teacher and the pupil.

It is often the patient self-sacrificing love that will hold these rough children off the street, when a hundred addresses or Sunday school lessons will not touch them. Once get their love and respect and it is wonderful what can be done with them.[17]

Similarly the Revd T. P. Stevens advised a meeting of Sunday school teachers gathered at the Anchor Mission Hall, Southwark in 1928 to aim for the highest ideal of gentleness, courtesy, and kindness.[18] The oral evidence indicates that these specifically Christian elements of teaching remained a dominant and distinguishing element in recollections of Sunday school. Many memories centre on biblical stories, hymns, the act and habit of prayer, the impact of certain religious images, and personal contact with teachers. These include memories of particular beliefs such as the love of God, punishment of the wicked, hell and heaven. Bertha Thornton, the daughter of a journeyman bricklayer from Kennington, for example, recorded in her written reminiscence her belief in Hell, her assurance of the love of God, and the necessity of personal salvation from sin through faith which were kindled within the context of a local Sunday school.[19]

Similarly, A. T. Collinson, born in 1893 in Drury Lane,[20] and W. Horwood of Walworth[21] both describe their Sunday schooling in relation to the memories of the main tenets of the Christian doctrine which were taught at Holy Trinity and the St John's College Mission respectively. A number of recollections specifically associated the Sunday school with memories of the person and character of Christ. Barbara Luke, for instance, described in her interview how

    [16] *South London Chronicle*, 21 Apr. 1888.
    [17] Southwark Sunday School Society, *Annual Report* (1903), 3.
    [18] *South London Press*, 10 Jan. 1928.
    [19] SLSL, B. Thornton, 'Memories of Childhood' (1987), 5–6.
    [20] Brunel University, Burnett Collection, A. T. Collinson, 'One Way Only' (1966), n.p.
    [21] SLSL, W. Horwood, 'A Walworth Boy Looking Back on the Years 1922–1939' (1977), 86–91.

We would pray to Jesus. Jesus was the thing when you went to Sunday School they talked about Jesus all the time. I think it was God when we went to church but in the afternoon it was Jesus, you know, when we had to sing 'Jesus loves you yes I know . . .' but um . . . it was all about Jesus and if you was good you would be sitting with him . . . all that kind of thing.[22]

Many of those interviewed in Southwark, when asked about Sunday school, immediately recalled Bible stories and texts. When Lilian Tims was asked what she learnt at Sunday school, she replied: 'All about Jesus. I used to like the stories, I think they're lovely stories. I've got a Bible today that they gave me for attendance, a New Testament. I've still got them.'[23]

Helen Westall's main memory of Sunday school was also the texts and the text cards she received from her teacher. Philippa Ivy recalled how each week she would spend her pocket money on the texts at Sunday school, 'Used to have about 6d pocket money and I used to spend it on texts'.[24] She went on to describe how 'If you went to Sunday school they used to give you a text and then you would get a big one . . .'[25] She recalled in particular memories of specific texts from the book of Samuel which she had learnt in Sunday school. Some of the texts which she had received she continued to carry in her bag throughout her adult life.[26] Mrs Croft also described how

If you went to Sunday school regular they used to give us a little text . . . you had to save them until you got half a dozen you'd take it back to the Sunday school and they'd give you a big one instead. That was regular attendance and at the end of the year we used to get a prize.[27]

This evidence is reinforced by the Essex material. Earnest Perkins, for example, described how he attended Sunday school each week at three o'clock: 'And you had a little text. The Lord is my Shepherd and a little picture, or something. And you had to take it home to prove to your mam that you'd been to Sunday School.'[28]

Mrs L. Epps, born in 1903, the daughter of a cabdriver from Peckham, described in her interview with the Essex Oral History Project the nostalgia evoked by the memory of these texts.[29]

And when we went to Sunday School we used to get books like what they put the stamp, the star in and we always had to show 'em when you come home. Was no getting out of it you know . . . Yes, yes and we used to get a little text card with

[22] SCW, Int. 6.   [23] SCW, Int. 23.   [24] SCW, Int. 17.
[25] Ibid.   [26] Ibid.   [27] SCW, Int. 18.
[28] EOHA, Int. 113, 13.   [29] EOHA, Int. 392.

them. Funny thing is a friend gave me a Bible the other day Oh couple or three months ago and it was all these little texts brought back memories to me of when I was a kid 'cos we always got 'em from Sunday School.[30]

Similarly, Lucy McLelland, born in 1900, the daughter of a waterman from Greenwich, described how,

Well Sunday School we used to sing choruses and they used to talk to us and give us a text. And then we had to bring it next time and then when you got so many we got a prize, a hymn book or something. Oh yes we always had got to go to Sunday School.[31]

The collection of these texts appears to have been taken very seriously by many individuals. Many would do considerable amounts of work in order to receive what they considered to be the high accolade of a completed card or a Sunday school prize. Elizabeth Merritt went so far as to learn entire chapters from the Bible by heart and was rewarded for her efforts with prizes of books: 'She used to make me learn a chapter by heart. I did that and she used to get me books for prizes.'[32]

For many, these stories and texts appear to have established the Bible as an authoritative repository of truth. Most of those who attended Sunday school received a Bible and these were often kept carefully and respectfully and passed down in the family.

For others Sunday school was recalled in relation to the habit and act of prayer,[33] the singing of particular hymns, or a repertoire of powerful visual images associated with religious teaching and ideas. The recollection of visual images was a striking feature of the oral testimonies. Religious paintings, prints, or limelight slides along with the small texts which included scenes from Bible stories often formed the focus of a range of memories associated with the teachings which they communicated or the circumstances under which the images were received. The memory of these pictures often precipitated the recollection of biblical stories.[34] Sunday school teaching material contained in the John Johnson Collection specifically employed vivid colour illustrations such as Carmel and Babylon overshadowed by forbidding clouds and an atmosphere of brooding evil, while the pictures of Mount Zion and

---

[30] EOHA, Int. 392, 42.

[31] EOHA, Int. 391, 45.

[32] SCW, Int. 21.

[33] SCW, Int. 7; EOHA, Int. 257, 14.

[34] See e.g. Arthur Harding's description of the murals on the wall of the mission in Nichol. R. Samuel, *East End Underworld: Chapters in the Life of Arthur Harding* (1986), 26–30.

Bethlehem were draped in light.[35] The illustrations found in Bunyan's
The Pilgrim's Progress formed a recurrent feature of many of the recollections. Elizabeth Rignall, born in 1894, the daughter of a painter and
decorator from Clapham Common, described in her written reminiscence how she was drawn each Sunday without fail to their family copy
of *The Pilgrim's Progress* and to the page where Christian wrestles with
Apollyon.[36] Similarly, J. H. Bennett was much impressed by the image of
Pilgrim advancing towards the angels at the entrance of heaven and he
would go out of his way to peer through the window of a local shop in
Walworth just to look at the illustration.

A little past Page's Walk was a picture shop and in the entrance was a picture
showing the straight and narrow path with Pilgrim advancing towards the angels
at the entrance to heaven and the winding broad highway with numerous
temptations leading to the fires of hell. This had quite an effect on me. I used to
gaze and stare at this every time I passed as a small boy.[37]

The limelight slides, which were often shown as part of a Sunday
school activity, were a powerful medium for the creation of lasting and
evocative images in the minds of Sunday school children. For Barbara
Luke recollections of Sunday school led on to recollections of the limelight shows.

In the mornings we had to go to church and in the afternoons was like Sunday
school when you sit round and they tell you stories about Jesus and sing all their
songs . . . and in the evening we used to go over the stone church and they used
to put a magic lantern on.
Q: Tell me about them [the limelight concerts].
A: They were all about Jesus and what 'e done, but the last one we saw frightened
the living daylights out of me.
Q: Why was that?
A: Because he was all chained up and all you could hear was the chains and you
could see them, I don't know what it was, I think it was Jesus chained you know
where they were going to . . . I think it was that, um . . . we was really frightened
me and my two sisters were, the funny thing about it was when we came home
we was really frightened and we had to go upstairs and there was a full moon and
it was shining on the chamber and I screamed 'cos I said, 'look, it's Jesus here!'
and we fell down the stairs we were so frightened. My two sisters . . . I pushed
them down, oh we was so scared, my brother was courting his young lady on the

[35] These were produced by the Committee of General Literature and Education
Appointed by the Society for Promoting Christian Knowledge.
[36] Brunel University, Burnett Collection, E. Rignall, 'All so Long Ago', n.d., n.p.
[37] SLSL, J. H. Bennett, 'I was a Walworth Boy' (1977), 10.

door and he rushed in. My mother thought . . . she didn't half hit us 'cos we frightened the life out of her. It was really frightening.[38]

The power of these visual images was quickly harnessed as a medium in facilitating conversion. J. W. Clarke of Ringford Road, Wandsworth, designed special slides for 'winning souls'.[39] Mr Joseph Nix, of the West London Wesleyan Mission, was said to be

The first to select this method of conveying spiritual truths because he found that he could remember so much better things that had been seen than things that had been heard. 'I have come to the conclusion', said Mr Nix, 'that the magic lantern used in this way is the greatest agency for securing individual conversions in existence. I have never held a service with their assistance but such signs as the above have taken place.'[40]

Mr Nix went on to describe the power of the darkness to add a further dimension to the emotional impact of the slides. This was the case among adults as well as children: 'The darkness gives people the opportunity to give vent to their feelings. Strong men will weep in the dark who dare not allow their feelings to have free play in the light.'[41]

The limelight concerts were not always directly aimed at precipitating conversion; some were merely moral homilies. The message of *The Pilgrim's Progress* provided the theme for a series of limelight slides which was popular in London at this time. Simple moral homilies such as the 'Road to Heaven' series and 'Stories of the Lost Child' were graphically depicted in the slides. These visual images were powerful in shaping concepts of God as well as Christian teaching.

The material which has emerged from oral interviewing suggests that the Sunday schools rather than the day schools were at least perceived to be the formative centres for the dissemination of Christian instruction. Jeffrey Cox, however, in the same vein as Booth,[42] presents Sunday schools as ineffective mediums of Christian instruction. He compares them unfavourably with the elementary schools which, he argues, 'greatly strengthened diffusive Christianity'.[43] He concedes that the Sunday schools were 'virtually universal' but he pictures them as notoriously undisciplined. This lack of discipline was in marked contrast to the board schools and their successors the London County Council

[38] SCW, Int. 6.
[39] John Johnson Collection, Cinema Box 1, collection of advertisement handbills.
[40] 'The Magic Lantern Mission', *Review of Reviews* (1890), 5.
[41] Ibid.
[42] C. Booth, *Life and Labour* (1902), 'Religious Influences', vii. 12.
[43] Cox, *The English Churches*, 95.

schools, where religious teaching was carried out by 'trained teachers in a disciplined atmosphere'.[44] The oral evidence suggests, however, that the indiscipline of the Sunday schools did not necessarily preclude them from exercising a formative influence on local children. Even if the Sunday schools were weak in providing a disciplined acquisition of knowledge they appear to have provided a dimension which the day schools lacked: notably the personal contact between the pupil and the teacher and between church-based and popular culture. In this respect they were as important, if not more influential, than 'trained teachers in a disciplined atmosphere'. The strength of the relationship which sprang up between teachers and pupils in Sunday schools brought a personal dimension to contact between the church and the community. These relations appear, in general, to have inspired affection as well as deference. The Army and Religion Survey recorded that: 'Most men have had links with the church in their boyhood. If clergy or ministers have specialised in helping young men they are never forgotten. Bible class leaders have influenced many profoundly.'[45]

Particular Sunday school teachers were frequently remembered in terms of endearment. One of Bartlett's interviewees claimed, 'I loved her. I really did . . . I used to go up once a week and then we used to talk matters over and she used to speak to me about the Lord and that was the means of my conversion.'[46]

Stan Hall kept the birthday cards sent to him by his Sunday school teacher, Miss Webber, throughout his life: 'I still have two of those birthday cards, true they are seventy years old but I still get pleasure and warmth from them whenever I look at them'.[47]

Booth noted that these relationships were the chief strength of the Sunday schools and that they were of mutual benefit to both the pupils and the teachers alike.[48] The practice of recording the deaths of Southwark Sunday school teachers in the *Southwark Annual* also suggests their prominence as local figures. The personal and often quite intimate recollections which are given of Sunday school teachers are in contrast to the images put forward of schoolteachers. Stan Hall, for instance, gave an extended description of the contrast between the caning he received from his schoolteacher and the compassion shown

[44] Ibid.
[45] D. S. Cairns (ed.), *The Army and Religion: An Enquiry and its Bearing upon the Religious Life of the Nation* (1919), 115.
[46] Bartlett, 'The Churches in Bermondsey', Int. 2.
[47] SLSL, A. S. Hall, 'Reminiscences' (1988), 25.
[48] Booth, *Life and Labour* (1902), 'Religious Influences', vii. 12.

towards him by Miss Webber when his mother fell ill with a haemorrhage.

My mother who suffered from bad lungs had coughed the whole night . . . whilst
I was having my breakfast my mother suffered a haemorrhage . . . I went across
the road to a neighbour who came and helped my mother, then said I should go
to school, by now I was late so the result was the caning, no questions asked and
most important no compassion . . . mother spent Saturday in bed, insisted that
I went to Sunday School on Sunday, where Miss Webber heard my story. She had
compassion.[49]

A number of those interviewed by Age Exchange commented on a
similar distance in their relationship with schoolteachers. One interviewee described how

In our school years, we were much more in awe of our teachers, we were
terrified. You didn't dare run down a corridor. You did not dare eat in the street.
I can remember my geography mistress used to live near me and I was sucking a
lolly—you know in the bus queue, and I saw her come and I dropped this lolly
right in the gutter because I was terrified.[50]

Similarly, Dorothy Barton described her headmistress as 'a person
apart': 'When she came down the corridor you stood there with eyes
down—you didn't dare look at her, let alone do anything wrong'.[51]

Alexander Paterson gave an equally graphic description of the schoolteacher who appears to the child as 'master' not as 'man'.

The boy see his teacher walking briskly to school at a quarter to nine in the
morning, he sees him walk still more quickly back to the tram on the stroke of
half-past-four. Between these times there are five hours of lessons and two hours
in which the teacher is hidden away at the rest time in the teachers' room. It
follows that the boy associates him entirely with the class room, connects his face
with desks and ink pots, copy books, blue pencil and the cane. He knows him
just as a teacher but as a man, not at all.[52]

Sunday schools are recollected with an aura of nostalgia and familiarity. While the case should not be overstated, the material does suggest
a dimension of personal contact whereby the Sunday schools were integrated within the fabric of the community. The context or atmosphere
in which knowledge was obtained may well have been as important as
the content of that knowledge itself.

[49] Hall, 'Reminiscences', 22.
[50] Age Exchange, *Good Morning Children: Memories of School Days 1920 and 1930s*
(1988), 22.   [51] Ibid.
[52] A. Paterson, *Across the Bridges* (1911), 87.

The decision to send one's children to Sunday school was, therefore, in part a decision to identify the family with the teachings of the church and often with a specific individual associated with the institution. The Revd W. J. Somerville's phrase 'religion by deputy' also implied that the practice was to some degree a statement of personal belief in the importance of certain aspects of the churches' teaching on the part of the non-church-attending parents. When visiting a family, Somerville would invariably express the hope that the parents would attend church to praise God and to ask for his blessing, but his comments commonly solicited the reply, 'Well sir, I can't say I do but I send my children'.[53] Replies of this kind are echoed with a remarkable degree of regularity in the oral evidence, suggesting that some of them viewed the practice as one indication of their religious belief. They suggest that although parents did not go to church themselves they none the less identified themselves and their families, albeit indirectly, with particular elements of church-based religion. Their non-attendance is qualified by such comments and is carefully differentiated from both unbelief and hostility towards the church. It is, in this way, once again symptomatic of a conditional appropriation of church-based images, language and customs within popular culture. Non-church attendance did not necessarily mean a dissent from 'religion'. Popular religion of this kind merely involved a distinctive set of criteria and priorities. A large number of the interviewees responded to the question of whether their parents had attended church by saying 'no . . . but they sent their children'.

Q: Were your parents church-goers?
A: No, I don't think they were very interested, but they saw we were.[54]

Q: Were your parents at all interested in Church or chapel?
A: They weren't, but they saw we went, yes, yes they weren't non-religious I don't mean that . . . [55]

Q: Were your parents church-goers?
A: No, Mum and Dad were not church-goers—but we were made to go to Sunday school always.[56]

Emma Reynolds of Red Cross Street, Southwark also described in her oral interview how her parents did not attend church themselves but would send her to the church of the Most Precious Blood each Sunday

[53] St George-the-Martyr, *Annual Report* (1902), 14.
[54] EOHA, Int. 6, 11.
[55] EOHA, Int. 8, 7.
[56] EOHA, Int. 70, 16.

morning and afternoon without fail.[57] Similarly, George Webb from
Storks Road, Bermondsey, born in 1911, responded by stating that: 'no
my father and mother never went . . . no, no, no, but us kids had to go
to Sunday School'.[58]

Other interviewees claimed that 'well of course my parents wasn't
religious people. They didn't go to church but we children had to go'[59]
and 'Mother was not religious as I said but she made us go 'til we were
old enough to know our own mind'.[60]

When Elizabeth Merritt was asked whether her non-church-attending
mother brought her up to consider anything particularly important in
life she replied, 'She ur . . . didn't like me to miss Sunday school at all'.[61]
This point was reinforced by Miss Merritt a second time, later in the
interview, when she emphasized the point by saying, 'She liked me to go
regular'.[62]

Some interviewees specifically described this parental practice as
evidence of 'belief'. Helen Westall, born in Deptford in 1915, when asked
why her mother sent all her children to Sunday school while she herself
stayed at home to complete her washing, replied that it was specifically
to 'learn about God'.[63] She was careful to contrast her father's excessive
drinking habits with her mother's belief in God of which sending her
children to Sunday school and checking their weekly texts was an expression. Mrs Croft saw her mother's insistence on the attendance of all ten
of her children at Sunday school as an indication of her own commitment to church-based religion. When asked why her mother was so
strict in this matter, Mrs Croft replied: 'Well I think in her way she had
that religion touch . . . '.[64]

For some individuals, sending their children to Sunday school was
considered sufficient to fulfil a perceived religious duty towards the
family, to God, and also towards the church and the local vicar and it was
in this sense equivalent to their own attendance. It was the opinion of
the St Alphege Mission that those parents who practised 'religion by
deputy'[65] were not far from the church in terms of an assent to its teachings and values. The first to attend occasional missions in the parish were
those who sent their children to Sunday school,[66] while many of the

[57] SCW, Int. 4.   [58] SCW, Int. 3.
[59] EOHA, Int. 215, 15.   [60] EOHA, Int. 240, 16.
[61] SCW, Int. 21.   [62] Ibid.
[63] SCW, Int. 2.   [64] SCW, Int. 18.
[65] This amounted to a sizeable proportion of the parochial population of the parish as,
by 1883, 900 children attended the St Alphege Sunday school.
[66] St Alphege Mission, *Annual Report* (1883), 52.

mothers who were so insistent that their children attended Sunday school were themselves part of the regular core of attenders at the local mothers' meeting.[67]

Although the decision to send one's children to Sunday school could in this way be symptomatic of a personal attachment to many of the ideas taught within these institutions, this did not mean a full-scale association of a family with all the tenets of a particular church's teaching. Rather it was a decision to uphold a particular brand of the church's teaching from which specific denominational criteria had been extracted. The parents of Sunday school children appear to have been concerned to ensure that their children imbibed what they considered to be the essentials of Christianity but they were suspicious when a given Sunday school appeared to be taking their child beyond an acceptable limit. Miss Merritt's mother, for example, was most uncomfortable with the idea of her daughter voluntarily prolonging her childhood association with the church and joining the Bible class at the age of 15. This developed into open opposition when her daughter expressed her desire to be baptized and she was eventually prohibited from attending altogether.[68] The description given of Miss Merritt's mother suggests that she had a clear concept of what was a necessary foundation of Christian teaching to which she believed every child should be exposed. This teaching had clear boundaries. The kind of enthusiasm which led an individual to associate him- or herself too closely with church-based culture was as unacceptable as was the neglect which individuals showed when they failed to ensure that the basic foundation of Christian teaching was in evidence in the lives of their children.

This form of undenominationalism was a key feature of popular religion in Southwark. While the teaching given at a Sunday school was considered important, the denominational distinctions made by the teachers were often considered irrelevant to parents who insisted on the habit of Sunday school attendance for their children. A number of the recollections describe how various siblings attended schools of different denominations without arousing the censure of their parents, even when the Catholic/Protestant divide was crossed. This sentiment appears to have been a characteristic of popular religion which extended beyond Southwark. Mrs Newton of Shadwell, for example, recalled how she and her sisters attended the Church of England while her brothers went to the local Methodist Sunday school.

---

[67] SCW, Int. 15; SCW, Int. 18.   [68] SCW, Int. 21.

'cos my mother used to say it doesn't matter where you go as long as you go . . . those that wanted to go to chapel went to chapel, if you wanted to go to church you went to church. We had to go but didn't matter to her where we went so long as we went somewhere.[69]

The general ideals of the Christian faith were upheld as important within popular culture, but the specifics were seen as subsidiary if not irrelevant. When describing the Metropolitan Tabernacle, Dora Bargate wrote,

The name somehow has a Jewish ring to it but I believe it was Baptist although I just accepted the teaching because I liked the place and I never thought about asking the denomination it belonged to. It was simply Sunday School to me.[70]

This kind of blurring was found particularly among second-generation Catholics such as those inhabiting the courts and alleys around Red Cross Street, Southwark. Where a mixed Catholic-Protestant marriage had taken place, the type of Sunday school attended by the offspring of that marriage was often irrelevant to the parents, though it could rouse the protest of the grandparents. The children themselves frequently described their religion as either Protestant or Catholic or both at the same time. Edith Anders's father, for example, was a Catholic and her mother a Protestant. It did not trouble her parents that the children attended the local Methodist Central Hall in Bermondsey each Sunday.[71] Mr Mahoney of Poplar was the son of a stevedore whose own parents were Irish Catholics. Mr Mahoney's father had married a Protestant and Mr Mahoney attended a Church of England Sunday school and remarked that it did not matter either to him or to his parents as there were few distinctions between Protestants and Catholics: 'Oh, no, no there was no religious—oh no, no, no no, we had none of that what so ever, no we have none of the, Catholics and Protestants got on alright'.[72]

The arguments put forward by Sheridan Gilley for the earlier nineteenth century support this evidence. He described the religious instruction received by the children of mixed Protestant-Catholic marriages as 'not divisible into Catholic or Protestant'.[73] The oral material suggests that certainly by the beginning of this century individuals classified

[69] EOHA, Int. 331, 23.
[70] Brunel University, Burnett Collection, D. Bargate, 'Memories', n.d., n.p.
[71] SCW, Int. 5.
[72] EOHA, Int. 70, 30.
[73] S. Gilley, 'The Roman Catholic Mission to the Irish in London 1840–1860', *Recusant History*, 10 (1969), 138–9.

themselves primarily as cockneys and that general Christian training was seen as sufficient for all.

The undenominationalism of non-church-attending parents with respect to their children's Sunday schools was symptomatic of a more general attitude which underpinned all the beliefs considered. Religion was defined by the participants in terms other than specifically doctrinal or denominational ones. The Revd R. J. W. Pitchford, vicar of St Jude's Church, Southwark argued that the difference of church standpoint did not make the least difference to the hold of the church upon the people: 'The vast majority are ignorant of the differences of standpoint and would not care two pence about them if they did know'.[74]

This attitude may account for the relative absence of the ritual of confirmation among the population of Southwark. The importance of rituals such as churchings, baptisms, and church weddings is in sharp contrast to the relative absence of confirmation in popular practice. This ceremony signified a statement of commitment to the church and a denominational association, just as conversion was seen as the exchange of one value system for another by the individual. In St Alphege, confirmation was seen strictly as evidence of conversion and admission into a community of believers;[75] and the Revd R. B. Harrison of All Saints Surrey Square argued that it was confirmation which implied and demanded a higher standard of association and a much 'stricter life'.[76] Alan Bartlett interviewed one woman in Bermondsey who described how seriously confirmation classes were taken in the early 1900s. If a class was missed the rector would come and inquire as to the reason: 'When we were confirmed we promised that we'd do something in church you see. Take something on. That's when I began to be a Sunday School teacher . . .'.[77]

The Annual Report and Statement of Accounts of St George-the-Martyr parish church, Southwark specifically claimed that the decline in the number of confirmation candidates was due to the undenomination-alism of the local people.

The number of confirmation candidates this year was 39 as against 81 last year. The difficulty of procuring suitable candidates is very great and one of the most curious features in our church life is the very great reluctance which many parents evidence to carry out the plain directions of the prayer book and have

[74] LSE, Booth Collection, B269, 177.
[75] St Alphege Mission, *Annual Report* (1883), 15.
[76] All Saints Surrey Square, *Annual Report* (1899), 8.
[77] Bartlett, 'The Churches in Bermondsey', Int. 5.

their children brought forward for confirmation. This is doubtless one of the fruits of undenominationalism, which seems so popular now-a-days.[78]

The Rochester Diocesan Society also complained in 1902 of the difficulty of procuring suitable candidates for confirmation and attributed it likewise to the undenominationalism of the people[79] rather than to the lack of suitable clothing which was more popularly blamed by the *South London Press* in 1913.[80] In contrast to baptism and church marriage which involved no doctrinal or denominational statement, confirmation was seen as one of the distinguishing marks between popular culture and church-based culture. An occasional and distinctly conditional conformity to orthodox practice was incompatible with the strictures of confirmation in urban Southwark. There is no evidence in Southwark to suggest that confirmation appealed to the irregular attender as a folk remedy such as a cure for rheumatism as it did in South Lindsey.[81] To identify this undenominationalism as a key feature of the popular religious repertoire is not to suggest, however, that individuals did not believe sincerely, and often quite vehemently, in the basic constituents of Christian teaching to which they exposed their children.

The practice of sending one's children to Sunday school was closely associated with the practice found in many non-church-attending families of teaching their children to pray before going to bed, of saying grace at mealtimes, and of showing particular respect for Sundays as a different day. These were seen as indicators of either a personal form of religious devotion or at least as a facet of respect for the value and importance of religion within society at large. W. Horwood of Walworth describes in his recollections how his non-church-attending parents taught him to pray each night.[82] The oral evidence suggests that this custom was widespread in families where neither parent attended church. All but two of those interviewed in Southwark had been taught to say their prayers. In the majority of cases it was a parent who taught them to pray, but in a few cases the habit was enforced through the Sunday school.[83] Parents showed regularity and persistence in establishing this principle with their children: 'We always had to kneel beside our

---

[78]   St George-the-Martyr, *Report and Statement of Accounts* (1906), 10.
[79]   Rochester Diocesan Society, *A Short Account of Twenty-five Years of Church Mission Work in South London 1878–1902* (1903), 5.
[80]   The *South London Press*, 14 Mar. 1913.
[81]   J. Obelkevich, *Religion and Rural Society in South Lindsey 1825–1875* (Oxford, 1976), 264.
[82]   SLSL, Horwood, 'A Walworth Boy Looking Back 1922–1939', 10.
[83]   SCW, Int. 3; SCW, Int. 10.

bed and ask God to forgive us all our sins and all that sort of thing at night'.[84]

Mrs Scott of Walworth smiled when asked about prayer and described how she was taught to pray every night,

Oh yes at night. We used to say,

> I go to my bed as to the grave,
> I hope the Lord my soul doth save,
> If I die before I wake
> I hope the Lord my soul will take.[85]

Mrs Croft described how her mother's insistence on her children's attendance at Sunday school was firmly linked to her equally strict insistence on teaching her children to pray.[86] This widespread habit was selected for particular mention by Geoffrey Gorer in his study of the English character during the 1950s: 'Quite a number of English parents who do not go to church or pray themselves teach their children to do so'.[87]

Gorer specifically connected this practice with the faith of the parents which, he argued, was of greater influence in determining this practice than their own habits or actions:[88] 'Prayers before going to bed are part of the ritual of the end of the day for most English children almost independently of whether their parents say a prayer or attend a church service or not'.[89]

Likewise, many parents were in the habit of teaching their children to say grace before eating. Mrs Croft went on to describe how her mother would conduct the ritual of grace at each meal, insisting that every child take a turn in thanking the Almighty.[90] Saying grace was not always a mere formality; for some it appears to have been a genuine act of thanking God. Jane Willshers, for example, born in 1896, the daughter of a carter from Limehouse, related praying at mealtimes to a wider personal habit of prayer at other times of the day.[91] Similarly, Mrs Graig remembers saying grace as part of being taught to be thankful. Her description of grace led her on to a discussion of prayer in general.[92]

In much the same way that these habits were encouraged, so Sunday was still presented as a day worthy of particular respect. In most of the homes recalled in the Essex Oral History Survey, recreation was carefully

84 EOHA, Int. 13, 12.   85 SCW, Int. 19.   86 SCW, Int. 18.
87 G. Gorer, *Exploring English Character* (1955), 244.
88 Ibid. 248.   89 Ibid. 249.   90 SCW, Int. 18.
91 EOHA, Int. 298, 14.   92 EOHA, Int. 6, 12.

dictated on a Sunday. Mrs Blackhall of Queen's Park and Henry Elder of Grey's Inn Road, described how their parents, though they did not attend church themselves, thought it 'wrong' to play games on a Sunday:[93] 'We has to be very good on a Sunday as a rule. We could look at books on a Sunday.'[94] Henry Elder was prohibited from playing games in the street on a Sunday: 'Only like indoors but never in the street or anything like that. We could play as I say ordinary—ordinary games indoors.'[95]

Similarly, Mrs Blackman of Battersea said

Oh no, you weren't allowed to play, no, no you couldn't have a ball or any toy of any sort and you wasn't allowed to play, you could go out for a walk, yes, see. Then you walked sedately in the park or something like that. And you had to be careful that not too many people saw you laughing.[96]

Alan Bartlett's interviewees said much the same thing: 'Oh you wasn't allowed to play ball or anything like that. You wasn't allowed that, no you wasn't allowed to play ball and you wasn't allowed to play five stones or anything like that.'[97]

Particular clothes were worn on a Sunday[98] and special foods were eaten, while the tablecloth was often placed on the table though it remained unused during the rest of the week. In some cases, as Ellen Ross has pointed out, the solemnity of the day was heightened by the use of the parlour for the consumption of the main meal.[99] Alf Westall described dressing for a Sunday: 'anybody see you go out on Sunday they'd say oh look she's got beautiful clothes on, look at that girl . . . You had to make yourself look nice and neat Sundays'.[100]

Miriam Moore's overwhelming memory of her grandmother was her cape: 'Sundays she used to wear a beautiful cape all sequins and a bonnet and that . . . beautiful. But on week days it wasn't so elaborate naturally. The Sunday one was only worn Sundays and very special occasions.'[101]

When asked if Sundays were any different from the rest of the week, Phillippa Ivy immediately replied, 'Oh yes, 'cos you had your best clothes on'.[102] For Jim Bower, Sundays stood out from the rest of the

---

[93] EOHA, Int. 76. [94] EOHA, Int. 76, 14.
[95] EOHA, Int. 71, 17. [96] EOHA, Int. 96, 26.
[97] Bartlett, 'The Churches in Bermondsey', Int. 5.
[98] Ibid., Int. 6.
[99] E. Ross, *Love and Toil: Motherhood in Outcast London 1870–1918* (Oxford, 1993), 38.
[100] SCW, Int. 2. [101] SCW, Int. 15.
[102] SCW, Int. 17.

week because of a 'nice baked dinner' and 'bread and dripping'[103] and
Winifred Till, the daughter of a machinist at a locomotive works in south
Lambeth, described how her non-church-attending parents would insist
that they ate watercress and winkles for Sunday afternoon tea.[104]

In some cases the concern with clothing and food extended into a
more specific Sabbatarianism. Elsie Barralet, born in 1891 in Waltham-
stow, regarded Sunday as specifically a day of rest, despite the infrequent
attendance of her parents at church.

Q: Did your parents think it wrong to play on Sundays?
A: Oh yes it was a day of rest.
Q: Did they ever attend church?
A: My mother might go sometimes, but my father didn't.[105]

Arthur Newton, a shoemaker from Hackney, described in his autobiography how his family, whom he described as not 'exactly religious',
would sing the popular songs of the day on a Saturday night, but when
twelve o'clock midnight came such revelry was seen as inappropriate and
the party would congregate around the piano and sing only hymns from
then on.

As I said, if they were having a party on a Saturday you could sing the popular
songs you could drink beer even get tipsy, you could enjoy yourself but when 12
o'clock midnight came that was the finish there was no more singing after that
unless you wanted to sing hymns. And I believe that I have heard my father say
that at Sunday dinner time there was always a reading from the Bible. But I
wouldn't call them religious people. They weren't church goers let's put it that
way.[106]

Lilian Westhall, a domestic servant, born in the King's Cross area,
explained how she judged lying better than offending against the
sabbath. She was shocked when her employer asked her to buy a newspaper on a Sunday: 'I thought this was wrong and came back without it,
saying the shop was shut. It seemed better to lie than to offend the
Sabbath by buying papers'.[107]

Both the insistence on children's attendance at Sunday school and the
responsibility for teaching them to pray appears to have lain primarily

---

[103] SCW, Int. 1.
[104] Brunel University, Burnett Collection, W. Till, 'The Early Years of a Victorian
Grandmother', n.d., n.p.
[105] EOHA, Int. 216, 16.
[106] A. Newton, *Years of Change: The Autobiography of a Hackney Shoemaker* (1974), 9.
[107] Brunel University, Burnett Collection, Lilian Westhall, 'The Good Old Days', n.d.,
n.p.

with the mother, just as the folk customs outlined in the previous chapters were particularly prevalent among women. They were in most cases the initiators of the Sunday school habit in their children. Helen Westhall specifically recalled that it was her mother who would check the children's text and attendance cards each week to ensure that they had gone to Sunday School: 'And we used to have to take them home and show them to mum, that we'd been'.[108]

The oral evidence is consistent on this point with a range of other material. The annual report of the Southwark Sunday School Society for 1897 recorded how a meeting for parents of Sunday school children was held in the Mint near St George-the-Martyr church, Southwark, on 2 March. The attendance of fathers at this meeting was so poor that the vicar decided to arrange an additional fathers' meeting in May.[109] His efforts, however, were largely unsuccessful. Mr Mennie, born in 1870, the son of a barber from Shadwell, expressed this pattern more boldly than most when he was asked in his interview for the Essex Oral History Project whether he sent his own children to Sunday school. His reply was: 'Well, the wife looked after that'.[110]

In households where neither parent attended church it was nearly always the mother who taught her children to say their prayers before going to bed: 'She used to make us kneel down; say our prayers. Everyone say their prayers 'cos she'd say it with us and then into bed.'[111]

W. L. Fraser records how it was his mother who taught him to say his prayers at night.[112] Barbara Luke described how her non-church-attending mother would teach her children to say their prayers at night and even sing hymns and choruses with them such as 'Jesus loves me this I know'.[113] Similarly, in such households it tended to be the woman who would lead the family in grace at mealtimes.[114] This pattern is in contrast to families where both parents attended church. In these cases the father would both say grace and often hear his childrens' prayers at bedtime. Margaret Axham's parents both attended church regularly and in her household it was the father, a painter from King's Cross, who would conduct the prayers of his family.

[108] SCW, Int. 2.
[109] Southwark Sunday School Society, *Balance Sheet and Reports of Schools for the Year 1897* (1898), 7.
[110] EOHA, Int. 346, 8.
[111] EOHA, Int. 126, 17.
[112] W. L. Fraser, *All to the Good* (1963), 21.
[113] SCW, Int. 6.
[114] SCW, Int. 18; EOHA, Int. 126, 33.

And father used to read a Bible passage of scripture out of the Bible, say two or three passages from the Bible from a chapter. And if we wanted to stay up late we used to ask him, we got it you know, we took it all in but we could stay up a bit late if he read a bit more.[115]

The distinctive character of Sundays, however, tended to be upheld more rigidly by the father than by the mother. It was the father within a non-church-attending family who would insist that Sunday be kept special: 'Thought it wrong to play, thought it was wrong to my father, mind you my mother was different, Father wouldn't let you spend money on Sunday.'[116]

Charles Josland, the son of a compositor from Scovell Road, Southwark specifically mentioned his father in relation to the censuring of behaviour on a Sunday: 'Although my father wasn't religious we weren't allowed to play games'.[117] Likewise Mrs W. E. Sykes, the daughter of a sign writer from Muswell Hill, born in 1900, recorded how it was her father who would never let them play on a Sunday: 'Once I just rinsed a pair of stockings out and put them on the line, he just cut the line down. Never allowed anything like that on a Sunday.'[118]

The attendance of children at Sunday school, the centrality of prayer in non-church-attending families, and the rituals associated with Sundays cannot simply be dismissed without considering some of the wider implications of such practices in terms of the character and content of popular religion. These practices were carried out within a context in which both the church and its associated values continued to hold an important place within popular memory and heritage. The oral evidence suggests that for many parents to send their children to Sunday school and to teach them to pray was infused by a sense of nostalgia associated with these practices in their own childhood. It suggests that the memories, values, and images retained an evocative emotional power for individuals, which, although they remained untranslated into a tangible commitment to attend church regularly, still emerged as vitally important in the upbringing of their children as well as at significant turning-points in life or in periods of personal or communal crisis. Above all the material suggests that there existed a personal, familial, and corporate familiarity with a series of religious images, teachings, and symbols which remained a vital part of popular heritage. Church-based symbols were passed down from one generation to another as part of the fabric of family and communal life through the medium of the practices

115 EOHA, Int. 284, 58. 116 EOHA, Int. 125, 24.
117 EOHA, Int. 229, 54. 118 EOHA, Int. 297, 27.

described above. This created a sense of church-based religion as part of a corporate and individual past. These images had the power to draw some back to the church later in life and they bound individuals and families to certain aspects of the church institution with an emotional identification which extended far beyond the realms of formal commitment. Elizabeth Merritt's mother, for instance, not only sent her child to Sunday school but demonstrated a nostalgic love of certain aspects of church-based culture. Miss Merritt's testimony illustrates her mother's respect and her love of the church in a number of ways, not least in her careful preservation of her own Sunday school Bible which she passed down as a family heirloom to her daughter. Other women, despite their non-attendance at church, retained an atmosphere of prayer and hymn singing in the home. Barbara Luke and Louise Codd, born in 1910, the daughter of a carman from Jamaica Road, Bermondsey, as well as Elizabeth Merritt, recall their mothers' frequent hymn singing.

and of course at the same time when she was machining she was singing away at the top of her voice. Tell me the old, old story, you know and it, up and down, oh yes.
Q: Always hymns?
A: Yes always hymns mostly. She said she thought she had got the hymns from her own mother.[119]

   She went on to describe how the family would join in the hymns with their mother at home.

We all used to join in at home with mum and her hymns. Tell me the old old story. Yes, up from the grave he arose, she used to choose those that had a—long—crescendo, you know what I mean. Up and down. All the while she was threading.[120]

   These recollections communicate an aura of nostalgia which surrounded such practices. The widespread knowledge and love of hymns was symptomatic of the incorporation of aspects of symbolism and imagery within popular culture. Hymns had the power to arouse strong memories which were closely related to memories of home, the family, and particularly the mother. During the war hymns and prayers were said to form a 'link with home',[121] and at such moments of crisis the remnants of church-based religion taught at Sunday school took on a particularly powerful role among the men.[122] Attendance at Sunday

---

[119] EOHA, Int. 235, 11–12.
[120] Ibid. 46.
[121] A. Wilkinson, *The Church of England and the First World War* (1978), 153.
[122] Cairns, *The Army and Religion*, 14.

school was said to have left its mark among the soldiers in the knowledge of hymns which the men would 'sing with delight'.[123] These hymns drew them together via a common medium through which they were brought in touch emotionally with the world at home. F. T. Bullen described how, among sailors, hymn singing served to 'revive pleasant memories of emotional delights'.[124]

Praying was surrounded by a similar nostalgia. It is often associated in the oral recollections with a feeling of security, safety, and home. It was a significant and persistent element at turning-points in life and an attitude communicated to future generations. During the war, the Army and Religion Survey claimed that 'The value of prayer is the memory of childhood which most men retain and to which they turn in time of crisis'.[125]

Arthur Lambert, a private soldier who enlisted in 1914, described how in his mind when he went into combat 'There was always a confused mixture of prayer and thoughts of home'.[126]

Such prayer was seen as part of 'days in Sunday School'.[127] In the letters of soldiers during the war, phrases such as 'God bless you' or 'praying that God will keep the mites safe'[128] were common. Such language was associated with the same sense of familiarity and with the home.

Hymns, in particular, were closely interwoven with the fabric of familial and communal life. This is seen by the extent to which they acted as vehicles through which the memories and associations of communal and family life were aroused. S. S. Tamke has suggested in her study of Victorian didactic hymns that

The effect of the memorizing process could be profound. For many the hymns learned in childhood made a deep and lasting impression. In adulthood they could remember the lyrics automatically and even more important, that recall often included a recapitulation of the emotional climate surrounding the original learning process.[129]

This is strongly supported by much of the material considered in Southwark. Hymns were a powerful medium through which individuals could be brought in touch not merely with the world of home but also

124 F. T. Bullen, *With Christ at Sea* (1901), 26.
125 Cairns, *The Army and Religion*, 162.
126 A. Lambert, *Over-the-Top* (1930), 54.
127 Cairns, *The Army and Religion*, 161.
128 Ibid.
129 Tamke, *Make a Joyful Noise*, 78.

with the Sunday school and the church. Some respondents considered a love of hymns symptomatic of an emotional attachment to the church among those who did not formally ally themselves with the ecclesiastical institution. When asked whether her mother attended church, Elizabeth Merritt replied in the negative but qualified her statement with the caution: 'She didn't disbelieve'.[130] She went on to illustrate her point by citing her mother's love of the hymns as adequate evidence of the sincerity of her belief.

She believed in God and all that yeah, she believed in all that 'cos she used to join in the hymns indoors, oh yes, she liked all that she told me the old hymns she used to sing when she was young at Sunday school, yes she used to sing. She'd open this book and point out the ones and sing.[131]

Similarly, Barbara Luke gave a description of her mother's knowledge of the hymns as evidence of her 'belief': 'Oh, yes she was always singing the hymns and that on the wireless, yea always singing my mum at home, always singing the hymns, she'd turn the wireless on and she'd know all the hymns'.[132]

These hymns were drawn on or evoked by particular situations or events. Their role during the war has already been noted. This was no less the case at home than it was at the front. While soldiers in the trenches faced death singing 'Jesu Lover of My Soul',[133] the crypts of Southwark, which doubled up as air-raid shelters during the First and Second World Wars, rang with the sound of hymn singing: 'I was only young but I can remember sitting on my mum's lap . . . and they used to sing the hymns'.[134]

As Mrs Croft put it: 'they made you feel better'.[135] Hymns also remained prominent at the deathbed. Mrs Cotton described the importance of hymns for her mother at the hour of death.

And before she went into that coma she held my hand and my sister's hand and those hymns she was singing . . . 'sing up with me Ivy' . . . I had such a lump in my throat, my sister who's older, she was singing with her, then she went into a coma.[136]

This supports the descriptions given of deathbed scenes in the 1880s

[130] SCW, Int. 21.
[131] Ibid.
[132] SCW, Int. 6.
[133] C. E. Playne, *Britain Holds On* (1933), 208–9.
[134] SCW, Int. 21.
[135] SCW, Int. 18.
[136] SCW, Int. 22.

by T. C. Garland, a Wesleyan Missioner in the Port of London. He describes how hymns were frequently requested by the dying.[137]

Hymns were not only drawn on in certain situations; they were also stimulated by key events. The open-air and watch-night services were significant in this respect. On such occasions the nostalgic power of the hymns was sufficient to facilitate a powerful emotional response from some of the participants or onlookers. At Mr Rounsfell's services at the Old Vic the hymns played a prominent role, as they did in most of the open-air services recorded in Southwark. The open-air services held by James Flanagan's church in Trinity Street, Southwark were described as a 'means of good to many'. At such gatherings it was the singing of gospel hymns which was said to have 'awakened the heart, new hopes, desires, new purposes for a godly and righteous life'.[138]

The description of the services shows the favourable reception given in the Queen's Buildings, near Scovell Road and borough High Street in the northern part of the Borough. Five or six hundred people crowded onto the seven-storied balconies on a Monday morning.

One of the most marvellous and grandest sights to be seen in London is the crowds that attend our open-air services at the Queen's buildings—five or six hundred people looking on and attentively listening to the music, singing, speaking, praying by the bandsmen. The windows, balconies and doors are thronged and the people do not attempt to move until the band moves to another street.[139]

One of the inhabitants of this court told Flanagan of the effect of the hymns on his invalid wife.

Those beautiful hymns that Flanagan's band plays make my old woman happy and starts her off singing. Although, she cannot get out of bed because of pain she rejoices when she can hear them a' coming. Ted'n hark they are coming open the window so that I can hear them dear men play and speak.[140]

It was reported that when the old woman died she said, 'God Bless the band, they have brought such blessings to me'.[141] Open-air services held by the Salvation Army in the same place were sufficiently striking for a former inhabitant of the Queen's Buildings to mention them in his interview for the Essex Oral History Project.[142]

[137] T. C. Garland, *Leaves From My Log: Christian Work in the Port of London* (1882), 148–51.
[138] The South East London Mission, *Notes and Financial Accounts* (1898–9), 12.
[139] Ibid.
[140] Ibid.
[141] Ibid.
[142] EOHA, Int. 229, 29.

The sound of hymn singing on such occasions was sufficiently powerful to precipitate the conversion of individuals. James Bryant, a local farrier, recorded in his autobiography how the sounds of open-air hymn singing precipitated a dramatic conviction of sin, and his conversion to Christianity from a state of indifference.[143] Similarly, Henry Paterson, a private soldier recently returned from the Boer war, described in a short letter to the Collingwood Working Men's Mission, Webber Street in the New Cut how his conversion was facilitated by an open-air service at the corner of New Road, Bermondsey. Preaching and singing played a prominent part in this service.[144] The success of a ten-day mission at Christ Church, Blackfriars in 1883 was also attributed by the *Church Review* to the large contingent of working men who, under the leadership of Mr C. Powell and accompanied by a cornet player, paraded the streets and alleys of Southwark and managed by 'stirring addresses and soul-moving hymns . . . to bring in large bodies of the poor and outcast'.[145] This description is in contrast to the lack of success of open-air meetings in the streets leading to East Street Market in Walworth in 1896–7. This failure was attributed to the lack of a band.[146]

The power of hymns on such occasions as the open-air service was due largely to their familiarity. The tenacious support given by a number of churchmen at the turn of the century to the maintenance of 'old style gospel preaching', with its attendant emphasis on hymn singing, was based not only on a theological objection to various strands of modern doctrine but also on the recognition that it was the dimension of familiarity which had a transforming effect on the listener. The chief complaint of those interviewed in Southwark against the contemporary church was the tendency to sing 'new fangled modern songs' instead of the old favourites. Many of the interviewees described their lack of familiarity with these modern songs as a symptom of the departure of post-Second World War Christianity from its traditional roots and, by implication, as a symptom of their own alienation from the Church with which they and their parents had been familiar.[147]

The assimilation of hymns by the wider population during the late nineteenth and early twentieth centuries was aided by the character of the hymns themselves. S. S. Tamke has described how from mid-

---

[143] E. W. Jealous, *Happy Jim: An Autobiography of James Bryant the Converted Farrier* (1937), 24.

[144] The Working Men's Mission, *Annual Report* (1902–3), 23.

[145] *Church Review*, 15 Feb. 1883.

[146] Browning Settlement, *Annual Report* (1896–7), 22.

[147] SCW, Int 1; SCW, Int. 6; SCW, Int. 22.

century onwards the new type of hymn became prominent. These were simple, catchy, and often contained a rousing chorus. Tamke argues that their close resemblance to popular secular songs of the period made them far more readily assimilated by the unchurched. A simple catchy tune was said to account for the startling success of the 'Glory Song' which was introduced to London at the Torrey-Alexander Mission in 1906. The song was said to be sung by thousands.

> You hear it every where. Not only is it sung at the Torrey-Alexander mission but on the bus and in the street, in trains and in the house one hears it sung and played and whistled. There is no getting away from it. For months copies of it have been hawked on the streets and these are selling in the thousands.[148]

When Mr Alexander was asked to account for this success he replied, 'Because it is in the compass of the average voice. It does not grow monotonous . . . the words appeal to any man or woman.[149]

Similarly, George Murphy's collection of Popular Tunes and Melodies for Temperance meetings which appeared in 1870 are remarkably similar in style and presentation to the songs printed as penny songsters. Ira Sankey's American-style Gospel hymns were also extremely popular in England at the end of the nineteenth century. They were known far beyond the circle of the church and beyond those who attended the Moody evangelistic campaigns of the 1880s. At the successful St Alphege Mission the Moody and Sankey hymn book was used with 'everybody joining in with heart and voice'.[150] Similarly, Mr D. J. Rounsfell specifically mentioned how many of those attending limelight services at Victoria Hall knew the hymns, especially those in the Moody and Sankey hymn-book, *Songs and Solos*.[151] Rounsfell also noted that these hymns were sung more heartily in the dark where people felt more able to enter emotionally into the singing of their favourite hymns. He noticed that people often entered after the hall was darkened for the lantern slides: 'The singing was also more hearty when the gas was down. People did not like to be seen singing but joined in heartily in the obscurity of the darkened room.'[152]

Gipsy Smith recounted how the hymn 'Count Your Blessings' achieved enormous popularity in the borough of Southwark during the 1890s.

[148] *The British Workman Annual*, 51 (1906), 39.
[149] Ibid.
[150] St Alphege Mission, *Annual Report* (1883), 6.
[151] LSE, Booth Collection, B270, 29–31.
[152] Ibid. 31.

The hymn attained extraordinary vogue during my mission campaign at the Metropolitan Tabernacle. Wherever one might go—in the street, in the trams, in the trains—someone was humming or whistling or singing 'Count Your Blessings'. The boys pushing their barrows along, the men driving their horses and the women rocking their cradles, all these had been caught by the truth and melody of the hymn.[153]

The power of these hymns was their ability to tap an emotional reserve within popular culture in which certain images, teaching, and symbols were drawn to the surface. This familiarity was reinforced through their transmission from one generation to another. As Hugh McLeod has argued, 'In Victorian England hymns were the most universally popular art-form and the nearest thing to a cultural inheritance common to women and men, working-class and middle-class, old and young, the sceptical and the devout'.[154]

Such images and associations stood alongside a wider notion of the importance of the church and the religious figure within the community. Chapter 4 has highlighted how the communities within Southwark, whether a street, an alley, or a larger area of the borough, had an 'our church'. This was more than a mere phrase; it signified an identification within that community with a particular church building and through that building with its representative religious figure. It encompassed a set of expectations, associations, and attachments as well as ideals and beliefs based on a concept of the reciprocal relationship between communal culture and the Deity, the church, and the religious figure. The presence of religious institutions could be closely interwoven with a sense of community which was reinforced when all the children in a street attended the Sunday school together. Lilian Tims described how all the children of Massinger Street, Southwark would set off together at two o'clock every Sunday afternoon for Sunday school at St Mary Magdalene.[155] Helen Westall recalled that 'We lived in a street and a lot of people went to church and all the children went to the Ragged School and Sunday School'.[156]

Sydney Barry gave a similar description of the children on his street who would go together to the Ragged School in Long Lane Camberwell. 'We went together, we used to call for each other'.[157] These descriptions echo the picture given by the Revd Mackrell of the streets in St Alphege

---

[153] Gipsy Smith, *His Life and Work* (1903), 349.
[154] McLeod, *Religion and Society*.
[155] SCW, Int. 23.
[156] SCW, Int. 2.
[157] SCW, Int. 12.

parish during the 1880s: 'The streets are crowded in the afternoon with Sunday School children carrying their books and pictures with the innocent cry of 'teacher, teacher', it touches the heart'.[158]

Sunday school at the local church could act as an extension of communal street culture. The local mission hall could play a vital communal function.

We find that often the children of the poorest do not care to go to the buildings in the main thoroughfares but they will flock to ours and often love them better than the places they call home which are blighted by poverty and alas frequently cursed by drink.[159]

Where the Sunday school or the church club succeeded in rooting itself within the local street or alley as a forum in which the children of the area entertained themselves, then the notion of 'our church' became an ideal which was endowed with reality within popular culture, in support of Booth's comment that: 'If a mission is built nearby they will come to it as "It shall be their own"'.[160]

A number of the interviews suggest that the experience of community took place against the backdrop of the church, club, or mission hall. Sydney Barry of Merrow Street, Walworth described in his oral interview how he spent most of his childhood, during the late 1920s and 1930s, at the Augustus Johnson Boys Club run by the Trinity College Mission in Albany Road;[161] and Edith Anders described how, when the children of Decimer Street were not playing in the road, they were at Bermondsey Central Hall watching a limelight show or attending a Band of Hope meeting together.[162] Similarly, William Belcher, born in Marylebone in 1884, described in his autobiography how he and his sister found interest and amusement at the local mission in the Thrift Hall in Upper Holloway.[163] His memories of childhood friendships and family life were set against the backdrop of the mission concerts and limelight lectures as well as the mission hall itself which acted as an extension playground. Likewise, Norman James described how the Catholic church in Union Street acted as a communal focus: 'We'd meet down there . . . with all the various families. We'd meet down there for a party, birthdays, celebrations whatever.'[164]

[158] St Alphege Mission, *Annual Report* (1883), 52.
[159] Southwark Sunday School Society, *Annual Report* (1903), 6.
[160] Booth, *Life and Labour* (1902), 'Religious Influences', vii. 45.
[161] SCW, Int. 12.
[162] SCW, Int. 5.
[163] Brunel University, Burnett Collection, W. Belcher, 'An Autobiography', n.d., n.p.
[164] SCW, Int. 16.

The Sunday school treat was the archetypal event in this respect. The entire Sunday school, often comprising children of a group of intersecting streets, would take off on the outing together. Local papers gave notice of forthcoming Sunday school treats as major communal events and full reports were given of the success of each outing. L. J. Carter argued that in Walworth during the late 1920s the Sunday School treat was the most eagerly anticipated annual event.[165] Recollections of Sunday school treats often form the highlight of childhood experience. Dora Bargate, for example, gaves a detailed description of the Arch Mission Sunday School, the Manor Mission Bermondsey, and the Metropolitan Tabernacle Sunday School, but of all her memories, the Sunday school treat formed the highlight of her childhood as it did for Henrietta Burkin[166] and others. In these recollections, personal memories combined with communal and religious associations.

The association of the church club, Sunday school, or society such as the Band of Hope[167] with childhood communality goes a long way towards explaining the emotional hold of the church on individuals long after they had ceased to attend regularly (or if they later became regular churchgoers). These associations were perpetuated among adult women through institutions such as the mothers' meetings. Alan Bartlett has shown the incorporation of these meetings within the local working-class community in Bermondsey to the extent that they may be defined as 'popular religious institutions'.[168] The mothers' meetings provided another setting for female sociability of a more structured kind than the informal interchange of ideas over the back wall, fence, or in the street. Here drinking tea and talking with one another combined with prayers and hymns and the occasional short address. In this way communality combined with an expression of corporate worship suited to the tastes of the attenders. Booth associated the mothers' meetings with the insistence among poor women on the propriety of the rites of passage.

The women, however, have nearly all of them a strong though rather indefinite sense of religion which the Mothers' Meeting does something to satisfy and

[165] L. J. Carter, *Walworth 1929–1939* (1985), 56–8.

[166] Brunel University, Burnett Collection, H. Burkin, 'Memories', n.d., n.p.

[167] Charles Booth considered the Band of Hope to be an institution on a par with the Sunday school in terms of its influence in children's lives. Booth, *Life and Labour* (1902), 'Religious Influences', vii. 14. A large number of those interviewed by the Essex Oral History Project and in Southwark attended the Band of Hope as well as the Sunday school.

[168] Bartlett, 'The Churches in Bermondsey', 168.

which finds expression in other ways such as in the proprieties of the marriage and of churching and in respect for baptism.[169]

The reverent attitude which was maintained towards the Bible and prayer[170] at these meetings along with the specific emphasis on communality allied them closely with the central characteristics of popular religion. They were particularly popular where prayer and hymn singing took place against a backdrop which emphasized the dimension of communality. The annual report for St Paul's Church, Southwark for 1898–9 described the success which followed a rearrangement of the structure of these meetings. The ordinary mothers' meetings which, from the photograph collections at Southwark Local Studies Library, appear to have consisted of large numbers of women sitting in rows in an orderly fashion to be addressed from the front, were changed at St Paul's to a mothers' own. These meetings were more informal gatherings on a Monday afternoon at which the seats in the hall were arranged on the basis of small circles, known as 'home circles'.

In the middle of each circle is a small table laid with cups and saucers and a plant upon it to give it a home like appearance and at each table a lady is seated ready to welcome and entertain the mothers as they come in and to entertain them during the afternoon.[171]

Memories of Bible stories, texts, individual Sunday school figures, and hymns were in this way surrounded by a corporate experience among children and women in particular. This took on a particular significance during the war and interwar period. Mothers' meetings such as those organized by the South East London Mission became a focus of female camaraderie during the war years. They provided a social focus, a context in which grief and loss could be expressed, and the forum for mutual prayer and support both between the organizers and the participants and among the women themselves. The *Light and Truth* magazine declared in 1914 that 'In all our meetings at St.George's Hall we have scores of women whose eyes speak of heart agony, silently and bravely borne. Never were women's meetings more appreciated than now.'[172]

During the course of the war this magazine was increasingly tailored to suit the tastes of a community of women centred around the local

---

[169] Booth, *Life and Labour* (1902), 'Religious Influences', vii. 19.

[170] Ibid. 277.

[171] *A Record of One Year's Work in the Parish of St. Paul's Westminster Bridge Road 1898–1900* (1899), 9–10.

[172] *Light and Truth*, 15 (Nov. 1914), 1370.

mission. From 1915 onwards most of the articles were written by women and most were designed to appeal to specific issues in their lives. 'Faces We Miss', 'An Afternoon's Visiting', 'They also Serve', and 'Child Life' are but a few examples of articles. The withdrawal of male personnel from missions and church-based organizations during the war period was accompanied by a gradual adaptation of the focus of the missions around providing for the needs of women and children. The war tended to accelerate the dislocation of the male population from the church and from regular association with the church.

One of the results on Crossways of the war was a great loss of some two-hundred volunteering their services for king and country. This loss was felt in almost every department: the sunday school, brotherhood, Band of Boys' Brigade, church institute—each rendered its fair share of men and practically every part of our work suffered.[173]

The absence of regular male members meant a diminution in the income from subscriptions. In addition, there was a decline in the amount of money received from voluntary contributions and gifts. This forced mission projects to concentrate on their strengths rather than weakness and produced churches tailored predominantly to the needs of female and youth culture. Interwar church records focus closely on social provision and domestic and youth culture, medical missions, and child welfare projects. In 1922 the South London Mission announced its intention of setting up a baby clinic and free breakfasts for the youth of the area. The war also accelerated the burgeoning Boys and Girls' Brigades Movement. The twenty-third London Company of the Girls' Life Brigade was set up in 1914 at East Street Baptist Chapel in Walworth. Sports clubs abounded in this period. Southwark football club, for example, was established at the Pembroke College Mission.

By the end of the century, therefore, there was an overarching sense of the presence and accessibility of the church within the community—a sense which was strengthened by the close geographical proximity of churches and religious agencies to the home and workplaces of the working classes in Southwark.[174] It was considered one's duty not only to be good to one's fellow man but also to uphold the concept of the church

[173] Crossways Central Mission, *Annual Report* (1914), 1.
[174] The obtrusive presence of both the philanthropic network and the physical accessibility of religious institutions in the lives of working-class people is described by Colin Marchant in his thesis 'The Interaction of the Churches and Society in an East London Borough' (London University Ph.D. thesis, 1979), as 'spatial symbolism' which he argued had considerable effect on the mentality of the inhabitants of West Ham.

in the community. Although individuals might rarely step over the threshold of a church from one year to the next, they might none the less have identified themselves with the local church to the extent that they would ardently defend the religion proclaimed within it. Irregular or non-church-attenders appear to have retained a defined set of beliefs about the correct code of behaviour expected on either side of the reciprocal relationship between the representative of the church and the community. Booth, for instance, described how non-church-attending sections of the population would 'fight for the parson against the secularist', who was said to 'threaten their religion'.[175] If a vicar won the respect of the community they might not fill the pews of his church but they would defend him against the attacks of outsiders. A number of the records describe how the vicar or the missioner was defended by the people against the attacks of elements considered hostile to religion.[176] The Revd Richard Free described how, when he was preaching in the East End, he was defended against the attacks of secularists by his audience which consisted of those 'Who made no sort of profession of religion'.[177] Ted, for example, an inhabitant of one of the courts in the northern part of Southwark, which was regularly visited by the South East London Mission brass band, threatened, 'If I was to see any man raise his hand against Flanagan and his men I would knock them down'.[178]

Conversely, if affection was not won, the position or the office was defended from violation by an unworthy personage.[179] Walter Southgate described how the boundaries of acceptability were crossed when a local religious man claimed that he was the second Christ and even the religiously indifferent took offence, forcing him out of the area.[180] Thus, as Alexander Paterson argued, 'Though they may never enter church through the year yet they will view with little favour the new vicar who departs from old ways'.[181]

The notion of 'our church' appears to have had substance in terms of a series of expectations which related to both sides of the equation in the relationship between the people, the church, and its religious figure. In return for this kind of loyalty it was expected that the church would be

[175] Booth, *Life and Labour* (1902), 'Religious Influences', vii. 35.
[176] Ibid.
[177] R. Free, 'The Very Poor', in W. K. Lowther Clark (ed.), *Facing the Facts* (1912), 121.
[178] South East London Mission, *Annual Report* (1898), 12.
[179] Booth, *Life and Labour* (1902), 'Religious Influences', vii. 209.
[180] W. Southgate, *That's the Way it Was* (1982), 41.
[181] Paterson, *Across the Bridges*, 209.

there when the people needed it, that the religious man would pray and
represent them in the ways described in Chapter 4. These expectations
involved the intermingling of social, communal, and spiritual responsibilities within the community. They were, however, subject to clearly
defined limits. Personal loyalty to that religious figure was considered
quite compatible with doctrinal indifference[182] and, as has been seen,
loyalty to his person did not extend to regular church attendance nor did
it involve an acceptance of remonstrations regarding certain kinds of sin.
The definition of 'our church' and the concept of religious duty which
lay behind it was consequently in marked contrast to the concept of
religious duty upheld by the regular church-attender. The occasional
attendance of many women at the mothers' meetings, alongside their
failure to go to services on a Sunday, is seen as highly dubious by some
churchmen and regular attenders. Complaints were frequently made
that the churches were used by the working classes merely to extract
material relief and entertainment while the duties and responsibilities of
association were not met. Some churchmen were cynical of the mothers'
meetings. These were depicted as institutions exploited for the goose
clubs and Christmas food hand-outs but ineffective from a 'religious'
point of view. Yet these descriptions oversimplified the relationship
between the church and the local community. A mixture of motives may
well have prevailed, but a mercenary desire did not necessarily nullify the
sense of personal and communal identification with the church. Such
labels may have been applied to behaviour which arose not simply from
indifference and apathy, but as a result of a re-definition of the standards
of association within popular culture.

The development of these notions of 'our church' were characteristic
of the late nineteenth century in particular. A marked change appears to
have taken place in the attitudes of the local population towards the
churches during the last two decades of the nineteenth century. Many of
the churchmen of Southwark described the transition from an attitude
of hostility and suspicion to that of cordial acceptance.[183] The annual
report of All Saints Surrey Square in 1900 insisted that 'A much better
feeling exists towards us personally, the clergy, sisters and other workers
than was the case a few years ago'.[184]

When the South East London Missioners first began to hold open-air

---

[182] Booth, *Life and Labour* (1902), 'Religious Influences', vii. 35.
[183] Bartlett makes the same point regarding Bermondsey in this period, 'The Churches
in Bermondsey', 129.
[184] All Saints Surrey Square, *Annual Report* (1900), 4.

services in the courts and alleys of Southwark in 1873, they were regularly interrupted by various kinds of physical and verbal assault: 'bruised faces, indecent remarks and leers were the order of the day'.[185] The descriptions of the early days of the mission are in marked contrast to the cordial reception given by the inhabitants of the Queen's Buildings, such as Ted, to Flanagan and his band at the turn of the century. The respect paid by the crowd to individuals such as Flanagan and Father Cadman was in contrast to the hatred of London's working class towards the clergy about which G. M. Murphy was warned before commencing his position as a city missioner during the 1850s. The Revd Newman Hall wrote to George Murphy in Birmingham 1856 to point out that

The working men of London hate all parsons until they know personally as a particular individual but there is always prejudice against them as a class. Therefore the city missionaries are most suicidal in dressing as if they were ministers.[186]

During the 1860s W. Carter wrote in a similar tone of the working men of London: 'In my own personal knowledge of the working class I am persuaded that there are tens of thousands who are prejudiced against clergymen and dissenting ministers'.[187]

Father Goulden traced a gradual change from attitudes such as these in the parish of St Alphege during the 1880s. He described the trend towards incorporation and association which had taken place among the local population to the extent that by the end of the 1880s it was generally believed that 'The church is a power known and recognised in court and alley, in street and shop'.[188] In 1897 the St Alphege Mission claimed confidently that 'As a rule the people love their church and come to it'.[189]

This chapter has highlighted a number of customs which were practised within popular culture and which formed part of the outworking of a particular notion of what it meant to be a good, moral, and Christian person within the community. The tendency among contemporary middle-class observers was to define religiosity on the basis of the criterion of direct church involvement. In doing so, however, they overlooked many more complex elements of the interaction between

[185] *Programme for the laying of the foundation stone at St. George's Hall* (1898).
[186] Correspondence of G. M. Murphy as quoted by Annie Taylor, *The Life of G. M. Murphy* (1888), 58.
[187] W. Carter, *The Results of Theatre Preaching* (1863), 31.
[188] St Alphege Mission, *Annual Report* (1883), 6–7.
[189] St Alphege Mission, *Annual Report* (1897), 10.

church-based and popular culture. The pattern of irregular church attendance did not necessarily imply the absence or the irrelevance of church-based images, symbols, and hymns within popular culture. Beyond the realms of formal church attendance there existed a network of association, attachment, and identification whereby church-based symbols were incorporated as part of a distinct popular identity and heritage. Sunday school attendance, hymns, and prayers were ascribed particular meaning as a part of familial culture. These meanings were distinguished from a full-scale association with church-based religion. They involved a conditional and partial incorporation of both Christian teaching and the local church. Historians have tended to isolate a number of the practices considered in this chapter and to consider them in so far as they related to the institutional churches. Yet in doing so it is easy to lose sight of the role which these practices played within a wider repertoire of religious belief, of the connections which were made with a broader definition of religiosity, and of the ways in which the church was seen and its presence felt beyond the parameters of the institutional church within popular culture.

7

Patterns of Change

We are dealing with a field of experience where there is not a single conception that can be sharply drawn. The pretention under such conditions to be rigorously 'scientific' or 'exact' in our terms would only stamp us as lacking in understanding of our task. Things are more or less divine, states of mind are more or less religious, reactions are more or less total, but the boundaries are always misty and it is everywhere a question of amount and degree.[1]

William James's words are scarcely more apt than when it comes to concluding this study of popular religion. In moving away from assessing the social effects of orthodox and institutional religion and considering instead the character and content of the attitudes, ideals, and 'habits of mind'[2] which shaped popular culture, the preceding chapters have entered the often intangible arena of belief where qualitative impressions rule. While some of the ends of such a study will, perhaps inevitably, remain tantalizingly untied, the material considered in Southwark does point in a number of clear directions. First, it challenges the association of irregular church attendance with religious indifference by suggesting that the patterns of behaviour described by contemporary religious observers such as Charles Booth arose from divergent definitions of religious belief. The apparently incongruous passion among local families for having their children baptized and for attending church at various ceremonial occasions in life, along with their loose affiliation to religious agencies such as the mission[3] arose from different concepts of religious duty, from varying expectations of the demands of the religious life, and from contrasting ideals and images of goodness and morality. These constituted a distinctly popular religious response which emerged with the greatest clarity when these expectations were challenged or contravened; when, for instance, a 'good neighbour' was accused of sin or when regular church attendance was demanded as a necessary

---

[1] W. James, *Varieties of Religious Experience*, 2 vols. (1902), ii. 39.
[2] V. Branford, *Interpretations and Forecasts: A Study of the Survivals and Tendencies of Contemporary Society* (1914), 72.   [3] Ibid.

requirement for a moral life. At such cultural boundary points an agreed code can be discerned based on a conditional acceptance of church-based religious practices. Many of those interviewed in Southwark suggested that their absence, and their parents' absence, from regular church services was not a product of 'unbelief' but rather the assertion of a different set of value criteria in which their ideal of the true believer and of genuine religion remained independent of the authority of the church as the arbiter of true morality. 'Religion by deputy', that is, the practice of regularly sending one's children to Sunday school was considered to be evidence of religious commitment and belief, as were the associated customs of teaching one's children to pray, of saying grace at meals and of showing particular respect for Sundays as a separate and special day. Oral interviewing has suggested that these customs were overarched by a sense of nostalgia associated with these practices in the parents' own childhood. They were not merely the product of a desire to maintain or assert social respectability; in many cases they were carried out within a context of sincerity and even devotion whereby the church and many of its values continued to hold an important place within popular memory, heritage, and nostalgia. This pattern of religiosity reflected a vibrant system of belief which retained its own autonomous existence within popular culture. It drew on elements, images, and ideals of church-based religion, but these were appropriated, reinterpreted, and internalized in a distinctly popular manner in combination with a folk idiom. Hymns, religious phraseology, and forms of private religious devotion continued to hold an evocative power. They formed part of a perceived heritage to be passed on to subsequent generations. An association with the church remained part of this heritage but the form which this association took was highly specific and it was expressed within parameters conditioned by a peculiarly popular concept of religious duty. In many of the cases considered in Southwark individual families identified themselves with specific local churches, and through them with religious figures in the community. They continued to defend these individuals against what they considered to be the threatening attacks of secularists and to seek them personally for both advice and prayer.

In this sense the characterization of popular religion in Southwark is similar to the descriptions given by Jeffrey Cox of diffusive Christianity in Lambeth: 'The people of Lambeth thought of themselves as Christians but insisted upon defining their own religious beliefs rather than taking them from clergymen'.[4]

---

[4] J. Cox, *The English Churches in a Secular Society: Lambeth 1870–1930* (Oxford, 1982), 92.

But what this study has shown secondly, in addition to these descriptions, is the construction of this popular expression of religiosity on the basis of a composite model of two kinds of religious discourse. These church-based elements of the popular religious repertoire cannot be considered in isolation from a second discourse of folk religion. In this idiom the Deity was amenable and accessible to immediate and private forms of address and manipulation through charms, amulets, and superstitions. Individuals positioned themselves in relation to the super-empirical sphere through a discourse which remained partially independent of both the church and of orthodoxy. The Lovett material presented in Chapter 3 demonstrates the persistence of these kinds of beliefs in south London. Superstitious customs which were readily accepted as features of the countryside were also incorporated within the fabric of popular urban culture in the period before and after the First World War. These were not a mere residue of former ages but a valid response to the particular issues of the modern human situation with credibility in their own right. They were most widely diffused, though not exclusively so, among women.

These beliefs were characterized by a commitment to the present. Superstitious charms and efficacious magic rituals were used primarily to ensure luck in the present, power over another, or the relief and prevention of sickness. The supernatural was thus evoked or placated in so far as it was believed to have an immediate bearing on everyday life. The afterlife was seen as an attribute or an extension of the present life, rather than the present being seen as a preliminary to the future state. This did not involve, however, an absence of belief in an other-worldly state or in a notion of heaven, nor did it negate the possibility of worshipping and contemplating a personal God who could intervene to administer reward and retribution. These beliefs were regulated and legitimated by an appeal to an authoritative tradition which was believed to be in some sense historical. This notion of the past existed over-whelmingly in oral tradition, in stories, and in folklore. It was a notion of history that was subservient to the present rather than contingent upon it. It involved a selective construction of the past resembling at times a kind of folk history, myth or meta-history; that is, a directive for action in the present deriving its legitimacy from its association with a perceived cultural past. 'Rightness' was thus conferred on contemporary actions by extending to them the sanctity of tradition and folklore. Anthropologists have long noticed that societies in periods of transition generate atavistically some apparently traditional forms, giving to them new meaning in contemporary circumstances.[5] Such reactions are frequently described as syncretistic marriages of tradition and modernization. These are seen clearly in modern London in motor-car mascots, witch balls in modern house decoration, and lucky jade stone charms imported from New Zealand. Entrenched customary forms were used in this way in radically changed circumstances to manage the experience of change so as to minimize disruption and to make sense of new circumstances through a recourse to familiar folk idioms.

The coalescence of folk and official religious discourses is found in popular attitudes to the rites of passage, in the incorporation of Christian symbolism in the form of certain charms and amulets, and in the ideals of the true believer. Their duality suggests a continuity between the patterns of popular belief found in urban Southwark and those identified in rural areas in earlier periods, but it argues in favour of its consideration as a distinct religious expression which should not simply be equated with the pre-modern and rural world. The specific content of popular religious belief was, no doubt, adapted over time and within different situations, but the basic coalescence of types of belief continued to form the central feature of its expression with a remarkable degree of resilience.

This model of the interaction of religious idioms should not be confused with the idea of the confrontation between discursive worlds on the basis of a crude power struggle between an élite and a subordinate class. This study has challenged James Obelkevich's identification of popular religion with forms of social and economic configuration which vie for power with those of an élite. It cautions against the tendency to see one discourse as the indigenous language of belief and to view the other as an alien formulation which is imposed by an outside élite. Both discourses were internalized within popular culture. Church-based religious values were not appropriated simply as a medium through which to ape the manners and customs of a social élite in the process of *embourgeoisement*. Church-based religious values were understood as the territory of the people and incorporated as part of their perception of identity and tradition. Moreover, they were accepted critically within popular culture, they were reinterpreted and invested with new meaning as a result of their interaction with a folk religious discourse and a range of attitudes and presuppositions which remained peculiarly popular in their emphasis. Furthermore, to consider church-based values in order simply to assess the degree to which an evangelical middle-class minority

[5] A. Cohen, *The Symbolic Construction of Community* (1992), 44–53.

succeeded in asserting their cultural hegemony is to misrepresent the way in which individuals understood their religious value system and to oversimplify the interaction between types of religious language in Southwark during the later nineteenth and early twentieth centuries. For the participant there was no divide between the religious idioms which structured popular religion. The people were not the passive receivers of external agencies which shaped and manipulated their understanding of the world.[6] They were the makers of their own culture in religion, as other historians have shown was the case in leisure, in economics, and in popular politics.[7]

This characterization of popular religion, therefore, qualifies previous descriptions of urban working-class religiosity in a number of respects. Although it agrees with the basic characterization of popular belief given by both Jeffrey Cox and Alan Bartlett, it extends their discussion by considering more diffuse aspects of belief which extended beyond the sphere of the institutional church and orthodox Christianity. In Southwark as in Lambeth, popular religion consisted of a general belief in God, a belief that this God was just and benevolent, a confidence that good people would be judged favourably by Him with regard to the life to come and a belief that the Bible was a special book to which children in particular should be exposed.[8] Yet the material considered in Southwark also suggests that, in addition to this general pattern and contrary to Cox's claim,[9] these dimensions of belief were amalgamated within a repertoire of religious language in which 'survivals of semi-pagan magic'[10] remained important in the late-nineteenth-century urban environment. The socio-economic changes of the nineteenth century did not totally cleanse popular religion of its 'centuries old non-Christian accretions'.[11] The evidence presented qualifies Cox's description of popular concepts of God as remote from everyday concerns by suggesting that the super-empirical sphere could be manipulated through the use of charms, amulets, and mascots and on occasions through more overt spells and

---

[6] F. M. L. Thompson, 'Social Control in Victorian Britain', *Economic History Review*, 34 (1981), 189.

[7] H. Cunningham, *Leisure in the Industrial Revolution c.1780–1880* (1980); E. P. Thompson, *The Making of the English Working Class* (1963); E. F. Biagini and A. J. Reid, *Currents of Radicalism: Popular Radicalism, Organised Labour and Party Politics in Britain 1850–1914* (Cambridge, 1991).

[8] Cox, *The English Churches*, 94; A. B. Bartlett, 'The Churches in Bermondsey, 1880–1939' (Birmingham University Ph.D. thesis, 1987).

[9] Ibid. 95.

[10] Ibid.

[11] Ibid.

rituals, and that God could be appealed to directly within the context of ordinary life through prayer.

Furthermore, the characterization of popular religion given in the preceding chapters also qualifies Gareth Stedman-Jones's view that late-nineteenth-century working-class culture was impervious to church-based religion.[12] It challenges Patrick Joyce's argument that the people lacked an attachment to the institutions and dogma of organized religion[13] and it attacks Joanna Bourke's dismissal of religion from her study of working-class cultures on the basis of the 'failure' of the churches.[14] It does so by showing the incorporation of church-based Christianity within popular culture. Chapter 6 in particular demonstrated that south Londoners did not remain unaffected by their inter-action with church-based culture; rather, certain features of this culture were deeply engrained and embedded within popular language, identity, and morality. It showed the sincerity of belief which was attached to certain of the ideals and values of orthodox Christianity and in the nostalgic love of 'our church'. An intermediate and more textured position is put forward whereby the selective and conditional nature of the incorporation of church-based religion within popular culture is appreciated and where the character and content of the ideals and attitudes to which individuals remained attached, are assessed in relation to an autonomous tradition of popular religiosity rather than in relation to the relative success or failure of the institutional church to win the masses.

In this way, the study has shown the need to consider both religious belief and popular culture in a more integrated fashion. On the one hand social historians have expressed dissatisfaction with a crude base–super-structure model of socio-economic change and have placed an emphasis on popular culture as an alternative to social and economic typologies based on class and class consciousness. There has been an appreciation of the continuity and complexity of popular cultural phenomena and a willingness to consider more elaborate ways of understanding the social order in terms of social identity and discourse. But studies of popular culture have rarely incorporated a careful consideration of the religious dimension which operated as part of the community of values of which that culture was composed. On the other hand religious historians have

[12] G. Stedman-Jones, 'Working-Class Culture and Working-Class Politics of London 1870–1900', *Journal of Social History*, 7 (1974), 460–508.

[13] P. Joyce, *Work, Society and Politics: The Culture of the Late-Victorian Factory* (1980), see esp. 178–9, 243–8.

[14] J. Bourke, *Working-Class Cultures in Britain 1890–1960* (1994).

tended to neglect the wider symbolic sphere of popular culture in their efforts to shed light on the religion of the working classes. Their considerations of religiosity have remained attached to a structural and institutional focus and they have been far slower to incorporate a thorough consideration of participant descriptions of popular belief into an understanding of the nature of cultural phenomena and the symbolic dimension of community. The material unearthed in Southwark has suggested a bridge between these two emphases. It emphasizes the religious dimension within popular culture while at the same time appreciating the diffuse and para-institutional expressions of religiosity which are treated as part of the experience of community as a bounded symbolic whole, rather than as a sign of a traditional and outmoded social structure.

Adaptation and continuity, rather than dislocation, characterize the popular beliefs described in this book. Those changes in popular religion which did come about at the end of the nineteenth century and during the interwar period were complex and amorphous and they cannot be classified simply as 'decline'. The 1880s witnessed the crystallization of the concept of 'our church', the acceptance of local vicars or missioners as benevolent or holy figures within the community, a corresponding decline in sectarianism, and the development of a common brand of undenominational popular religion which joined both Catholic and Protestant in an adherence to general 'Christian principles'. A notion of 'religion by deputy' became a common feature of familial and popular heritage. This rested on a sincere belief in the importance of inculcating in the next generation the virtues of a blend of Christianity in which the distinctions between types of church-based religious doctrine had been largely removed. These developments, although far more clearly pronounced from the 1880s onwards, were not new in themselves; they drew on many pre-existing aspects of belief which were endowed with renewed meaning in the modern urban situation as communities established more clearly defined local links. The First World War is frequently described as the harbinger of change, yet in Southwark the experience of international conflict in the 1914–18 war tended to act as a catalyst to pre-existent trends of thought and feeling. During the war the religious responses of the people were marked by their incorporation of familiar and traditional aspects of behaviour, devotion, and supernaturalism. A familiar folk theodicy was prominent in the use of charms, mascots, and amulets both at home and at the front. The war encouraged the tendency to look beyond the churches for supernatural

and super-empirical explanations and solutions and strengthened the
incorporation of a folk discourse within the popular religious repertoire.
The great majority of the responses given to the Army and Religion
Survey describe how the experience of war precipitated a reawakening of
religious convictions which churchmen regarded as unmediated by the
churches and by Christianity. The rise of popular spiritualism affords a
good example of the way in which unorthodox religious narratives were
drawn on with renewed vigour in a period of uncertainty. Speculations
and pronunciations which followed in the wake of the war on the
character of the afterlife were significant for descriptions of the human
condition which few churchmen would have classified as orthodox.

At the same time the war vindicated the ethical and moral principles
upon which popular religion was founded. Incidents of heroism and
camaraderie appeared to offer conclusive evidence of the goodness
of most men's instincts. The 'active good will'[15] which thrived independently of orthodox moral teaching and outside the sphere and
influence of the church was taken to indicate the prevalence and virtues
of 'latent Christianity'. As Arthur Newton wrote in his autobiography,

It is a paradox of war that whatever the position of a man or a woman, whatever
the attitudes of others towards him in times of peace, he suddenly seems to be
elevated and mysteriously becomes a better person in times of war. What I am
trying to say is that a hard working, relentless, uncompromising employer
suddenly finds that the man he previously treated like dirt is not such a bad
person after all.[16]

The generation who fought for their country found the notion of the
'true Christian' a particularly pertinent ideal which was obtainable in a
context other than that of the church.

It is a paradox, however, that while weakening some features of the
interrelationship between the popular religious repertoire and the
churches, the war also strengthened certain aspects of the incorporation
of a church-based religious discourse. Prayer and hymn singing, for
example, took on a renewed significance both at home and at the front,
and among women in particular these dimensions of the religious
repertoire were strengthened within the context of the local community.
Where the experience of war tended to dislocate men from the church it
strengthened the relationship between female culture and the local
church. The notion of 'our church' became a tangible reality for many

[15] D. S. Cairns (ed.), *The Army and Religion: An Enquiry and its Bearing upon the
Religious Life of the Nation* (1919), 60.
[16] A. Newton, *Years of Change: The Autobiography of a Hackney Shoemaker* (1974), 48.

women during the war years. In this respect the war encouraged the association of religion with the home and with the mother in particular and exacerbated the process of the 'privatisation' and 'domestication' of religion which had preceded it.

A number of developments during the interwar period also appear to have strengthened this trend. The widespread popularity of the wireless, for example, provided a mechanism by which private forms of religious devotion were given wider and more formalized expression. Llewellyn Smith described how by the 1930s

The wireless has now become a very general adjunct of the amenities of working-class life in London, nor was it limited to the homes of the better paid artisans. It looks as if the wireless, though an entirely post-war development, has already come to play a part in London working-class life not less important than that of the cinema.[17]

The wireless was a prominent feature of home life in Walworth during the 1920s and 1930s. L. J. Carter described how wirelesses were often built by Walworthians from plans in amateur radio magazines and the aerials doubled up as washing lines in the day time.[18] Religious broadcasts of various kinds were popular in the interwar period, as indeed some argue they still are today. During the 1920s and 1930s Sunday on the BBC began with a religious service in the morning between 9.30 a.m. and 10.45 a.m. There was silence from then until 12.30 p.m. and thereafter a selection of serious musical pieces and talks were played until the eight o'clock religious service began. This was followed by more serious music until the end of the day at 11.30 p.m.[19] Even after Radio Luxembourg began to broadcast a more lively Sunday programme from January 1934, people still tuned into the 8 p.m. service. Seebohm Rowntree noted in 1941 that in working-class households in York it was customary to switch on Radio Luxembourg first thing in the morning on a Sunday and to leave it on all day but with a deliberate break in the evening for the religious service. Many of those interviewed described how they enjoyed listening to the religious service on the radio—and later in the century watching *Songs of Praise* on the television—as part of their regular weekly routine. Religious programmes of these kinds stitched together the public and the private sphere and gave individuals access to a wide range of images, symbols, events, and ceremonies which

[17] H. Llewellyn Smith, *The New Survey of London Life and Labour*, ix. 8.
[18] L. J. Carter, *Walworth 1929–1939* (1985), 152.
[19] P. Scannell and D. Cardiff, *A Social History of Broadcasting: Volume 1 1920–1939* (Oxford, 1991), 232.

were relayed to audiences in a direct manner. During the 1920s, BBC engineers arranged broadcasts which specifically emphasized the sense of personal participation in the event being recorded. Broadcasters did not interfere to rewrite events such as church services. Most services observed real time, the length of the broadcasting corresponding to the duration of the event.[20] Paddy Scannell and David Cardiff have argued that

Radio sought to minimise its own presence as witness claiming simply to extend the distribution of the event beyond its particular context to the whole listening community. Their appeal, which was very great to an audience, unlike today's which takes such things for granted, was that they admitted listeners to public events in a way no previous technology had been able to do.[21]

Developments in school education also accelerated the divide between the values identified with the home and those of the wider society. Day-school education introduced an authoritative standard of knowledge which was independent of the family and the immediate community and it developed another concept of community which extended beyond the immediate confines of popular culture. The autobiographical evidence in particular suggests that one of the effects of this intrusion may have been a greater unwillingness on the part of children to accept their parents' traditions as authoritative. It also cultivated in individuals a broader perception of their relationship to a national culture expressed through the printed word. Many of the working-class autobiographies considered were written with an awareness of their interaction with a wider public and literate culture. The separation of the generations deepened on the basis of a cultural divide between those who could read, and thus had access to a wide range of other types of explanatory authority, and those who could not. W. Horwood's autobiography, for example, shows how the experience of school encouraged him to view his parents in a new light. The revelation that his father read the newspaper simply by way of the pictures developed a scepticism in Horwood's attitude towards the authority of his father's opinions.

But I was beginning to learn things for myself—other boys' parents had views of their own. Their ways were different from ours but none the worse for that. Our school teachers did their best to widen our horizons, teaching us to question things and not to accept something simply because someone said it was. I have said that my father was almost illiterate. He could read short newspaper

[20] Scannell and Cardiff, *A Social History of Broadcasting*, 277–8.
[21] Ibid. 278.

paragraphs only with difficulty. He had never read even the most simple book in
his life, yet he maintained that by looking at a few illustrations he could learn
more from them than someone else could by absorbing the whole text. This
picture method of learning led him to make all sorts of absurd assumptions and
generalisations which he would expound with loud authority.[22]

Such material hints at the wedge between the traditions enshrined in
a semi-literate culture and the advent of new forms of knowledge
and explanatory authority associated with education and 'progress'. A
similar pattern is found in the displacement of the cockney dialect.
A number of the autobiographies describe the process whereby the
native cockney tongue of the home was replaced by other forms of
language associated with the school. Walter Southgate, for example,
described how

For the first fourteen years of my life I heard and spoke very little but cockney
slang. But then I began to realise there was a difference between the language that
I read in books and the language of our teachers in the classroom and the
language of the cockney street. It required great effort and concentration to drop
the accent and so on going out into the outside world.[23]

This process encouraged the separation of the home from the school
and the private from the public, and with it the kinds of knowledge and
tradition peculiar to the community which had formerly derived much
of its identity from a distinctive cockney dialect.

Although these changes can be traced in some of the material considered, the case should not be overstated. The process by which this
transition took place was once again through the complex interweaving
of the old and the new, the public and the private. Once again assimilation and incorporation were the norm rather than dislocation. There
was no clear-cut divide in all cases between the literate and the illiterate
and between oral and written forms of explanatory authority. The two
overlapped in a manner which defies the notion of straightforward
linear change. Horwood's father may have spent a greater proportion of
his time looking at pictures, but he was still by his own definition 'reading the newspaper' and imbibing many of the basic currents of its
thought and argument. Furthermore, many of the opinions he formed
were shaped and reinforced with reference beyond the private arena of
his own reading of the newspaper in the public arena of the pub.
Horwood went on to point out that

[22] SLSL, W. Horwood, 'A Walworth Boy Looking Back on the Years 1922–1939' (1977),
70–1.
[23] W. Southgate, *That's the Way it Was* (1982), 45.

Another source of information gathered would be from men he met at work or in a pub. If they had travelled and had done things he didn't, he would carefully store up their sayings as he understood them and trot them out as indisputable facts whenever the opportunity arose.[24]

The opinion of the community as expressed in this way informed his reading of the newspaper and subjected his personal viewpoints to public confirmation. Similarly, although Southgate described the offensive waged by elementary education on the cockney dialect, he went on to describe how he none the less found himself returning to it in moments of uncertainty and crisis. 'In moments of strain and excitement it was easy to fall back into the old idiom of early speech'.[25]

The general picture that emerges is of the intermixing of oral and folk wisdom with written culture. The latter was appended to and interwoven with the former in a world of thought and presupposition which continued to mediate other forms of knowledge. David Vincent has shown the complex and erratic decline of the oral tradition in nineteenth-century popular culture. He highlights the coexistence of literacy and oral wisdom and challenges the classic dichotomy presented between oral and written, traditional and advanced, primitive and progressive cultures.[26]

In practice the two modes of communication had been an active presence in the mental universe of the labouring poor for generations before the period of this study. Thus literate and illiterate and their respective structures and artefacts had already formed a complex series of conflicting and mutually reinforcing relationships. The process of change was consequently uneven both in pace and direction.[27]

Similarly, Patrick Joyce has argued that verbal folk wisdom and folk knowledge along with the values and assumptions that clustered around linguistic custom continued to be important despite the inroads made on the oral nature of popular culture.[28] Both these writers demonstrate the links between linguistic customs and notions of popular history and collective memory and, as this study has shown, it is within this arena of heritage and identity, in particular, that religious values, traditions, and customs thrived and were perpetuated from one generation to the next.

[24] Horwood, 'A Walworth Boy', 71.
[25] Ibid. 45.
[26] D. Vincent, *Literacy and Popular Culture: England 1750–1914* (Cambridge, 1989), 8.
[27] Ibid. 13.
[28] P. Joyce, *Visions of the People: Industrial England and the Question of Class 1840–1914* (1991), 171.

Mothers, in particular, continued to exercise extensive influence over the socializing of subsequent generations and popular religion remained an essential core of values and presuppositions associated with the home which operated as a foundation from which people derived a basic understanding of truth and morality and to which they returned in periods of transition and crisis. The provision of such items as the wireless created further channels for the expression of religious devotion in the private context of the home. Even after the Second World War a church-based religious discourse continued to hold sway in the domestic arena and to influence the articulation of a sense of right and wrong. The Mass-Observation surveys of the 1940s and 1950s and the surveys carried out by Geoffrey Gorer and by Seebohm Rowntree and G. R. Lavers show a consensus on the social and cultural importance of generalized Christian values in the post-Second World War period. Rowntree and Lavers concluded that: 'People today still believe that Christianity is a relevant and vital force, although they no longer accept the idea that the church is the "chosen instrument" for the expression of that force'.[29]

In much the same way Mass-Observation described the importance ascribed to ethical teachings which were identified with Christianity. Most people argued in favour of the importance of undenominational religious instruction in schools.[30] These writers stressed the continued strength of belief in a personal God, in life after death, and in private devotional practices such as prayer. Geoffrey Gorer and David Martin in their studies of England in the 1950s and 1960s respectively also described the continuity in beliefs in ghosts[31] and in the employment of various kinds of superstitious belief in fate, magic talismans, and pre-Christian religion.[32] The recent work of Grace Davie on this period underlines this point. She points to the persistence of religiosity beyond the drop in formal religious observance. 'The sacred does not disappear, indeed in many ways, it is becoming more rather than less prevalent in contemporary society.'[33]

A narrative of change in which the diminution of religion is identified by isolating phenomena with reference to formal indices constitutes an inadequate method by which to understand and interpret popular

[29] S. Rowntree and G. R. Lavers, *English Life and Leisure* (1951), 367.
[30] Mass-Observation, *Puzzled People* (1947), 85.
[31] G. Gorer, *Exploring English Character* (1955), 262–70.
[32] D. A. Martin, *The Religious and the Secular: Studies in Secularisation* (1969), 116–17.
[33] G. Davie, *Religion in Britain since 1945: Believing without Belonging* (1994), 43.

religion in any period. We need to understand how successive generations continued to construct, communicate, and adapt religious language if we are to appreciate popular religion as a distinctive system of belief in its own right, persisting not only beyond the advent of the modern industrial world but also into the post-modern era in which we find ourselves today.

APPENDIX

The Oral Project

Twenty-nine oral interviews were carried out during the course of research in Southwark. As far as possible these were with former inhabitants of the Metropolitan Borough but in many cases the problems of finding suitable candidates forced the sample to be extended to those who resided in the wider geographical area of present-day Southwark which includes Bermondsey, Camberwell, Peckham, and Dulwich, as well as Southwark proper and Walworth.

The interviews were carried out at two day centres in Southwark; the Beornude Centre in Abbey Road, Bermondsey and The Southwark Age Concern Centre in Crawford Road, Camberwell Green. The interviews took the form of form of free-flowing conversations. A series of questions was drawn up but this was used merely as a stimulus for discussion, not as a questionnaire. Certain key questions were asked to introduce themes but within these subject areas questioning proceeded on the basis of conversation as naturally as possible.

A deliberate effort was made to contact and talk, in a context other than that of the churches, to interviewees who were not necessarily churchgoers. This approach is in contrast to that used by Alan Bartlett in Bermondsey. His interviewees were all churchgoers who had lived in Bermondsey for the majority of their adult lives. They were contacted through local churches and via the recommendations of clergy. In Southwark, however, the criterion of church involvement was entirely subsidiary. The day centres drew together a diverse sample of former inhabitants of Southwark on the basis of geography rather than the criterion of church involvement. The centres were run on an informal basis in large halls where it was possible to sit and talk to individuals for extended periods of time with little interruption.

These interviews were considered in conjunction with a number of the transcripts of Alan Bartlett's interviews in Bermondsey which are deposited at Southwark Local Studies Library, with the original transcripts of interviews with the forty-five former inhabitants of the Greater London area carried out by the Essex Oral History Project, and with the oral surveys carried out by the Age Exchange Centre in Blackheath.

Brief details of each interviewee are given below. Pseudonyms are used throughout to protect the privacy of individuals.

THE INTERVIEWS

Interview 1:   Jim Bower; born in 1919 in Abbey Street, Bermondsey. He was the son of a Bermondsey docker.

Interview 2:   Helen and Alf Westall; born in 1915 and 1910. Helen was born in Deptford and grew up in Camberwell. Alf was born in Rockingham Street, Southwark. Helen's father was a labourer.

Interview 3:   George Webb; born in 1911 in Storks Road, Bermondsey.

Interview 4:   Emma Reynolds; born in 1911 in Red Cross Street off Borough High Street, Southwark. Her father was a butcher who worked in Battersea.

Interview 5:   Edith Anders; born in 1919 in Decimer Street off Tower Bridge Road, Bermondsey. She was the daughter of a costermonger.

Interview 6:   Barbara Luke; born in 1921 in Peckham, the daughter of a ladies' tailor.

Interview 7:   Anna Telby; born in 1905 in Colbar Square, Marylebone. She was the daughter of an Italian immigrant who died while she was still in infancy and of a domestic servant who had been brought up in an unspecified northern village by an elderly woman. Her grandparents were unknown. Her parents met while her mother was in service in Manchester and they moved to London to the above area when she was a tiny baby.

Interview 8:   Sid Venables; born in 1913, in Camberwell. His father was a greengrocer and florist but he was brought up by his grandparents who also lived in Camberwell. His grandfather was a cooper and his grandmother kept a local vegetable stall.

Interview 9:   Mrs Sawyer; born in Ireland in 1892. She came to London at the time of her marriage in 1924 and lived in Rodney Road, Southwark. Her husband was a Catholic who was born in Bermondsey.

Interview 10:   Emily Smith; born in 1920 in Coldharbour Lane, Camberwell. Her father was a regular soldier.

Interview 11:   William Bevis; born 1903 in Peckham. His father was an employee at the Peckham Gas works.

Interview 12:   Sydney Barry; born in 1921 in Merrow Street, Walworth. His father was a bookmaker in the West End until he lost all his money quite early on in Sydney's childhood and from then on he was irregularly employed in Walworth.

Interview 13:   Second interview with Anna Telby.

Interview 14:   Esther Annenberg; born in 1903 in Queen's Street, Upton Park, Peckham. Her father worked as a busman. She was from a Jewish family who had lived in England since the seventeenth century.

Interview 15:   Miriam Moore; born 1904. Her father was in the Navy and away at sea. Her mother worked in a laundry. She was brought up by her grandmother in the Peabody Buildings, Blackfriars Road.

Interview 16:   Norman James; born in 1921 in the Old Kent Road but grew up in Union Street, Southwark. His father was a local carman.

Interview 17:   Philippa Ivy; born in 1904 in East Dulwich. Her father was a solicitor's clerk who drank heavily and left his family impoverished.

Interview 18:   Mrs Croft; born in 1908 in Dulwich where she lived all her life. Her father was in the army and away from home most of the time. He left ten children in the care of Mrs Croft and her mother.

Interview 19:   Mrs Scott; born in 1901 in Westmoreland Road, Walworth. Her father was a compositor.

Interview 20:   Molly Layton; born in 1911 in South Street, Walworth. Her father died while she was very young and she was brought up by grandparents. Her grandfather was a docker and her mother went out to work while her grandmother looked after the children. Her mother and all her aunts worked in Walworth polishing golf clubs.

Interview 21:   Elizabeth Merritt; born in 1912 in Kinglake Street, Walworth. Her parents were also from Walworth. Her father was a carpenter and her mother peeled onions.

Interview 22:   Mrs Cotton; born in 1910 in Peckham. Her father was a compositor.

Interview 23:   Lilian Tims; born in 1918 in the Old Kent Road, the daughter of a printer.

Interview 24:   Harry Rea; born in Camden Town in 1910. He lived on the Old Kent Road from the time of his marriage in 1939.

Interview 25:   Bob Giles; born in 1907 in Camberwell.

Interview 26:   Mrs Mayhead; born in 1921 in Camberwell, the daughter of a porter at Borough Market.

Interview 27:   Mrs Duncan; born in 1905 in East Street, Walworth, the daughter of a wheelwright.

Interview 28:   Mr and Mrs Turner; born in 1913 and 1917. They lived on the Old Kent Road from the time of their marriage and prior to that in Bermondsey.

Interview 29:   Mrs W. Fleming; born in 1908. She was brought up in an orphanage in Dulwich. She did not know her parents.

BIBLIOGRAPHY

PRIMARY SOURCES

(A) *Manuscript*

Brunel University Library, Burnett Collection of Working Class Autobiographies

Ashley, J., 'Autobiography' (1908).
Balne, E., 'Autobiography of an Ex-workhouse and Poor Law School Boy' (1972).
Bargate, D., 'Memories', n.d.
Belcher.W., 'An Autobiography', n.d.
Brown, E., 'Reminiscences', n.d.
Burkin, H., 'Memories', n.d.
Castle, J., 'The Diary of John Castle' (1871).
Clark, E. M., 'Their Small Corner', n.d.
Collinson, A. T., 'One Way Only' (1966).
Doniton, D. M., 'Reminiscences', n.d.
Edwards, J., 'The Lean Years' (1970).
Goring, J., 'Autobiographical Notes' (1938).
Ireson, A., 'Reminiscences' (1930).
James, A. G., 'A Soul Remembering', n.d.
Metcalfe, S., 'One Speck of Humanity', n.d.
Mockford, G., 'Wilderness Journeyings and Gracious Deliverences' (*c.*1880).
Raymont, T., 'Memories of an Octogenarian 1864–1949', n.d.
Rignall, E., 'All so long Ago', n.d.
Seymour, A., 'Childhood Memories', n.d.
Till, W., 'The Early Years of a Victorian Grandmother', n.d.
Westhall, L., 'The Good Old Days', n.d.
Young, H., 'Harry's Biography', n.d.

Essex University Library, The Essex Oral History Archive

John Johnson Collection, Oxford

The London School of Economics, The Booth Collection

Interview Notebooks: B269, B270, B273, B274, B267, B276, B277, B278, B283.
Parish Notes: A45, A46, A47.
Police Notebooks: B364, B365.

Ruskin College Oxford, Working-Class Autobiographies

Joel, C. E., 'Autobiography' (1906).
Wallis, B., 'Yesterday', n.d.

Southwark Local Studies Library, Reminiscences of Local Inhabitants

Bennett, J. H., 'I was a Walworth Boy' (1977).

Bustin, P., 'My Two Square Miles of London' (1974).

Davis, A. C., 'Heatherstone and Vinegar' (1979).

Fish, M., 'Reminiscences of Southwark' (1985).

Hall, A. S., 'Reminiscences' (1988).

Horwood, W., 'A Walworth Boy Looking Back on the Years 1922–1939' (1977).

Mayhew, F., 'Memories of Good and Bad Days of Childhood' (1976).

Thornton, B., 'Memories of Childhood' (1987).

Worthy, D., Manuscript notes (1980).

(B) *Printed*

All Saints Surrey Square, Walworth, *Annual Reports* (1897), (1898), (1899), (1900), (1901).

All Souls Grosvenor Park, *Church Magazine* (1894–1902), (1938–40).

The Aquarium Songster, pub. W. S. Fortey (*c*.1888–90).

Arch Mission Rotherhithe, *Annual Reports* (1869–70).

Armstrong, C., *Pilgrimage from Nenthead: Autobiography* (1938).

Armstrong, G. G., *Memories of G. G. Armstrong* (1944).

Ash, D. L., *Memories of a London Childhood* (1984).

Ashton, J., *Modern Street Ballads* (1888).

Atkinson, J. C., *Forty Years in a Moorland Parish* (1891).

Ball, W. D., *The Sermon on the Mount and Other New Testament Extracts* (1896).

Barclay, T., *Memories and Medleys: Autobiography of a Bottlewasher* (1934).

—— and Perry, T., *Report and Survey of Housing Conditions in the Metropolitan Borough of Southwark* (1929).

Bell, E. W., *Theosophy and Home Life* (1903).

Bermondsey Young Men's Catholic Club, *Annual Report* (1884).

Besant, A., *Theosophy and the Law of Population* (1891).

Besant, W., *South London* (1899).

Blackburne, H., *This Also Happened on the Western Front* (1932).

Blacker, H., *Just Like it Was: Memories of the Mittel East* (1974).

Blakeborough, R., *Wit, Character, Folklore and Customs in the North Riding of Yorkshire* (1898).

Booth, C., 'The Inhabitants of the Tower Hamlets (School Board Division), their Conditions and Occupations', *Journal of the Royal Statistical Society*, 1 (1887).

—— *Life and Labour of the People of London*, 1st edn. 1898 (1902), 'Poverty', i, ii.

—— *Life and Labour* 1st edn. 1900 (1902), 'Industry', iv.

—— *Life and Labour* (1902), 'Religious Influences', i–vii.

Booth, M., *Charles Booth: A Memoir* (1918).

Brairstow, J. O., *Sensational Religion in Past Times and Present Day* (1890).

Branford, V., *Interpretations and Forecasts: A Study of the Survivals and Tendencies of Contemporary Society* (1914).

Britten, J., *Bermondsey Young Men's Catholic Club* (1984).

Browning Settlement, *Annual Reports* (1896–97), (1898), (1900), (1904).

Bullen, F. T., *With Christ at Sea* (1901).

Bumpus, T. F., *London Churches Ancient and Modern* (1907).

Burne, C. S., *Shropshire Folklore: A Sheaf of Gleanings*, edited from the collections of G. F. Jackson (1883).

Cairns, D. S., (ed.), *The Army and Religion: An Enquiry and its Bearing upon the Religious Life of the Nation* (1919).

Campbell, J. R., *The New Theology* (1907).

Carlisle, J. C., *My Life's Little Day* (1935).

Carpenter, M. L., *Angel Adjutant* (1921).

Carter, L. J., *Walworth 1929–1939* (1985).

Carter, W., *The Results of Theatre Preaching* (1863).

Cassell's Saturday Journal (1899–1906).

Caudwell, F., *The Cross in Dark Places and Among All Sorts and Conditions* (1903).

Cay, A., *Anti-Christ: A Sermon delivered in the Parish Church of St. Mary Newington* (Nov. 1865).

Census for England and Wales, County of London 1871 (1872).

—— *County of London 1881* (1881).

—— *County of London 1891, presented to the House of Commons 1893–4.*

—— *County of London 1901* (1902).

—— *County of London 1911* (1914).

—— *County of London 1921* (1922).

—— *County of London 1931* (1937).

Charlton, I. W., *The Revival in Wales, Some Facts and Figures* (1905).

Chevalier, A., *Before I Forget* (1901).

—— *Limelight Lays* (1903).

Christ Church Blackfriars Road, *Parish Magazine* (1909–14).

The Church of St Michael's Lant Street, *Statement of Account and Balance Sheets for 1899* (1899).

Clifford, J., *The Demands of the Twentieth-Century: An Address given at the Baptist Union*, (26 April 1900).

The Colleges of St Saviour's Southwark, *Annual Reports* 1905, 1907.

Comte, A., *The Positive Philosophy*, 2 vols., trans. by H. Martineau (1853).

Critchley, G., *Three Sermons* (1899–1900).

Crossways Central Mission, *Annual Reports* (1913), (1914).

Crossway Church New Kent Road, *Church Magazine* (1912–15), (1928–32).

Dan Leno's Songster, pub. W. S. Fortey (*c.*1890–2).

Dash, J., *Good Morning Brothers* (1969).

Davies, C. M., *Orthodox London* (1873).

—— *Unorthodox London* (1874).

Deenah-Dinah Do Songster, pub. W. S. Fortey (*c.*1890–2).

Dickens, C., *Oliver Twist* (1837).

Donovan, M., *A History of St. Paul's Lorrimore Square* (1930).

Dulwich College Mission, *Annual Report* (1926).

Durkheim, E., *The Division of Labour in Society*, trans. by G. Simpson (1893, repr. New York, 1964).

—— *The Elementary Forms of Religious Life*, trans. by J. W. Swain (1915, repr. New York, 1965).

East Street Walworth, *Annual Report* (1895).

Edge, H. T., *God in Man* (1897).

Edwards, A. W., *Souvenir of Brunswick Methodist Church 1835–1934* (1935).

Ellerton, A., *When the Gentle Breezes Blow* (1909).

Foote, G. A., *Dr. Torrey and the Bible* (1905*a*).

—— *An Open Letter to Dr. Torrey* (1905*b*).

Free, R., 'The Very Poor', in W. K. Lowther Clark (ed.), *Facing the Facts* (1912).

Friar Street Mission Hall, *Annual Report* (1899).

Gabbot, E. R., *The Sins of the Salvation Army* (1987).

Garbett, C. F., *In the Heart of South London* (1931).

Garland, T. C., *Leaves From My Log: Christian Work in the Port of London* (1882).

Gibbs, H., *Autobiography: Box On* (1981).

Gipsy Smith, *From Gipsy Tent To Pulpit: The Story of My Life* (1901).

—— *His Life and Work* (1903).

Goode, G. R., *The Book of Songs* (1911).

Graeme. A., *The Dairy of a Dead Officer: Being the Post Humous Papers of A. Graeme* (1919).

Graves, R., *Goodbye to All That* (New York, 1930).

Greenward, J., *The Seven Curses of London* (1982).

Gorser, W. H., *Hundred Years Work for the Children: Being a Sketch of the Operations of the Sunday School Union* (1905).

Greenwood, J., *The Seven Curses of London*, ed. J. Richards (Oxford, 1981).

The Grove Mission, *Annual Reports* (1902–3).

Gwyer, J., *Gwyer's Life and Poems* (1877).

Harland, J. and Wilkinson, T. T., *Lancashire Folklore* (1867).

—— —— *Lancashire Legends* (1873).

Harrington, J. P., *Top Hat Everytime* (1910).

Harris, H., *Under Oars: Reminiscences of a Thames Lighterman, 1894–1909* (1974).

Head. A., (ed.), *Mrs Charlotte Hanbury* (1903).

Heathcote, W. J., *My Salvation Army Experience* (1891).

Henderson, W., *Notes on the Folklore of the Northern Counties of England and the Borders* (1879).

—— *Victorian Street Ballads* (1937).

Heren, A., *Growing Up Poor in London* (1908).

Hickman, C. D., *On a Bright Summer's Day* (1902).

Higham, F., *Six Years On: The Story of Southwark Cathedral and Diocese 1905–1965* (1965).

Hollingshead, J., *Ragged London* (1861).

Holloway, H., *A Voice from the Convict Cell or Life and Conversion* (Manchester, 1877).

Holy Trinity Southwark, *Church and Monthly Magazine* (1912–18).

Hopps, J. P., *The Inviting* (1892).

Horsley, J., *I Remember* (1911).

Housman, L., *War Letters of a Fallen Englishman* (1930).

Hunt, R., *Popular Romances of the West of England* (1865).

Hughes, H. V., *A London Childhood in the 1870s* (1977).

Hume, A., *Condition of Liverpool, Religious and Social* (1858).

James, W., *Varieties of Religious Experience*, 2 vols. (1902).

Jealous, E. W., *Happy Jim: An Autobiography of James Bryant the Converted Farrier* (1937).

Jeffs, E. H., *The Cause of Crossway: The London Central Mission, New Kent Road* (1910).

Jephson, A. W., *Peace Thanksgiving: A Sermon Preached in St. John's Walworth* (8 June 1902).

Jephson, A. W., *My Work in London* (1910).

John Street Methodist Sunday School, *Annual Report* (1911–22).

Keeling, E., *The Greatest Need of the Age: Paper Delivered to the Pembroke Literary Society* (20 November 1895).

Kent, W., *The Testament of a Victorian Youth* (1938).

The King's Own Mission, *Annual Reports* (1897), (1898).

Knight, G. S., *The History of Manor Chapel* (1899).

Knowles, R. G., *Of Stories Just a Few* (1904).

Lambert, A., *Over-the-Top* (1930).

Lax, W. H., *Lax and His Book: Autobiography* (1937).

Leather, E. M., *The Folklore of Herefordshire* (1912).

Leighton, H., *Nature* (1904).

—— *Look at the Time you Save* (1903).

Leo, F., *What a Fine Old Game you're Having* (1900).

—— *Where's the Gold in London* (1900).

—— *The Eagle* (1907).

Light and Truth Magazine: Monthly Organ of the Primitive Methodist South East London Mission (1908), (1912), (1913), (1914), (1915), (1919), (1920).

Linda, C., *Call Him Back Before its too Late* (1907).

Lipton, D., *Let the Good Work go on* (1915).

Llewellyn Smith, H., *The New Survey of London Life and Labour* (1930–4), i–ix.

Loane, M., *The Queen's Poor* (1906).

—— *Neighbours and Friends* (1910).

—— *The Common Growth* (1911).

Lockfields Methodist Chapel, *Rodney Road Handbills of a Special Mission* (1899).

London Borough of Southwark Official Guide (1967).

London City Mission Addresses (1882).

Lovett, E., 'The Ancient and Modern Game of Astragals', *Folklore*, 12 (1901), 280–93.

—— 'The Vessel Cup', *Folklore*, 12 (1902), 94–6.

—— 'Specimens of Modern Mascots and Ancient Amulets in the British Isles', *Folklore*, 19 (1908), 288–303.

—— 'Difficulties of a Folklore Collector', *Folklore*, 20 (1909), 227–8.

—— 'Superstitions and Survivals among Shepherds', *Folklore*, 20 (1909), 64–70.

—— 'Amulets and Coster Barrows in London, Rome and Naples', *Folklore*, 20 (1909c), 70–1.

—— 'English Charms, Amulets and Mascots', *Croyden Guardian*, 17 Dec. 1910.

—— 'Folk Medicine in London', *Folklore*, 24 (1913), 120–1.

—— 'The Belief in Charms', *Folklore*, 28 (1917), 99–100.

—— *Magic in Modern London* (1925).

—— 'Londoners still Believe in Superstitions', *The Evening News*, 1 Oct. 1926.

—— 'Old Fashioned Witchballs in Modern House Decoration', *Daily Mail*, 29 Dec. 1926.

—— —— 'London Witch Doctors', The *Star*, 23 Apr. 1927.

—— *Folklore and Legend of the Surrey Hills and Sussex Downs* (1928).

The Lyric Songster, pub. W. S. Fortey (*c.*1890–2).

McCree, G. W., *His Life and Work with Extracts from his Journal* (1893).

MacDonagh, M., *In London During the Great War* (1935).

Mallock, W. H., *Studies of Contemporary Superstition* (1895).

Mann, W. F., *Recollections of the Years 1884–1911* (1975).

Martineau, J., *The Bible and The Child: Tracts for the Times* (1898).

Marx, K., *Karl Marx: Early Writings* (1844, repr. London, 1963).

—— and Engels, F., *On Religion* (Moscow, 1957).

Mass-Observation, *Puzzled People* (1947).

Mass-Observation, *Meet Yourself on Sunday* (1949).

Mass-Observation, *Contemporary Churchgoing* (1949).

Mayhew, H., *London Labour and the London Poor*, 3 vols. (1851).

Mead, A., (ed.), *Charlotte Hanbury: An Autobiography* (1901).

Meakin, H. T., *A Practical Solution to the Problem of Slumdom* (1908).

Mearns, A., *The Bitter Cry of Outcast London* (1883).

Mills, A. J., *Give us a Bit of Your Kilt* (1908).

Money, A., *Old Songs for Young Voices* (*c.*1888–90).

Morton, R., *Aunt Mandy* (1904a).

—— *She's Mine, I'm Hers* (1904b).

—— *Come and Kiss Your Honey on the Lips* (1905).

Mowark Minstrels Songs and Ballads, pub. Francis, Day and Hunter (1890–2).

Mudie-Smith, R., *The Religious Census of London* (1904).

Murphy, C., *The Coloured Millionaire* (1902).

Murphy, G. M., *Parental Aid or Speed the Plough: An Address to the Parents of Sunday School Scholars* (1863).

—— *The Downfall of the Dagon Drink: an Argument and An Analogy* (1864).

—— *Ten Years of the Southwark Mission* (1866).

—— *Popular Melodies and Hymns for Temperance Meetings* (1870).

The Music Hall Songster, pub. W. S. Fortey (1892).

The Navvy Mission, Industrial Christian Fellowship, *Annual Reports* (1895–6), (1896–7), (1897), (1899–90), (1890–1), (1905–6), (1912), (1914).

Navvy Mission Society, *Annual Reports* (1877–96).

The New Pavilion Songster, pub. W. S. Fortey (1890–2).

Newton, A., *Years of Change: The Autobiography of a Hackney Shoemaker* (1974).

Noel, C., 'The Working Classes', in W. K. Lowther Clarke (ed.), *Facing the Facts* (1912).

Orford, E. J., *The Book of Walworth* (1925).

Osbourne, C., *Where's My Two Bob Gone?* (1907).

Oxford & Bermondsey Mission, *Annual Report* (1939).

The Oxford Songster, pub. W. S. Fortey (*c.*1890–2).

Padfield, E. J. *A Plea for the Children of Bermondsey* (1912).

The Paragon Songster, pub. W. S. Fortey (*c.*1890–2).

Parsons, P., *Structure and Process in Modern Societies* (New York, 1960)

Paterson, A., *Across the Bridges* (1911).

Pembroke College Mission, *Annual Report* (1898).

Philcox, H. N., 'Reminiscences of the Strict and Particulars', *The Baptist Quarterly* (1936).

—— 'The Early Days of East Street Chapel, Walworth', *The Baptist Quarterly*, (1938).

Playne, C. E., *Britain Holds On* (1933).

The Popular Songster, pub. W. S. Fortey (*c.*1890).

Popular Stories for the Home, pub. S. W. Partridge (1891), ii–vi.

Price-Hughes, K., *The Story of My Life* (1945).

Pym, T. W., and Gordon, G., *Papers From Picardy* (1917).

The *Quarterly Review, St. Saviour's Southwark* (1890).

A Record of One Year's Work in the Parish of St. Paul's Westminster Bridge Road 1898–1899 (1899).

The *Religious Census of London*, repr. from the *British Weekly* (1888).

Richmond Street Mission, *Annual Report* (1897).

Rick, A. E., *There's no Harm in Kissing a Lady* (1907).

Ritchie, J. E., *Days and Nights in London* (1880).

Roberts, R., *A Ragged Schooling: Growing Up in a Classic Slum* (Manchester, 1976).

Rochester Diocesan Chronicle (1892–9), (1901–5), (1911–18).

Rochester Diocesan Society, *A Short Account of the Spiritual Needs of the Metropolitan Boroughs Comprising South London* (1902).
—— *A Short Account of Twenty-Five Years of Church Mission Work in South London 1878–1902* (1903).
Rosenbaum, M., *History of Borough Synagogue* (1917).
Rowntree, B. S., and Lavers, G. R., *English Life and Leisure* (1951).
Ryle, J. C., *Sheet Tracts* (1881).
St Alphege Mission, *Annual Report* (1883), (1893), (1897).
—— *Twenty Years Work among the Masses* (1893).
—— *Monthly Paper* (1911–15), (1925–39).
St George-the-Martyr, *Report and Statement of Accounts* (1898), (1906), (1905), (1902).
—— *Parish Magazine* (1915–24).
St George's Parish Magazine (1915), (1918), (1920–4).
St John's College Mission, *Annual Report* (1896).
St Jude's Parish Magazine (1922–7).
St Luke's Working Lad's Club, *Annual Reports* (1909–11).
St Mark's, *Annual Report* (1884–5).
St Mark's Parochial Magazine (1885).
St Mary Magdalen's, *Parish Magazine* (1912), (1924–6).
St Mary Newington Parish Magazine (1866), (1870–6), (1879–87), (1892–1941).
St Matthew's, *Annual Statement of Parochial Accounts* (1895), (1891), (1892), (1890), (1886), (1889).
—— *Annual Report and Balance Sheets* (1899), (1902).
St Matthew's Parish Magazine (1896–7), (1903–10), (1937–40).
St Paul's Lorrimore Square, *Yearbook* (1903).
—— *Parish Magazine* (1906), (1912–19), (1939).
St Peter's Walworth, *Parish Magazine* (1886–94), (1906–40).
St Stephen's Walworth, *Parish Magazine* (1910–18).
Scannell, D., *Mother Knew Best* (1974).
See and Serve Quarterly Journal of the Methodist Union for Social Service (Oct. 1909)
Shaftesbury Memorial Mission and Hall, *Annual Report* (1898).
Shelly, H., *Hi Diddle-Diddle* (1902).
—— *The Old Straw Hat* (1902).
—— *I Always Wears an Orchid next to me Heart* (1902).
—— *The Little Things that Gold Can't Buy* (1903).
—— *The Old Oak Wall* (1906).
—— *The Newsboy's Song* (1906).
Sheridan, M., *Nursery Rhymes or Oh Be Careful* (1900).
—— *At the Football Match Last Saturday* (1907).
Simpkinson, C. H., *A South London Parish* (1894).
Smith, E., *Three Years in Central London* (1889).

South East and South London Auxiliaries of London City Mission, *Annual Report* (1899), (1901).

South East London Mission, *Notes and Financial Accounts* (1898–9).

South London and Deptford Mission and Settlement, *Annual Report* (1916–17).

South London Auxiliary Sunday School Society, *Annual Report* (1882–5), (1888).

South London Chronicle (1875), (1876–90), (1891–3), (1895–1907).

South London Mail (1896–1904), (1888–1940).

South London Mission, *Annual Report* (1897), (1919), (1920), (1921), (1922).

—— *The Children's Church* (1918).

South London Press (1880–1940).

South London Wesleyan Mission and Settlement, *Annual Report* (1909).

Southgate, W., *That's the Way it Was* (1982).

Southwark and Bermondsey Recorder (1882–4).

Southwark Annual (1893–1906).

Southwark Auxiliary Sunday School Society Union, *Annual Report* (1883), (1885), (1888).

Southwark Boys Aid Association, *Annual Report* (1912).

Southwark Sunday School Society, *Annual Reports, Rules and Regulations* (1821–1934).

—— *Annual Report* (1897), (1903).

—— *Balance Sheet and Reports of Schools for the Year 1897* (1898).

Southwark Sunday School Union, *Annual Report* (1885).

Spurgeon, C. H., *Illustrated Almanack and Christian Companion* (1863–1917).

—— *Evening by Evening: Or Readings at Eventide for the Family or the Closet* (1868).

—— *John Ploughman's Pictures: Or More of his Plain Talk for Plain People* (1880).

—— *A Good Start: A Book for Young Men and Women* (1898).

—— *The Gospel Extract* (1899).

The Standard Songster, pub. W. S. Fortey (1890–2).

Stead, W. T., (ed.), *Coming Men on Coming Questions* (1905).

Steele, H., *Harry Steele's Song Book* (*c.*1888–90).

Stephen the Yeoman Mission, *Annual Report* (1933).

Stevens, T. P., *The Story of Southwark Cathedral* (1922).

—— *Cassock and Surplice: Incidents in Clerical Life* (1947).

Stouffer, S. A., *The American Soldier: Combat and its Aftermath* (Princeton, 1949).

Stovin, J., *Journal of a Methodist Farmer 1871–1875* (1982).

Stratton, E., *Songster* (1894).

Surrey Chapel Central Mission, *Annual Reports* (1904–5).

Surrey Gardens Memorial Hall, *Annual Report* (1913).

The Surrey Tabernacle Witness (1899).

Stuart, C. D., and Park, A. J., *The Variety Stage* (1895).

Ta-ra-ra-boom-de-e Songster, pub. W. S. Fortey (1890–2)

Tarrant, W. G., *The London Unitarians and the Churches where they Worship* (1900).

Taylor, A., *The Life of G. M. Murphy* (1888).

Thompson, F., *Lark Rise to Candleford* (Oxford, 1939).

Tönnies, F., *Community and Society*, trans. by C. P. Loomis (Michigan, 1964).

Turner, I., *Bang Went the Door* (1890).

Turner, J. A., *The Life of a Chimney Boy* (1901).

Vaux, J. E., *Church Folklore* (1894).

Walker, H., *Sketches of Christian Work and Workers* (1896).

Wallace, H. C., *Reverence Sermon* (1904).

—— *The Holy Catholic Church Sermon* (1904).

—— *Foes of Progress* (1904).

—— *The Fall of Jericho* (1904).

Walworth Club for Working Girls, *Annual Report* (1905).

Walworth Herald (1887–8).

Walworth Road Chapel, *Church Manual* (1897).

Walworth Young Men's Christian Mission, *Annual Report* (1898).

Watson, D., *I was a Parson* (1948).

Weber, M., *The Protestant Ethic and the Spirit of Capitalism* (1904–5, repr. Allen & Unwin, 1930).

—— *The Sociology of Religion*, trans. by E. Fischoff (1922, repr. Boston, 1963).

—— *The Theory of Social and Economic Organisation* (1922, repr. Oxford, 1947).

Wellington College, *Annual Report* (1896), (1899).

West, A., *The Brothers Maloney* (1903).

Willis, F., *Peace and Dripping Toast* (1950).

Woodsmith, W. M., *A Revival Call to the Churches* (1902).

The Working Men's Mission, *Annual Report (1898–9)*, (1902–3), (1907–8).

Wright, T., *The Great Unwashed* (1868).

—— *The Great Army of the London Poor* (1882).

—— *Our New Masters* (1973).

SECONDARY SOURCES

(A) *Manuscript*

Bartlett, A. B., 'The Churches in Bermondsey 1880–1939' (Birmingham University Ph.D. thesis, 1987).

Bennett, G., 'Aspects of Supernatural Belief, Memorate and Legend in a Contemporary Urban Environment' (Sheffield University Ph.D. thesis, 1985).

Chadwick, R., 'Church and People in Bradford and District 1880–1914' (Oxford University D.Phil. thesis, 1986).

Dickie, J. G., 'College Missions and Settlements in South London 1870–1920' (Oxford University M.Litt. thesis, 1975).

Field, C. D., 'Methodism and Metropolitan London' (Oxford University D.Phil. thesis, 1974).

McLeod, H., 'Membership and Influence of the Church in Metropolitan London 1885–1914' (Cambridge University D.Phil. thesis, 1971).

Marchant, C., 'Interaction of Church and Society in an East London Borough' (London University Ph.D. thesis, 1979).

Marrin, A., 'The Church of England in the First World War' (Columbia University Ph.D. thesis, 1968).

Rose, G., 'Locality, Politics and Culture: Poplar in the 1920's' (London University Ph.D. thesis, 1989).

Rycroft, P., 'Church, Chapel and Community in Craven, 1764–1851' (Oxford University D.Phil. thesis, 1988).

Williams, S. C., 'Religious Belief and Popular Culture: A Study of the South London Borough of Southwark *c.*1880–1939' (Oxford University D.Phil. thesis, 1993).

(B) *Printed*

Abercrombie, N., Barker, J., Brett, S., and Foster, J., 'Superstition and Religion: The God of the Gaps', *Sociological Yearbook of Religion*, 3 (1970), 93–129.

Age Exchange, *Can We Afford the Doctor?* (1985).

—— *Good Morning Children: Memories of School Days 1920s and 1930s* (1988).

—— *On the River: Memories of the River* (1989).

Allport, G., *The Individual and His Religion* (1951).

Ainsworth, A. J., 'Religion and the Working-Class Community and the Evolution of Socialism in Late Victorian Lancashire: A case of Working-Class Consciousness', *Histoire Sociale*, 10 (1977), 355–80.

Anderson, M., *Family Structure in Nineteenth-Century Lancashire* (Cambridge, 1971).

Anderson, O., 'The Growth of Christian Militarism', *English Historical Review*, 86 (1971), 46–72.

—— 'The Incidence of Civil Marriage in Victorian England and Wales', *Past and Present*, 69 (1975), 50–88.

Avis, P., *Gore, Reconstruction and Conflict* (Worthing, 1988).

Baddeley, A., 'The Limitations of Human Memory', in Moss and Goldstein (eds.), *The Recall Method* (1979).

Badone, E. (ed.), *Religious Orthodoxy and Popular Faith in European Society* (Princeton, 1990).

Bailey, P., *Leisure and Class in Victorian England: 1830–1885* (1978)

—— *Music Hall: The Business of Pleasure* (Milton Keynes, 1986).

Baker, M., *Folklore and the Customs of Rural England* (1974).

Baker, T., *Music Hall Records* (1978).

Barrow, L., *Independent Spirits: Spiritualism and the English Plebeians 1850–1910* (1986).

Bebbington, D., *The Nonconformist Conscience* (1979).

—— 'City, Countryside and Social Gospel in Late-Victorian Non-conformity', *Studies in Church History*, 16 (1979), 415–27.

—— *Evangelicalism in Modern Britain* (1989).

Bell, C., *Ritual Theory: Ritual Practice* (Oxford, 1992).

Bell, D., 'The Return of the Sacred: The Argument on the Future of Religion', *British Journal of Sociology*, 18 (1977), 419–49.

Bellah, R., 'Religious Evolution', *American Journal of Sociology*, 29 (1964), 358–74.

—— *Beyond Belief, Essays on Religion in a Post-Traditional World* (New York, 1970).

Bendix, R., *Max Weber: An Intellectual Portrait* (1959).

Bennett, G., 'Ghosts and Witches in the Sixteenth and Seventeenth Centuries', *Folklore*, 97 (1986), 3–15.

—— '"And I Turned Round to Her and Said . . . ": A Preliminary Analysis of Shape and Structure in Women's Story Telling', *Folklore*, 100 (1989), 167–84.

—— and Smith, P. S., *Contemporary Legend* (Sheffield, 1990).

Benson, J., *The Working Class in Britain 1850–1939* (1989).

Berger, P. L., *The Social Reality of Religion* (1967).

—— *The Sacred Canopy—Elements of a Sociological Theory of Religion* (1967).

—— and Luckmann, T., *The Social Construction of Reality: A Treatise in the Sociology of Knowledge* (New York, 1966).

Best, G. F. A., *Temporal Pillars: The Crisis of Church Reform 1820–1835* (1964).

Biagini, E. F., and Reid, A. J., *Currents of Radicalism: Popular Radicalism, Organised Labour and Party Politics in Britain 1850–1914* (Cambridge, 1991).

Billington, L., 'Popular Religion and Social Reform: A study of Revivalism and Teetotalism 1830–50', *Journal of Religious History*, 10 (1979), 266–94.

Blumer, H., 'What is Wrong with Social Theory?' *American Sociological Review*, 19 (1954), 3–10.

—— *Symbolic Interactionism* (Engelwood Cliffs, NJ, 1969).

Bonser, W., *A Bibliography* (1961).

Bourke, J., *Working-Class Cultures in Britain 1890–1960* (1994), 145–8.

Briggs, A. (ed.), *They Saw it Happen: An Anthology of Eye-witness Accounts of Events in British History 1897–1940* (Oxford, 1960).

—— 'The Salvation Army in Sussex', in M. J. Kitch (ed.), *Studies in Sussex Church History* (Brighton, 1981), 189–208.

Briggs, J., 'Charles Haddon Spurgeon and the Baptist Denomination in the Nineteenth Century', *The Baptist Quarterly*, 31 (1986), 218–40.

Brookes, P., *The Pearly Kings and Queens of England* (1975).

Brose, O. J., *Church and Parliament 1828–1860* (Oxford, 1959).

Brown, C. G., *The Social History of Scotland since 1730* (1987).

Brown, C. G., 'Did Urbanisation Secularise Britain?' *Urban History Yearbook*, 15 (1988), 1–15.

—— 'A Revisionist Approach to Religious Change', in S. Bruce (ed.), *Religion and Modernisation* (1992), 36.

—— *The People in the Pews: Religion and Society in Scotland since 1780* (1993).

Brown, K. D., 'An Unsettled Ministry: Aspects of Nineteenth-Century British Nonconformity', *Church History*, 56 (1987), 204–24.

Bruce, S., *Religion in the Modern World: From Cathedrals to Cults* (Oxford, 1996).

Budd, S., *Sociologists and Religion* (1973).

—— *Varieties of Unbelief: A Sociological Account of the Humanist Movement in Britain 1850–1916* (1977).

Burke, P. (ed.), *Lucien Febvre—A New Kind of History* (1975), 34.

Cardwardine, R., 'The Welsh Evangelical Community and Finney's Revival', *Journal of Ecclesiastical History*, 28 (1978), 463–80.

Chadwick, O., *The Secularisation of the European Mind* (Cambridge, 1975).

—— *The Victorian Church*, 2 vols. (1972).

Chamberlain, M., and Richardson, R., 'Life and Death', *Oral History Journal*, 11 (1983), 31–44.

Chinn, C., *And They Worked all Their Lives: Women and the Urban Poor in England 1880–1990* (Manchester, 1988).

Clark, D., *Between Pulpit and Pew: Folk Religion in a North Yorkshire Fishing Village* (1982).

Cohen, A., *Two-Dimensional Man: An Essay on the Anthropology of Power and Symbolism in Complex Society* (1974).

—— *The Symbolic Construction of Community* (1992).

Collinson, P., *The Religion of the Protestants: The Church in English Society* (1979).

Connolly, G. P., 'Little Brother be at Peace: the Priest as Holy Man in the Nineteenth-Century Ghetto', *Studies in Church History*, 19 (1982), 191–206.

Cox, J., *The English Churches in a Secular Society: Lambeth 1870–1930* (Oxford, 1982).

Cronin, J. R., 'Language, Politics and the Critique of Social History: Languages of Class', *Journal of Social History*, 20 (1986), 177–84.

Crossick, G., 'The Labour Aristocracy and its Values: A Study of Mid-Victorian Kentish London', *Victorian Studies*, 19 (1975–6), 301–28.

—— (ed.), *The Lower Middle Class in Britain* (1977).

—— *An Artisan Elite in Kentish London 1840–1880* (1978).

Cunningham, H., *Leisure in the Industrial Revolution c.1780–1880* (1980).

Currie, R., *Methodism Divided: A Study of the Sociology of Ecumenicalism* (1968).

—— Gilbert, A., and Horsley, L., *Churches and Churchgoers: Patterns of Church Growth in the British Isles since 1700* (Oxford, 1977).

Davie, G., *Religion in Britain since 1945: Believing without Belonging* (1994).

Davis, R. W., and Helmstadter, R. J. (eds), *Religion and Irreligion in Victorian Society* (1992).

Dean, W., 'The Methodist Class Meeting and the Significance of its Decline', *Proceedings of the Wesleyan Historical Society*, 43 (1981), 41–8.

Demerath, N. J., *Religion in Social Context* (1969).

Dixon, K., *The Sociology of Belief* (1980).

Dorson, R. M. (ed.), *Folklore and Folklife: An Introduction* (Chicago, 1972).

Douglas, M., *Natural Symbols: Explorations in Cosmology* (1982).

Duthie, J. C., 'The Fisherman's Religious Revival', *History Today*, 33 (1983), 22–7.

Dyos, H. J. 'The Slums of Victorian London', *Victorian Studies*, 11 (1967), 5–41.

Ellis, A., *Educating Our Masters* (1985).

Ellis-Davidson, H., 'Myths and Symbols in Religion and Folklore', *Folklore*, 100 (1989), 120–1.

Ellsworth, L. E., *Charles Lowder and the Ritualist Revival* (1982).

Epstein, J., 'Understanding the Cap of Liberty: Symbolic Practice and Social Conflict in Early Nineteenth Century England', *Past and Present*, 122 (1989), 75–118.

Evans, G. E., *Where Beards Wag All: The Relevance of the Oral Tradition* (1970).

Evans-Pritchard, E. E., *Witchcraft, Oracles and Magic among the Azande* (Oxford, 1937).

—— *Theories of Primitive Religion* (Oxford, 1965).

Fentress, J., and Wickham, C., *The Social Memory: New Perspectives on the Past* (Oxford, 1992).

Field, C. D., 'A Sociological Profile of English Methodism 1900–31', *Oral History Journal*, 4 (1976), 73–96.

—— 'The Social Structure of English Methodism', *British Journal of Sociology*, 28 (1977), 199–225.

Fielding, S., *Class and Ethnicity* (1995).

Fraser, W. L., *All to the Good* (1963).

Fukuyama, Y., 'The Major Dimension of Church Membership', *Review of Religious Research*, 2 (1961), 154–61.

Gailey, A., 'The Nature of Tradition', *Folklore*, 100 (1989), 143–61.

Gardiner, J., *What is History Today?* (1988).

Garfinkel, H., *Studies in Ethnomethodology* (New York, 1967).

Geertz, C., 'Religion as a Cultural System', in M. Banton (ed.), *Anthropological Approaches to the Study of Religion* (1966), 1–46.

Gerth, H., and Mills, C. W., (ed.), *From Max Weber: Essays in Sociology* (1906, repr. 1946).

Gibson, R., *A Social History of French Catholicism 1789–1914* (1989).

Gilbert, A. D., *Religion and Society in Industrial England: Church, Chapel and Social Change 1740–1914* (1976).

—— *The Making of Post-Christian Britain* (1980).

Gilley, S., 'The Roman Catholic Mission to the Irish in London 1840–1860', *Recusant History*, 10 (1969), 123–45.

—— 'Protestant London, No Popery and the Irish Poor', *Recusant History*, 10 (1970), 210–30.

—— *The Irish in Britain 1815–1939* (1989).

—— *A History of Religion in Britain* (1994).

Glock, C. Y., *Religion and the Face of America* (Berkeley, 1958).

—— 'The role of Deprivation in the Origin of Religious Groups', in R. Lee and M. E. Marty (eds.), *Religion and Social Conflict* (Oxford, 1964), 24–36.

—— and Stark, R., *Religion and Society in Tension* (Chicago, 1965).

Goody, J., 'Religion and Ritual, the Definition Problem', *British Journal of Sociology*, 12 (1961), 142–64.

Gorer, G., *Exploring English Character* (1955).

Green, S. J. D., 'Religion and the Rise of the Common Man: Mutual Improvement Societies, Religious Associations and Popular Education in Three Industrial Towns in the West Riding of Yorkshire c.1850–1900', in D. Fraser (ed.), *Cities, Class and Communication: Essays in Honour of Asa Briggs*, (Hemel Hempstead, 1990), 25–43.

—— *Religion in the Age of Decline: Organisation and Experience in Industrial Yorkshire 1870–1920* (Cambridge, 1996).

Grittins, D., 'Let the People Speak: Oral History in Britain', *Victorian Studies*, 26 (1983), 431–41.

Griffiths, E., *The Printed Voice of Victorian Poetry* (Oxford, 1989).

Haig, A., *The Victorian Clergy* (1984).

Hall, S., and Jefferson, T. (eds.), *Resistance Through Rituals* (1976).

Halsey, A. H., (ed.), *British Social Trends since 1900* (1972).

Hammond, P. C., *The Parson and the Victorian Parish* (1977).

Harrison, B., 'Religion and Recreation in Nineteenth-Century England', *Past and Present*, 38 (1968), 98–125.

Heeney, B., *A Different Kind of Gentleman: The Clergy as Professional Men in Early and Mid-Victorian Britain* (1976).

—— *The Women's Movement in the Church* (Oxford, 1988).

Heimann, M., *Catholic Devotion in Victorian England* (1995).

Hennock, E. P., 'Poverty and Social Theory in England: The Experience of the 1880s', *Social History*, 1 (1976), 67–91.

Herberg, W., *The Protestant Catholic Jew* (1960).

Herberg, W., 'Religion in a Secularised Society', *Review of Religious Research*, 3 (1962), 145–58 and 4 (1963), 33–45.

Hilton, B., *The Age of Atonement: The Influence of Evangelicalism on Social and Economic Thought 1795–1865* (Oxford, 1988).

Hoover, A. J., *God, Germany and Britain and the Great War* (New York, 1989).

Hopkins, C. H., *The Rise of the Social Gospel in American Protestantism* (New Haven, 1967).

Hughes, J. A., *The Perspective of Ethnomethodology* (1983).

Humphries, S., 'Steal to Survive: The Social Crime of Working-Class Children, 1890–1940', *Oral History Journal,* 9.1 (1981), 24–35.

Inglis, K. S., 'English Nonconformity and Social Reform', *Past and Present,* 13 (1958), 73–88.

—— *The Churches and the Working Classes in Victorian England* (1963).

Jahoda, G., *The Psychology of Superstition* (1969).

Jay, E., *Faith and Doubt in Victorian Britain* (1986).

Jefferson, A., and Robey, D., *Modern Literary Theory: A Comparative Introduction* (1986).

Jones, G. S., *Languages of Class 1832–1982* (Cambridge, 1983).

Joyce, P., *Work, Society and Politics: The Culture of the Late-Victorian Factory* (1980).

—— *Visions of the People: Industrial England and the Question of Class 1840–1914* (1991).

—— 'The End of Social History', *Social History* (Jan. 1995).

Kent, J. H. S., 'The Role of Religion in the Culture of the Late-Victorian City', *Transactions of the Royal Historical Society,* 23 (1972), 175–220.

—— 'Feelings and Festivals: An Interpretation of some Working-Class Religious Attitudes', in H. J. Dyos and M. Wolff (eds.), *The Victorian City,* 2 vols. (1973), i. 855–72.

—— *Holding the Fort: Studies in Victorian Revivalism* (1978).

Kitson-Clark, G. S., *Churchmen and the Condition of England 1832–1885* (1973).

Kluckholme, C., 'Values and Value Orientation in the Theory of Action', in T. Parsons and E. Shils (eds.), *Towards a General Theory of Action* (New York, 1962).

Kniffka, J., *Das Kirchliche Leben in Berlin-Ost in der Mitte der Zwanziger Jahre* (Munster, 1971).

Langton, J., and Morris, R. J. (eds.), *Atlas of Industrialising Britain 1780–1914* (1986).

Laqueur, T. W., *Religion and Respectability: Sunday Schools and Working-Class Culture 1780–1950* (1976).

Lenski, G., *The Religious Factor—A Sociologist Looks at Religion* (Garden City, NY, 1961).

Lerner, L., *The Victorians* (1978).

Lewis, D., *Lighten their Darkness* (1986).

Lloyd, R., *The Church of England in the Twentieth Century 1900–1965* (1946).

Lovegrove, D., *Established Church, Sectarian People* (Cambridge, 1988).

Luckmann, T., *The Invisible Religion: The Problem of Religion in Modern Society* (New York, 1967).

Machin, G. I. T., *Politics and the Churches in Great Britain* (1977).

MacIntyre, A., *Secularisation and Moral Change* (1967).

McKelvie, D., 'Aspects of Oral Tradition and Belief in an Industrial Region', *Folk*

Life, 1 (1963), 77–94.

McKibbin, R., 'Social Class and Social Observation in Edwardian England', *Transactions of the Royal Historical Society*, 28 (1978), 175–201.

McLeod, H., 'Class, Community and Religion, the Religious Geography of Nineteenth-Century England', *A Sociological Yearbook of Religion*, 6 (1973), 29–72.

—— *Class and Religion in the Late-Victorian City* (1974).

—— 'Religion in the City', *Urban History Yearbook* (1978), 7–22.

—— 'Protestantism and the Working Classes in Imperial Germany', *European Studies Review*, 12 (1982), 323–44.

—— 'Religion in British and German Labour Movements c.1890–1914', *Bulletin of the Society for Labour History*, 51 (1986), 25–35.

—— 'New Perspectives on Victorian Class Religion: The Oral Evidence', *Oral History*, 14 (1986), 31–50.

—— (ed.), *European Religion in the Age of Great Cities 1830–1930* (1995).

—— *Piety and Poverty* (New York, 1996).

—— *Religion and Society in England 1850–1914* (1996).

Malcomson, R. W., *Popular Recreations in English Society 1700–1850* (Cambridge, 1973).

Malmgreen, G., *Religion in the Lives of English Women 1750–1930* (1985).

Mander, R., and Mitchenson, J., *British Music Hall* (1965).

Marrin, A., *The Last Crusade: The Church of England and World War I* (1974).

Martin, B., *A Sociology of Contemporary Cultural Change* (Oxford, 1981).

Martin, D. A., *A Sociology of English Religion* (1968).

—— *The Religious and the Secular: Studies in Secularisation* (1969).

—— *A General Theory of Secularisation* (Oxford, 1978).

Mayer, A. J., 'The Lower Middle Class as an Historical Problem', *Journal of Modern History*, 47 (1975), 409–37.

Mayor, S., *The Churches and the Labour Movement* (1967).

Mews, S., 'Urban Problems, Rural Solutions', *Studies in Church History*, 16 (1979), 449–77.

Minor, J. E., 'The Mantle of Elijah, Nineteenth-Century Primitive Methodist and Twentieth-Century Pentecostalism', *Proceedings of the Wesleyan Society*, 43 (1982), 141–9.

Mole, D. E. H., 'The Victorian Town Parish: A Rural Vision and Urban Mission', *Studies in Church History*, 16 (1979), 361–73.

Moore, R., *Pit-Men, Preachers and Politics: The Effects of Methodism in a Durham Mining Community* (Cambridge, 1974).

Morley, J., *Death, Heaven and the Victorians* (1971).

Morris, G. M., 'The Nonconformist Chapel and the Local Community', *Local Historian*, 10 (1973), 253–8.

Morris, J., 'Church and People Thirty-Three Years On: A Historical Critique', *Theology*, 94 (1991), 92–101.

—— *Religion and Urban Change: Croydon 1840–1914* (Bury St Edmunds, 1992).

Moss, L., and Goldstein, H. (eds.), *The Recall Method in the Social Sciences* (1979).

Neatby, W. B., *A Short History of the Plymouth Brethren* (1901).

Neuburg, V. E., *Chapbooks* (1972).

—— *Popular Literature: A History and Guide* (1977).

Newsome, D., *Godliness and Good Learning* (1961).

Norman, E., *The English Catholic Church in the Nineteenth Century* (Oxford, 1984).

Obelkevich, J., *Religion and Rural Society in South Lindsey 1825–1875* (Oxford, 1976).

O'Day, R., and Englander, D., *Mr. Charles Booth's Inquiry: Life and Labour of the People of London Reconsidered* (1993).

Opie, I., and Opie, P., *The Lore and Language of School Children* (1959).

—— and Tatem, M., *A Dictionary of Superstitions* (Oxford, 1989).

Orr, J. E., *The Second Evangelical Awakening in Britain* (1949).

Ortner, S. B., *Sherpas through their Rituals* (Cambridge, 1978).

Paredes, A., and Bauman, R., *Toward New Perspectives in Folklore* (1972).

Parkin, F., *Max Weber* (1982).

Passerini, L., 'Work, Ideology and Consensus under Italian Fascism', *History Workshop*, 8 (1979), 82–108.

—— *Fascism in Popular Memory: The Cultural Experience of the Turin Working Class* (Cambridge, 1987).

Payne, E. A., *A Short History of the Baptist Union* (1958).

Paz, D. A., *Popular Anti-catholicism in Mid-Victorian England* (1972).

Pelling, H., 'Religion and the Working Class', *Past and Present*, 27 (1964), 128–33.

Pfautz, H. W., 'The Sociology of Secularisation', *American Journal of Sociology*, 61 (1955), 121–8.

Pickering, W. S. F., 'Religion a Leisurely Pursuit', *Sociology of Religion Yearbook*, 1 (1968), 128–33.

Pugh, D. R., 'The Strength of English Religion in the 1890s; The Evidence of the North West', *Journal of Religious History*, 12 (1983), 250–66.

Rack, H., 'Wesleyanism and the World in the later Nineteenth Century', *Proceedings of the Wesleyan Historical Society*, 42 (1979), 35–54.

Reardon, B., *From Coleridge to Gore* (1971).

Reay, B., (ed.), *Popular Culture in Seventeenth-Century England* (Worcester, 1985).

Reddy, W., 'The Language of the Crowd at Rouen 1752–1871', *Past and Present*, 34 (1977), 62–89.

Richter, M., *The Politics of Conscience: T. H. Green and his Age* (1983).

Roberts, E., *Working-Class Barrow and Lancaster, 1890–1930* (Lancaster, 1976).

—— *A Woman's Place: An Oral History of Working-Class Women 1890–1940* (Oxford, 1984).

Roberts, E., 'The Working-Class Extended Family: Functions and Attitudes, 1890–1940', *Oral History Journal*, 12 (1984), 48–55.

—— *Women and Families: An Oral History 1940–1970* (Oxford, 1995).

Robertson, R., *A Sociological Interpretation of Religion* (Oxford, 1970).

Robson, G., 'The Failure of Success: Working Class Evangelists in Victorian Birmingham', *Studies in Church History*, 15 (1978), 381–93.

Ross, E., 'Fierce Questions, Angry Taunts: Married Life in Working Class London 1870–1914', *Feminist Studies*, 8 (1982), 575–602.

—— 'Survival Networks: Women's Neighbourhood Sharing in London before World War I', *History Workshop*, 15 (1983), 4–28.

—— *Love and Toil: Motherhood in Outcast London 1870–1918* (Oxford, 1993).

Rowell, G., *Hell and the Victorians* (Oxford, 1974).

Royle, E., *Victorian Infidels: The Origins of the British Socialist Movement* (1974).

Rule, J., 'Methodism, Popular Belief and Village Culture in Cornwall', in Storch (ed.), *Popular Custom* (New York, 1982).

Runciman, W. G., 'A Social Explanation of Religious Beliefs', *European Journal of Sociology*, 10 (1969), 149–91.

Rushton, P., 'A Note on the Survival of Popular Christian Magic', *Folklore*, 191 (1980), 115–19.

Russell, A., *The Clerical Profession* (1980).

Russell, W. M. S., 'Folktales and the Theatre', *Folklore*, 92 (1981), 3–24.

Samuel, R., *East End Underworld: Chapters in the Life of Arthur Harding* (Oxford, 1986).

—— and Thompson, P., *The Myths We Live By* (1990).

Samuelson, K., *Religion and Economic Action* (1961).

Scannell, P., and Cardiff, D., *A Social History of British Broadcasting: Volume 1 1920–1939* (Oxford, 1991).

Scotland, N. A. D., 'Methodism and the Revolt of the Field 1872–96', *Proceedings of the Wesleyan Historical Society*, 41 (1977), 39–42.

Sharock, W. W., and Anderson, R., *The Ethnomethodologists* (1986).

Shaw, C., and Chase, M., (eds.), *The Imagined Past: History and Nostalgia* (Manchester, 1989).

Sheppard, D., *Built as a City: God and the Urban World Today* (1974).

Shiner, L., 'The Concept of Secularisation in Empirical Research', *Journal for the Scientific Study of Religion*, 6 (1967), 207–20.

Shinman, L. L., 'The Band of Hope Movement', *Victorian Studies*, 16 (1973), 40–74.

Silverman, M., and Gulliver, P. H., *Approaching the Past* (New York, 1992).

Simey, T. S., *Booth the Social Scientist* (1960).

Smith, A. W., 'Popular Religion', *Past and Present*, 40 (1968), 181–7.

—— *The Established Church and Popular Religion 1750–1850* (1971).

Smith, M., *Religion and Industrial Society: Oldham and Saddleworth 1740–1865* (Oxford, 1995).

Spiegel, G. M., 'History, Historicism and the Social Logic of the Text in the Middle Ages', *Speculum*, 65 (1990), 59–87.

Spiller, B., *Victorian Public Houses* (1972).

Spufford, M., *A Cambridgeshire Community* (1965).

—— *Contrasting Communities* (1974).

—— *Small Books, Pleasant Histories* (1981).

Stacey, M., 'The Myth of Community Studies', *British Journal of Sociology*, 20 (1969), 134–47.

Stedman-Jones, G. S., 'Working-Class Culture and Working-Class Politics in London 1870–1900', *Journal of Social History*, 7 (1974), 460–508.

—— *Languages of Class 1832–1982* (Cambridge, 1983).

—— *Outcast London* (1984).

Stevenson, J., *British Society 1914–45* (1984).

Stone, L., 'History and Post Modernism', *Past and Present*, 131 (1991), 217–18.

Storch, R., *Popular Culture and Custom in Nineteenth-Century England* (New York, 1982).

Strauss, G., 'The Dilemma of Popular History', *Past and Present*, 132 (1991), 130–50.

Tamke, S., 'Separating the Sheep from the Goats', *Albion*, 8 (1977), 255–73.

—— *Make a Joyful Noise unto the Lord: Hymns as a Reflection of Victorian Social Attitudes* (Ohio, 1978).

Taylor, L. J., 'Languages of Belief', in Silverman and Gulliver (eds.), *Approaching the Past* (New York, 1992).

Tebbutt, M., *Making Ends Meet: Pawnbroking and Working-Class Credit* (New York, 1985).

Thomas, K., *Religion and the Decline of Magic—Studies in Popular Beliefs in Sixteenth- and Seventeenth-Century England* (1971).

Thompson, D. M., *Theological and Sociological Approaches to the Ecumenical Movement* (1978).

—— 'John Clifford's Social Gospel', *The Baptist Quarterly*, 31 (1985), 199–217.

—— 'Languages of Class', *Society for the Study of Labour History Bulletin*, 52 (1987), 54–7.

Thompson, E. P., *The Making of the English Working Class* (1963).

Thompson, F. M. L., 'Social Control in Victorian Britain', *Economic History Review*, 34 (1981), 189–208.

—— (ed.), *The Cambridge Social History of Britain 1750–1950*, 3 vols. (Cambridge, 1990).

Thompson, J., 'After the Fall: Class and Political Language in Britain, 1780–1900', *Historical Journal*, 39/3 (1996), 785–806.

Thompson, K. A., *Bureaucracy and Church Reform: The Organisational Response of the Church of England to Social Change* (1970).

Thompson, P., *The Voice of the Past* (1978).

—— *The Edwardians* (1991).

Thompson, P., Lummis, T., and Wailey, T., *Living the Fishing* (1983).

Thompson, T., *Edwardian Childhoods* (1981).

Tickner, L., *The Spectacle of Women* (1987).

Tiryakian, E. A., (ed.), *Sociological Theory, Values and Socio-Cultural Change* (1963).

Towler, R., *Homo Religiosus* (1974).

—— and Chamberlain, A., 'Common Religion', *The Sociological Yearbook of Religion in Britain*, 6 (1973), 1–28.

Trainor, R. H., *Black Country Elites* (Oxford, 1993).

Trudgill, P., *Socio-linguistics* (1974).

Tulloch, J., *Movements of Religious Thought in Britain During the Nineteenth Century* (1885, repr. Leicester, 1971).

Turner, V. W., *The Ritual Process* (1969).

Vansina, J., *The Oral Tradition as History* (1985).

Vaux, J. E., *Church Folklore* (1894).

Vigne, T., 'Parents and Children', *Oral History Journal*, 5 (1977), 6–13.

Vincent, D., *Bread, Knowledge and Freedom: A Study of Nineteenth Century Working Class Autobiography* (1981).

—— *Literacy and Popular Culture: England 1750–1914* (Cambridge, 1989).

Watts, M., *The Dissenters* (1995)

Werner, J. S., *The Primitive Methodist Connexion: Its Background and Early History* (1984).

Wickham, E. R., *Church and People in an Industrial City* (1957).

Wilkinson, A., *The Church of England and the First World War* (1978).

Williams, C. R., 'The Welsh Revival of 1904–5', *British Journal of Sociology*, 3 (1952), 242–59.

Williams, S. C., 'Urban Popular Religion and the Rites of Passage', in McLeod (ed.), *European Religion* (1995).

—— 'The Language of Belief: An Alternative Agenda for the Study of Victorian Working-Class Religion', *Journal of Victorian Culture*, 1/2 (1996), 303–17.

—— 'The Problem of Belief—the Place of Oral History in the Study of Popular Religion', *Oral History* (1996), 25–32.

Wilson, B., *Sects and Society* (1961).

—— *Religion in Secular Society* (1966).

—— *Contemporary Transformations of Religion* (Oxford, 1974).

—— 'Becoming a Sectarian, Motivation and Commitment', *Studies in Church History*, 15 (1978), 481–507.

—— *Religion in Sociological Perspective* (Oxford, 1982).

Winstanley, M., 'Some Practical Hints on Oral History Interviewing', *Oral History*, 5 (1977), 122–31.

Winter, J. M., 'Spiritualism and the First World War', in Davis and Helmstadter, *Religion and Irreligion* (1992).

Wolffe, J., *The Protestant Crusade in Great Britain 1829–1860* (Oxford, 1991).

Wood, H. G., *Belief and Unbelief since 1851* (Cambridge, 1955).

Wright, T., and Neill, S., *Interpretations of the New Testament 1861–1986* (Oxford, 1988).

Yeo, S., *Religion and Voluntary Organisations in Crisis* (1976).

—— 'A New Life: Religion and Socialism in Britain 1883–96', *History Workshop Journal*, 4 (1977), 5–56.

Yinger, J. M., *Religion, Society and the Individual* (New York, 1967).

Young, M., and Willmott, P., *Family and Kinship in East London* (1957).

INDEX